SONG OF THE WORLD BECOMING

By Pattiann Rogers

SONG OF THE WORLD BECOMING

New and Collected Poems
1981–2001

Pattiann Rogers

MILKWEED EDITIONS

Published 2001 by Milkweed Editions
Printed in the United States of America
Jacket and interior design by Dale Cooney
Jacket art by Petronella J. Ytsma
Author photo by Yvonne Mozee
The text of this book is set in Bembo.
01 02 03 04 05   5 4 3 2 1
First Edition

Milkweed Editions, a nonprofit publisher, gratefully acknowledges support from the Elmer L. and Eleanor J. Andersen Foundation; Bush Foundation; General Mills Foundation; Honeywell Foundation; Jerome Foundation; McKnight Foundation; Minnesota State Arts Board through an appropriation by the Minnesota State Legislature; Norwest Foundation on behalf of Norwest Bank Minnesota; Lawrence and Elizabeth Ann O'Shaughnessy Charitable Income Trust in honor of Lawrence M. O'Shaughnessy; Oswald Family Foundation; Ritz Foundation on behalf of Mr. and Mrs. E. J. Phelps Jr.; John and Beverly Rollwagen Fund of the Minneapolis Foundation; St. Paul Companies, Inc.; Star Tribune Foundation; Target Foundation on behalf of Dayton's, Mervyn's California and Target Stores; U.S. Bancorp Piper Jaffray Foundation on behalf of U.S. Bancorp Piper Jaffray; and generous individuals.

Library of Congress Cataloging-in-Publication Data

Rogers, Pattiann, 1940–
    Song of the world becoming : new and collected poems, 1981–2001 / Pattiann Rogers.—1st ed.
      p.   cm.
    Includes indexes.
    ISBN 1-57131-413-X (acid-free paper)
      I. Title

    PS3568.O454 S59 2001
    811'.54—dc21

                                                                00-067863

This book is printed on acid-free paper.

For moment and presence

SONG OF THE WORLD BECOMING

THE EXPECTATIONS OF LIGHT (1981)

THE TATTOOED LADY IN THE GARDEN (1986)

I

II

Legendary Performance (1987)

I

II

III

GEOCENTRIC (1993)

EARTHRISE

OLD SPIRAL OF CONCEPTION (1994)
(New Poems from Firekeeper)

ACKNOWLEDGMENTS

I thank first my country and my culture for the nurturing at-
mosphere in which I have lived; for the education it has been my
privilege to enjoy; for preserving the music, art, and literature, the
science, and the philosophy that have enriched my life; for allowing
me to believe, to announce my beliefs, and to constantly re-examine
and modify my beliefs; and for providing me with the freedom to
speak and to publish my writing.

I want to express my gratitude to those first editors who very
early gave me support and encouragement by publishing my poems,
offering me suggestions, and honoring my poems with awards from
their respective journals: David Wagoner at *Poetry Northwest* and as
editor of the Princeton Poetry Series, Joseph Parisi and the late
John Frederick Nims at *Poetry*, Hilda Raz at *Prairie Schooner*, David
Hamilton at the *Iowa Review*, Stephen Corey and the late Stanley
Lindberg at the *Georgia Review*, the late George Hitchcock at
Kayak. Thanks to teacher, editor, friend, and critic Peter Stitt at the
Gettysburg Review. I feel very fortunate to have had these talented
and dedicated people with me from the beginning. I want to thank
all editors of literary journals and small presses for their work in pro-
viding a venue for the poems of contemporary poets.

My thanks to Emilie Buchwald and Milkweed Editions for giving me a publishing home and for offering me the opportunity to gather my work over the past twenty years into this volume.

Gratitude always to my writing teachers, the late John Neihardt, the late Nelson Bentley, to Cynthia Macdonald, Stanley Plumly, and to Dr. William Jones, Professor of English at the University of Missouri-Columbia, now retired, for reading my first poems when I was an undergraduate student and encouraging me at that time. Thanks to Richard Howard for his friendship and his continuing interest in my work.

My appreciation to the Guggenheim Foundation, the National Endowment for the Arts, and the Lannan Foundation, for supporting me with financial assistance, validation of my poetry, and time to write. My gratitude to the Rockefeller Foundation for a residency at the Bellagio Study and Conference Center in Bellagio, Italy, during which I completed work on this volume.

Thanks to all my Texas friends and colleagues and to the Texas Institute of Letters for their recognition of my work and for their support of Texas writers. My gratitude for enlivening discussions with the members of our Meadows Book Club.

To my community of friends and writers, my love and thanks for your companionship, and for all of our conversations, during which we shared ideas and work, and for your loyal affection: Robert Michael Pyle and Thea, Richard Nelson and Nita Couchman, John Straley and Jan, Brian Doyle, Barry Lopez, Gary Nabhan, Alison Deming, Kurt Brown, Kim Stafford, Scott Russell Sanders, Ann Zwinger, John Daniel and Marilyn, Jane Hirshfield, Bill Kittredge, Annick Smith, Gary Holthaus, Claire Davis, Dennis Held, Cort Conley, Rick Bass, David James Duncan, Walter Pavlich, Sandra McPherson, Ralph Black, Jim Peterson, Alice Fulton, and the late Tom Watkins.

My gratitude to Marion Gilliam, Laurie-Lane Zucker, Chip Blake, and the staff of the Orion Society for enriching my life over the past several years, for giving me the opportunity to meet many wonderful and interesting people, and to visit parts of the country I would not have been able to visit otherwise. My thanks for their support of my work and for their steady friendship.

My gratitude to Christopher Merrill for his friendship, his energy and creativity, and for his support of my work in many ways over many years.

I appreciate the kindness shown me during my semesters at the University of Arkansas. Thanks to my friends and colleagues in Fayetteville, especially to Jim Whitehead, whose knowledge, originality, wit, and energy were a joy to me and benefited me greatly, and to Gen Whitehead for opening her home to me so often with such warm hospitality.

My thanks to those directors of conferences who have been so kind as to invite me more than once to join them: Carolyn Servid and Dorik Mechau at the Island Institute for Human Values in Sitka, Alaska; Jack Hicks at the Art of the Wild Writers Conference for including me in the Squaw Valley Community of Writers; Donald Sheehan at the Frost Place; and Celeste Mergens at Whidbey Island Writers Conference. My gratitude to all directors of writers conferences for their hard work in giving writers across the country the opportunity to meet together for discussion, work, and camaraderie.

Thanks to the visual artists with whom I've worked: Joellyn Duesberry, Robert Adams, Margot Voorhies Thompson, Mary Peck, and Jack Boynton, for friendship and for the perspectives their art has given me.

My thanks to the readers who have been so kind as to receive my work. We create together.

Love and gratitude always to my family: my brother, William E. Tall Jr., with appreciation for his curiosity, imagination, and ingenuity; my uncle and aunt, Floyd and Mary Keiter, for the fine people they are and the work they do; cousins Sue and Vernon Pfeiffer for keeping us in touch with Missouri, our first home.

In memoriam, my lasting gratitude and thanks for a rich and loving childhood to my parents, William Elmer Tall and Irene Christine Keiter Tall. And thanks to my other mother, my late mother-in-law, Roberta Frances Wilson Rogers, for her steady, serene, and wise spirit.

I am most grateful for those individuals dearest and closest to me: our inestimable sons, John Ashley Rogers and Arthur William Rogers, who have given me more joy than I could ever mention here, who have been perfect in every way, enriching and broadening my life, never ceasing to fill me with wonder and amazement and pride, and without whom these poems would never have come to be; and Lisa, our daughter-in-law, our daughter, who has so beautifully come to occupy a cherished place in our family and to offer generously her devoted companionship and care to all of us. My lasting love.

And finally to John, my dearest and oldest friend and companion, my loving husband of forty years, our histories are one history. There is not one without the other. This love in this life is the way we have defined and created it together. Faith is not abstract, for we have witnessed it in each other. We have touched it. These poems, their suppositions, their questions, their fears, their celebrations, their hope despite all ignorance, are document to our history and its time. You possess them in a way unlike any other.

SONG OF THE WORLD BECOMING

SONG OF THE WORLD BECOMING (2001)

I

A VERY COMMON FIELD

What is it about this grassy field
that's so familiar to me? Something
within the beings, the form of the place?
It's not within the foxtail, not within
the brome, not within oat grass or red clover
or yellow vetch or the lot of them as one
motion in the wind. It's not the morning
or even of the morning, or of the invisible
crickets, one near, one away, still sounding
in the damp after dawn.

What is it so resonant and recognized here?
A sense like nostalgia, like manner,
like a state felt but not remembered?
It isn't the center of the purple cornflower
or its rayed and fluted edges, not the slow
rise of the land or the few scattered trees
left in the fallow orchard, not the stone path,
not the grains and bristles of stems and seeds,
each oblivious in its own business,
but something impossible without these.

It's more than the increasing depth
of the day and the blue of its height,
more than the half-body of the lizard
turned upside down on the path, torn
and transfigured during the night, more
than the bells beginning their lesson
in the background.

Song of the World Becoming   5

It's not a voice, not a message,
but something like a lingering,
a reluctance to abandon, a biding
so constantly present that I can never
isolate it from the disorderly crows
passing over or from the sun moving
as wind down through the brief fires
of moisture on the blades of timothy
and sage, never separate it from the scent
of fields drying and warm, never
isolate it from my own awareness.
It is something that makes possible,
that occasions without causing, something
I can never extricate to name, never
name to know, never know to imitate.

––––––––––

BEING SPECIFIC

The beginning subject is narrowed
first to the yellow toe-claw on the left
front seven-segmented leg of this one
specific, totally bright yellow
spider misplaced, a small spectacle
moving across the damp, grey
gravel of the forest path.

Yet the subject, more specifically,
is the cellular tremble of pulse
in this particular toe-claw belonging
to this very spider I see, lost
from its yellow-orange flowerfield—
goldenrod, daisy, jessamine.

Still, to be more exact, the sole
subject here is one colorless shiver
of molecule inside the one-chambered
heart of this quite shiny, yellow-
eyed, golden pea-orb pausing
on rock at my feet.

But the focus, to designate
further, must be on one atom-
to-atom link inside this arachnid
heart this afternoon, and further,
within this spider-atom, one electron,
and beyond that, one hadron, one quark;
and further beyond that, the last
and finest specification possible,
which is naturally the only
underlying, indivisible universal
that thus possesses like the void
and exhibits like the boundless
and holds distance like the night
and serves like the sun and inhabits
like the stars and therefore exists
as this split-moment's revelation
inside the mind meeting itself
in the recognition of its own
most specific composition.

REITERATION

This contract is not singular.
It is present in each shaft
of the chickadee's chestnut feathers

holding to flesh. Part them
on the wing or on the belly down
to hot skin and touch the document.
The bonds of this contract are plural
and solitary, present in coon paw
and river print, in swallow and scat,
in rain falling on dry leaves,
like time in meter, chord
to arpeggio to chord.

Its terms are forest ashes and crystal,
scarlet persimmon and blood, the cave
and sunlit chamber of winter, wind
across corn tassel and granite.

One might believe this contract
to be invisible, invisible where
the disappearing points of the urchin's
spines appear as the motion
of the sea, where the shifting
reflection of the water willow
and the wavering shadow of the water
willow merge and part, where truth
and lie first draw together and link
from pre-death to presence.

Like anise-pleasure contained
in the seed-size dry fruits
of the fennel, so the binding
signature is contained in the agitation
of poplars taken by wind, in the sucker-
tipped tube feet of the slender purple
starfish, in the release of midnight's
cry by root cricket, by poaching owl.

Again and again, inside the purity
of tone in the ear of the mind
of the bell caster at his fire,
this signal tolling will continue
to repeat itself. Like the pause
of the winged ant stopped, extinct
and unbroken in rock amber, this contract
remains its own reiterated event,
from coming to coming.

Here is my hand on it.

THE NATURE OF THE HUCKSTER

Put on his garment of rain,
came swaying in silver across
the garden, his fragrance
of clarity preceding him. Put on
his garment of theft, stole
the seeds of the pecan, the eggs
of the horseshoe crab, roe
of cod, roe of mackerel, stole
the children's gold and purple
marbles, stole breath, stole fever.
Filled his pockets with blood.
Filled his pockets with charity.
Emptied his pockets of confetti-
feathers and bones. Emptied

his pockets of beetle menageries.
Over his garment of snow, donned

his garment of sun. Over his
many-colored coat of deception,
put on his many-colored robe
of verisimilitude. Under his attire
of aridity, wore his thunder cloak
of deluge. Put on his robe
of celibacy. Put on his jewelry
of prostitution. Traded his
garment of frivolity. Bartered
his overcoat of constancy. Shucked
his shawl of grief. Threw off
his hood of sanity. Under his silk

cape of surrender, clothed himself
in his steel vestment of siege.
Put on his garment of disdain. Covered
himself in his rags of spring. Wrapped
himself in his blankets of faith.
Discarded his garment of life. Donned
his garment of death. Put on his
garment of matter. Took off
his garment of light. Discarded
his garment of decay. Put on
his garment of lies. Paraded
back and forth, plain and invisible
in his ruse of apparel, hawking,
all the while, himself. Take him.

II

BORN ON NOAH'S ARK

Above my rocking cradle,
around the walls of the nursery,
the puffbirds and oilbirds,
the hornbills, swifts, and crimson
rosellas hung all day and all night
in their swaying, rocking cages.
And the grand cradle, of which
we were all a part, rocked too,
fell and rose, delving on the sweet,
rocking, rainwater sea.

What strange spheres, I wondered,
had formed these creatures
with whom we sailed? The soft-
soled, sharp-edged hooves
of the antelope-goats clearly
remembered an element unknown
to me. The blindness of mole
and mouse-tailed bat recalled a vision
and circumstance not present here.
The way the spider monkey once
climbed my crib, leaped to the eaves,
and settled, curling its black tail
around a cornerpost, suggested
knowledge of a missing presence
beyond my ken.

Sometimes the wind lifted and opened
locked surfaces of the sea. I saw
then many tiny suns and stars inside
the spray of waves that flew beside
the prow where I was placed for summer
air, secured to the railing in my little
chair with the wooden wheels.

Grains of salt could have been
the stars we ate with our porridge.

But the real stars above us
were the lanterns of many women
digging for clams, there on that shore
the color of the night sky, the only shore
I could understand. Did we really travel?
We never sailed close enough to call out
to the women, to hear their answer,
never sailed far enough from them
to see their lanterns fade, dwindle,
disappear. I didn't know where
we had been, where we were going.

But I watched to remember
a long-ago launching, a putting forth
from something rare, numerical,
simmering. And I learned to listen
for the foreign in the familiar, to lay
my head down on the boards
of the rocking deck, above the great
echoing hull, my ear pressed
to the thrum and scale, the creaking
and humming of that buoyant cradle
that kept and carried us on.

EYES AND THE SEA

I believe eyes were born of the sea,
for, similar to the sea, they are quick
to take in and give back with finesse
and ingenuity. Both the sea and the eyes
can bestow life and claim souls and enact
tragedy. In the right circumstances,
each can engender ice.

Surely related, the sea and eyes
alike establish distinctions simply
by being—the earth from the heavens,
the enfolded from the castaway,
the calm from the storm. And each
is composed of light at many levels,
holding depth and surface with equal
consideration. Both are so often
the color of the sky, clear and opaque.

I believe eyes were born of the sea.
How else could they have possessed
from the beginning the skill to multiply
the moon at every possible angle
above the horizon? How else could they
have known from the first how to accept
so graciously the ghostlike shadows
cast by birds passing over?

Or perhaps the sea was born
of the eyes, having inherited the same
essences of nightmare and reverie
that eyes possess during sleep.
If the sea was conceived by the eyes,

being their vision of the magnificent
made manifest, this could account,
as well, for the remarkable similarities.

Therefore, I couldn't say
with certainty which will return
at the end to save the other—whether
the eyes will be rescued from their dry
skeleton by the sea or whether the sea
from its parched bed will be preserved
and rendered immortal by the eyes
or whether salvation has always
existed in the continual genesis
of each by the other.

————————

ON THE WAY TO EARLY MORNING MASS

I entered the sea on the way
to early morning mass, walked
down deep along the rims of rock
coral caverns where my misstep
and consequent falling was most
slow and careful flying. I passed
over fields of slender, swaying
tubes of cuttlefish nests, supple
sheaves white and iridescent as pearl,
moved among the swift metal precision
of barracuda passion and shears.
A scatter of rain on the ceiling
of the sea above me appeared a sky-wide

scatter of stars struck to light
and snuffed in the same moment.

I rose from the sea on the way
to early morning mass, walked along
the wet stones of the path, through
the sunken-blue-eyed grasses and cat
peas of the pasture gauzed with drizzled
webs, shrouds and shells of beeflies
and seeds clinging to my feet,
along the two-rutted road, its frost-
fringed skims of water in shallow
delves, the fence ragged and tipsy
with wild rose, stripped blossoms,
crusty yellow leaves black-spotted.

On the way to early morning mass,
I entered the soft-spun skull inside
the curlew's egg, heard the echo
of chimes in that electric cellar
of sun, entered the knot of the witch's
pit, the sweet pulp pit of the lover's
intention, the knot of felicity,
the pit of vagary. Nothing was blacker
fire than the government of summer
collapsed in the knot of the coal.

I passed once a fragrance
of strawberries and orange simmering
for jam, once lavender and cedar
as from a spinster's trunk long
locked and suddenly opened, once
a sage wind down from the tops

of the pines. A door blew shut,
and a mongrel bitch on her chain
yipped to an empty window, circled
twice on her measured length.

On the way to early morning mass,
I followed the invisible corridor
of sky forged by swallows from river–
bank to bluff, followed the way
of my hand along the bones of his sleep
in the bed beside me, followed the way
of my eye following the way of winter
rain down the icy runnels of budded
oak, and every remembered motion
of succeeding motion was providential,
the way of making the way sanctum,
the proceeding the arrival,
the service continuing on
the continuing.

––––––––––

these horses never cease

     they pound and rumble like river–
bottom stones beaten hard and rolled
fast by spring rushes
                fall in galloping
    cascades like mountains collapsing,
like boulders up and over the backs
of one another and down rudely breaking
necks and spines and skulls, like rock–
chert tonnage in a rend of avalanche

                                        they run
          rearing and wheezing along the shore,
manes and muzzles and hooves flinging blown
strings of salt spray high against the icy
beachheads of metal scarps and cliffs
                                        they descend
          like vortexes spearing downward
to the dead end of the sea night, rise spinning
again in wide-eyed pillars careening like funnels
and geysers of steam

          they hump and kick like thunder
in a winter blow, veer like heavy rain
hit sideways by canyon winds, their backs
and withers
                    shine like summer bay waters
in a noon lull, blood/antiblood, candlelight
and chasm, they click
                              and beat together
          as constant and dependable as atomic
clocks, gather like a green canter of cedars
down an arid gorge
                         scream out
          independently like a wild whinny of larks
and pipits rippling the evening southward,
like a question of water beetles circling
the still surface of a back eddy
                              they graze,
          a moving pause of ripening berry patches
and hassles

          they speed round and round as if on tethers,
in rings like moons, like comets and stars

and committees of stars
                              they are horses,
       they are fire, they burn, they scatter
their ashes, their bones smoke, they roll
belly up in the ocean and swerve like prairie
grasses of blue fishes with wings
                              o my skies,
o my seas, my lands, my herds and herds
       of heavenly hosts

III

BELIEVING IN BLOOD

I don't know how fast the blood
must rush through the throat, up
the spinal column, round the gut
and lungs and ribs of the sparrow's
three-ounce body. I don't know how fast
it must speed, the color of fire unseen
below ground, maybe almost smoking,
that blood careening back from wing tip,
back from claw nail and brow, back
to the pow of the heart keeping
the body an ember in this Arctic blue
air that breaks and seizes with zero.

Maybe in harsh moments like these
the blood flies as fast inside a bird's
boundaries as a rock shot past a high
cliff plummets toward the sharp
water of the ice-rimmed rush below.
Maybe the blood winding inside a bird's
body in January cold moves as fast
and as forcefully as the arc of a whip
flicked high, sparking across a frozen
sky, melting the threatening strictures
of winter with the heat of its own racing.

The sparrow gleans and prims among the icy
weeds, hardly noticing, as if she knew
she were not merely herself, not pulse,

not marrow, not throbbing, but an eternal
equation of motion relative to belief
relative to loss that always results,
anywhere it figures in the heavens,
in a tight fist of feathers,
bone-red structures and breath.

The enduring, absolute math
of this sparrow must exist right now
elsewhere, replicated a billion other
times as wire feet, beak pricking,
shocking shaft of eye present
in the swirl of forces roaring
through the igniting star bombs
and radiances among which we float.

The intricate shadows of winter branches
networked across the snow plain
where I stand seem to me now the flat
black veins of missing birds who long ago
must have mistakenly abandoned forever
their faith in the calculation
of momentum and promise present
in a crimson of salt.

SPEAKING OF EVOLUTION: LUMINOSITY

For aren't we all the children
of the children of great-grandfathers
who called down lightning, who sought out

the tree struck and smoldering, who minded
the punk log day and night as if it
were alive? We are each of us the progeny
of grandmothers who guarded burning
rocks held in seashells, who cradled
coals in clay cups through windy mountain
journeys; the sons and daughters
of mothers who blew sparks on twisted
moss wicks floating in bowls of oil;
the family of those who peeled
bark strips from trailside trees,
twined and lit the funnels to burn
as torches on rainy night treks.
We are kin to the kin of fathers
who spun wood against wood until
the smoky heat ignited fine-thread
tinder of cedar hairs, charred
corn tassels, who fanned and coddled
and spoke to the warm light coming.

The old structures of these ritual
passions, kept deep in the genes,
in the heart—like precious scripts
preserved in the rock cellars of hidden
monasteries—these are eternal. They breathe,
alive in the seed of every coming child,
each tiny embryo skeleton bound
and forming to fit forever the bones
and powers of all past solicitors of light.

And during any cold, frightful time
when something of vision is missing,

these talents will appear, rising,
seeming of a sudden resurrected—
the way inert soil opened to sun seems
of a sudden to flower—the kindling,
the watchful nursing, the urging forth
of that first slight savior of flame,
the same close kissing of fire,
as if, in truth, the earth had never
been absolved without such religion.

DATA FROM THIS LINE OF LIGHT LABORATORY

This particular line of light
is the angle of the black mare's
neck as she bends to the evening
grasses. It is the same angle
composing the history
of the trajectory remaining
in the comet's wake, the same
angle inherent to the salt curve
of the wave falling into its fall.

The jiggling gold ball on the jester's
pointed hat is the shaking line
of circular light that occurs
whenever the king sits crying.
This line is similar to the sunside
circle of the orange tossed up
by the juggler so high its only being
is its fire shaking against the sky.
It is akin also to the trembling

the light makes in the tears
of the childless at night.

One certain light of line-clarity
is a single strand of cobweb
floating as its own sun across
the lawn. Another is the crack
in a cut crystal vase so fine
it is seen only when held
to the sky, which fine clarity
sounds like a violin replicating
the liquid line left by the sea's
advance on the moonlit sand.

This line of illumination was created
when thieves first forced the sealed
entrance to a desert tomb and starlight
fell at once straight to its stone floor.

Light lines of double vision
imply either parallel light
off the tines of silver pickle forks
or off the steel of railroad tracks
empty at high noon on the prairie,
or the sun divided in the vision
of the surface-floating whirligig
beetle, or the day divided
by the separately rotating eyes
of the vine green chameleon.

Two lines of light bisecting
at right angles can signify either
two search beams crossing at sea,
or a collision of sincerity and ruse

at the subatomic level, or hope,
or an apparition of hope created
by those investigating every sign
of light at any level.

———————

As Even Ever

Everybody knows the sun, every
body in the whole world, no matter who.
Even the moth of the moon knows the sun
it holds, just as a mirror holds the silver
it knows as its own light. And the hairy-
tailed mole and the silver-haired bat
know the sun to avoid it.

The sun may even be the very first
thing any one of us knows, apprehending
the full light of the boundless air. The full
light of the boundless air is always today.

I am strange about the sun,
how it is massively stupefying
no matter where it is in the sky. It burns
and blinds and roils wildly white heat
like boiling lava. It rends with rash
and constant explosions that spew
and arc, bellow and roar and sear
and make known against the blue
in all directions right above the serene
siestas of the quiet trees, the calm dozings

of the dogs. I have flinched, cowered
before the sun more than once.

Every language has a word
for the sun. Even dead languages
speak of the sun today within its full
light filling the boundless air. I like
its word, a foundation word, a core
thought. Even one-seed junipers
and water pipits and spur-throated
grasshoppers pronounce *sun* in the form
of their own languages. The sun
might even be the only song they
ever sing in constant unison.

I know the sun isn't god. But the sun
does initiate distinctions—the feathers
of the palm cockatoo from the feather
plumes of the sea lily from the feather
barbs of the walking catfish, for instance.
And it creates union. Green
needlegrass, white sweet clover,
and grey lark sparrow, by the sun,
become one gold in a clear dawn.
And the sun gives equally to each
its own shadow, thus establishing
a model for justice, even to the blind
dog a shadow, even to the earth.

The sun touches us, but we can
never touch the body of the sun
with our hands (the way we like

to touch). I am strange about the sun,
how it is blood of my blood, how
it creates the daylight in my sleeping
dreams. Even in the deep night
inside my doubts, it is solely
by the moon's source of light
that I see.

IV

PEACE ALL SEASONS, EACH NIGHT

The husk-thin skull of a hummingbird
or little pocket mouse, light as a leaf
of dry cotton grass, weightless as an empty
milkweed pod, can be cradled nicely
in the crook of one finger. The purple-
spotted grey egg of a pipit, the pale
blue egg of a bunting, each can be nestled
comfortably in the hand of a child.
And a smooth cherry pit or a pearl
button or a pea-sized pebble
can be taken up and held lovingly
in the soft curl of a tongue.

But no one alone could ever encircle
the horned head-bone of a triceratops
with both arms and draw it to the breast
for solace or soothe the moon
out of its stiff-starch routine
into an easeful rest against the heart.
An Arctic wind in a rock canyon,
with its waves and whips of snowy
dust, might likewise be considered
so deprived.

Some speak of the sargasso sea
as a cradle, because, in its largess,
it sways and rocks and appears to enfold
and nurture spikes and claws, fins,

fronds, slug strings, fishes
like porcupines, fishes like pipes.

Realms without names are crossed
sometimes inside the boundaries
of this cradling privilege, as when
the closed eyes wake at once to dawn
and the soul transforms itself;
as when one slight shudder shifts
the body from pulse to passion;
as when cradler and cradled suddenly
change places, passing through
one another to merge to neither
momentarily during the changing.

I don't know which brings more faith—
to hold carefully the small blossom
of a new body and drip water like milk
from the fingertip like a nipple
into its funnels, or to dream of existing
as an open sea with ceaselessly disappearing
arms and laps of comforting currents,
or to anticipate being held in death,
as never held in life, in the crook
of a steady finger, or to imagine being
a pearl still tasting of salt, taken up
and rolled all night in the bed
of your tongue.

THE MAKING OF THE WORLD

First and second violins and violas
in steady crescendo make themselves
possible in straight brass seams
of early morning sun coming through
a welter of sumac and sassafras hedge.

The orange-scarlet of rose moss,
the iris of purple, the white garden
moth captured and pinned to the board
become in reality this minor treble
chord when played in arpeggio, the last
note held to stillness.

This chord in bass, whenever struck
thrice and ringing in all its tones,
means murder.

The sound of bagpipes, organ
pipes, panpipes, and wooden
whistles takes its form from the rush
of stone stalactites in multiple
spears across a cavern ceiling. No,
rather it is a thematic wind
through dry thistles, nettles,
thorny grass blades and sparrow
shafts that is the soul born
spontaneously with bagpipes, organ
pipes, panpipes and whistles of wood.

The flicking swaggle of the racing
Sonoran lizard, the swelter of horseshoe
crabs mating in a rampage of ocean

salt and semen are, within what they are,
the event of melody played rapidly
in counterpoint by masters
of guitar, oboe, and horn.

This comes closer: glass chimes
and one cymbal with soft brush
create the night sky quietly
restless with stars, just as
the still surface of a pond
restless in slow rain creates
glass chimes and one cymbal
with soft brush.

To simplify: you and I side
by side in bed on the blue–
checked quilt—place fingers
on these strings, hold bow
at this angle, draw easily.

———————

BORN OF A RIB

Genesis 2:21, 22

Maybe it was actually from the delicate
rib of a piñon mouse put to a deep
sleep just for this purpose in his bed
of shredded juniper bark, or from
the steadfast bone of a snoring boar,
that chest stave as tough and stone-
mandatory as one of his searing tusks.

Sometimes it seems the making
must have originated in the edifying
rib of a fern leaflet drowsy
before dawn, because the satiating
taste of its earth-subtle sap
still lingers in the mouth. Yet
there is evidence that the forming
came from the marrow blood of a blue
whale's rib, because the regular
thunder of his near heart remains
permanent and dictatorial in the sound
of time passing in its orbits.

There are moments when I could imagine
emerging, gyring and firmament-rounded,
made soaring by the hollow bone
of a broad-winged hawk in his element,
or being turned upside down, born
subterranean, sun-denying and recalcitrant
from the dormant rib of a brown bat
in his cave hibernation.

Everything might be different today,
we could agree, if the rib chosen
had been taken from the shell
of the somnolent rosy cockle,
so steadfastly sculpted, so smoothly
sea-polished, so stoically pure,
or if the insistent, violet rib
of the rainbow had been the one selected,
or if the false transparent rib
of the night's vaulted sleep had been
the one extracted for the purpose.

But in truth—remember—from whatever
spine of creature, plant, or sky-cage
the said material rib was stolen,
to that alone must belong forever
all the blessing, all the blame.

———————

VENERATION

What is it in the body that wants
to go on living, that heals the wound,
that knits the bone even while the I
is sleeping, that takes air to blood
unnoticed while the singer prays
for grace, while the thief darts in
and out pedestalled doorways,
while the player plucks the guitar,
while the reader deserts his own
to enter the book?

Not summoned, what is it in the body
that quickens by itself, goes sharp
and dimensional at near thunder, that lifts
and lightens in the presence of laughter
across a lawn, purple and rose lanterns
strung through trees at dusk?

Is it just an emptiness, like the motion
of an empty cape that undulates
and flutters at its edges as it flies,
like the emptiness inside the cape
of the midnight wind, inside the fluttering

shadow-cape of the manta ray flying
across the ocean floor? Maybe it's just
a nothingness, like the vision of lightning
to the blind—never known, only remembered.

But it stays a place. It genders
warmth. It contrives. It is as tangible
and exact as the *stone* of a stone idol,
as straight and alert as a ghost riding
a riderless stallion. It creates like sunlight
on water makes fire. It maintains
as if its message were entire in simply
making message possible.

What is it in the body that wants
to stay alive, that itself has no name
except *keeper*, except *vigilance*, except
above all, except *undeniable?*

V

THE FUNNIEST CLOWN

Guilty in truth, he was hung
from the gibbet at the crossroads,
dangling there where everyone passed.

His tongue turned purple, cracked
to brown, was swollen tight, before
the first crow came. Over and off
each hair, into the corners and slits
of his extremities, the slow morning
fog-rain ran.

Three weeks, his neckbone
was neckbone.

Sometimes in ice and snow
it seemed he was the sun himself
hanging in the sky circling himself,
burning orange at dusk and dawn.

Month after month, and a seed,
soft green, rose in spring,
sprouting from the broken top
of his pelted pate, in the very way
I once saw a seed showing a single
leaf growing in the upturned bowl
of an old turtle shell turned white
on the forest floor.

And his eyes grew daily also,
deeper and blacker and deeper
than the devil's bible at the passage
of midnight, the only moment
when the devil may possess
a verse in any matter.

There were times in winds
when we watched him wave,
graceless but personable, times
in stasis when we saw him stiffly
bowed to his own amen, and there were
occasions in mercies when his arms
spread wide and his great carcass
grinned in its rags, empty with welcome.
And we laughed and laughed.

Afterward

I caress the bony, bald forehead
of his skull, soothing, riveling
along its cracked boundaries,
and trace his eye pits, round
and round each rim, penetrating
the nether black of those two
bottomless bolt holes.

I gather together and spread
his fleshless finger-sticks, open
and shut them like the staves
of a fan. They click together

with a sound like ivory dice shaken
in a wooden cup. Occasionally I push
the teeth apart, widen the jaw
and look in and out the other
side, the mossy white vertebrae
of his craggy neck.

Once the moon was in his mouth
like an apple in the mouth
of a roasted pig. Once a moment
of moth settled in the space
for his tongue. Once the shadows
and suns of cedars and fronds
were ancestries shining from the spaces
of his head. Was it the scholastic
current of the stars I then thought
he held in his hands?

I lick up and down and up
his spine, cuddle him, cradle him
on my lap, his bare pelvis bowl
slipping. I turn his clatter over
and turn it back. I bend his knee
joints, let his foot bones dangle
like fish on a line. I grip the grate
of his empty ribs and raise the whole
contraption of his being clacking
and rattling in its own confusion.
Down it tangles, bobbing and guttering.
Remember, it is I alone who enter
through the staves of his hollow
framework, rub and beat steadily
where his heart once rumbled.

His reason is the only form
of my madness; for, heaven ever above,
he is measure and I am flow, he is
earth and I am sea.

PAGANINI, AND RUMOR AS GENESIS

For John Straley

It could simply have been as reported—
one man going town to town
carrying a hatbox containing the head
of his deceased wife. And thus
the rumors began.

Yet there might actually have been
many men seen in mountain cities
and in cities by the sea, on roads
between, each carrying a hatbox
containing any of several parts
of the deceased: warthog tusk,
deer hoof handle, spiralled pearl
shell of conch, fossil fin of a jawless
fish, moon rock on a silver chain.

Perhaps the rumor began inside
the engraved silver hatbox of the moon
containing many smaller silver hatboxes
inside other silver hatboxes, the last
and smallest pearl-sized, containing
a naked man standing in the sun, waiting

with ten silver dollars to buy the hat
of a moon for his bald head.

But I think the beginning
really began with one ordinary woman
carrying through town one ordinary
cardboard hatbox containing an average
straw hat, witnessed, however,
as she passed, by a bored, half-moon
visionary of rumors selling pearl
hatpins on the corner.

A holy man has begun a rumor
asserting that a single hatbox containing
the head of his deceased god is being
passed man to man, town to town,
like a rumor.

In one child's text the final rumor
of genesis begins thusly:

Chapter 1, Verse 1. God rides
disguised as tissue paper in a hatbox,
wrapped ever protective in gentle folds,
like a rose, round and round the velvets,
furs and moon-silver jewels, the bluebirds
and brass whistles, the crinkled foil
butterflies and berry-colored flowers
of a singularly fine chapeau.

Still, if the true beginning were a rumor
telling of a moon-pated man carrying
nothing but his own bible yet unwritten
on the stone skull of his god sealed

inside the perfect holy hatbox not yet
in existence, then there might be
space aplenty for the genesis
of rumors of any kind.

THE BLESSINGS OF ASHES AND DUST

Cuckoo birds and putterings of wrens
bathe in them, showering themselves
luxuriantly, making small riots
in dry ditches or old, black campfires.
Web-footed geckos and sidewinders are glad
to bury in their powders, and the back-flip
spider weaves them into her web
then pulls it over her body
to hide on the desert from her prey.

Not at all like water, air, icy smoke
or fog, they both, while still basic
and elemental, can yet be held easily
in the hands. And most pleasantly
obscure, unlike fossils of mammoths
or jawless fishes, dust and ashes
hardly resemble in the least
what they used to be.

So totally dead, there's no fear
of more death in either. They thus possess
a sublimity far beyond the frenetic
wolverine, the nervous, ever-vigilant,
meerkats, and they can maintain a lasting

serenity never hoped for by a bloom
of yellow meadow rue or a powdery
blue wing of prairie ringlet.

And ashes and dust are esteemed,
being cited in scripture (ashes
over the body for anguish, dust shaken
off the heels for scorn). They are called on
by name often in grief, sometimes even kept
in honored marble jars in locked and honored
places. They have been wept over
by most everyone from the beginning.

Surely dependable, these two never change
their natures suddenly to something else
radically different, as a pignut
hickory seed is known to do, and likewise
a white, breast-warmed phoebe egg
in its mossy nest.

In a world of shift, fall, mirage,
hallucination, swindle, and evil
trickery, this certainty must be
considered a blessing: pure ashes
and dust alone forever remain
thoroughly themselves, so ever
and ever and ever.

VI

THE COMPOSER, THE BONE YARD

Across my work yard the bones lie,
a rubble in crests and waves, piled
white, grooved brown, ocean to ocean—
dirt, ash, bevel, hovel. The rib staves
maintain their swell like breath held.
Fetal vestiges curl, dead in their dead
pelvis bowls, hard seeds stopped
in fossil blossoms, pearl stones
in cracked shells.

I dig and scrape, horizon
to horizon, unearth, unheaven,
fasten and hinge great saber tusks
and broken mandibles, tiny notches
smaller than dormouse fang,
titmouse toe. I latch and lock
together the fractured pieces—ball,
joint, hammer—sew and seam
with brass threads, fit pegs
into their corresponding jigsaw
hooks, count my knotted strings
and bands. I untangle, match,
mend, lathe the past-to-come
in this graveyard where I work.

Sometimes I think I feel the splintered
herds beginning to emerge whole
and in motion, the fallen flocks

to sound and wing. Perhaps I see
dry fish skeletons come weaving
out of rock to water. Resurrection
is my work and belief my resurrection.

The composing pattern of these bones
is the only world I possess, the myth
of my eye, the measure of my ear,
the defined day of the definition to be
when finally fully assembled I can rise,
shaking off dust and rain, roaring,
many-voiced, many-bodied, and raucous
with new hungers.

FOSSIL TEXTS ON CANYON WALLS

1. *Astrophysical Dynamics*

There are fables and legends written
right on my bones, on the red grain
of my bones, visible plots, subplots,
captures and escapes, as decipherable
as black ink fictions scribed
on rolled parchments.

And finely needled tattoos—inked
permanently in trumpet creepers,
jungle canopies, moon-webs of winter,
bellflowers of blood—compose the inner
bowl of my skull. Ancient missas
and pre-earth percussions are recorded

inside every knuckle, engraved on the turns
and curls of my ankles and wrists.

By the spine, I am epic, its staff
and sway. I am an oratorio
of skeleton, an ave of stance. I carry,
by body, the chamber concert of birth,
the well-worn recital of death.

It's possible then for me to sink also,
a myth of sun buried, and to rise again
on earth as a parable spoken in stone
on a canyon wall.

I could truly relent now,
as if I believed bone were rock and rock
light and all boldering stars were fossils
of canyon histories, as if I knew stellar
stories were simply constellations
of the body and living blood were symphony,
all motions intergalactic, interheart,
being just the same and as easy to negotiate
as the swing and pulse I might make
from one ringing refrain to the next.

2. *This State of Stone*

This canyon is the place for sleep,
the sleep of one watching himself
sleep, an immobile rock sleep filled
with the jumble of one's own stone
bones and the constant roaring of old
seas, a fossil tangle of sleep curled
and kept inside bright angel shale,

coconino sandstone, squeezed
among algal remnants, seed fern,
armored fish, worm burrows.

And this sleep is a familiar reading
of sleep, the descending and rising
layers of language, low violet and rose-
orange murmurs and striations, stratas
of predators and prey captured together,
the sleeping limestone cries and curses
of a million murders.

In this place one might sleep a wise
sleep, seeing with eyes opened by stone,
a sleep watching its own breaking
revelation, as looking in a mirror
one is suddenly broken in two.

If I falter, I must remember
that from this sleep engaged in the present
study of its own ancient sleeping,
one need never wake.

———————

VARIATIONS ON BREAKING THE FAITH OF SLEEP

1.
By murdering, as Macbeth, someone sleeping.

By rising from bed sleeping, moving forward,
still sleeping, with scissors in hand
to murder.

By cursing an old woman on a soiled
couch complaining in her sleep.

By abandoning a son as he sleeps
in his crib; by leaving a lover sleeping
naked and renewed after love.

While sleeping, to murder a father
over and over in dream.

By murdering the sleeping unborn.

2.
By not recognizing sleep as the earth–
white underside of a blue butterfly's
skyside wings.

By not recognizing sleep as the lift
of a white skeleton of leaf mistaken
for the white bones of a blue butterfly
blown over white beaches mistaken
for dunes of snow.

By failing to sleep with the serenity of snow
so as not to disturb the congregation
of white butterfly bones covering
the body, their crowded flocking
fluttering like breath at rest on thighs
and breasts, throughout the frozen
grasses of the hair.

3.
To wake from sleep not thanking
the moment unwinding itself like the scrolled
fire of the rosa rouletti, not thanking

the weather rising in the spreading
sail of the moment, not thanking
the gold ring balanced on a stick
and set spinning by the moment,
for the astonishment given.

To wake from sleep not blessing
the deep hood beneath the wing
of the winter goose, not blessing
the lock of the sea floor
on its blindness, not blessing
the first and last blackness
kept inside the seed inside the pod
of the wild yucca, for the sweet
sleep taken.

STONE BIRD

I remember you. You're the one
who lifted your ancient bones
of fossil rock, pulled yourself free
of the strata like a plaster figure
rising from its own mold, became
flesh and feather, took wing,
arrested the sky.

You're the one who, though marble,
floated as beautifully as a white
blossom on the pond all summer,
who, though skeletal and particled

like winter, glimmered as solid as a bird
of cut crystal in the icy trees.

You are redbird—sandstone
wings and agate eyes—at dusk.
You are greybird—polished granite
and pearl eyes—just before dawn,
midnight bird with a reflective
vacancy of heart like a mirror
of pure obsidian.

You're the one who flew down
to that river from the heavens,
as if your form alone were the only
holy message needed. You were alabaster
then in the noonday sun.

Once I saw you rise without rising
from your prison pedestal
in the garden beneath the lime tree.
At that moment your ghost
in its haunting permeated every
regality of the forest with light,
reigned with disdain in thin air
above the mountain, sank in union
with the crosswinds of the sea.

I remember you. You're the one
who entered in through my death
as if it were an open window
and you were the sound of the serenade
being sung outside for me, the words
of which, I know now, are of freedom
cast in stone forever.

VII

Disunion: Moonless Hound Monologue

The moonless hound in his night
rambles can only swallow the empty
rumble of the starving heavens,
can only take into the paltry shell
of his musing the pale and worthless
crumbs of the stars, can only steal
occasionally a grey and shriveled
fragment of light—lone leaf of forest
phosphorescence, luminarias of mushroom,
glow bug. The petty crimes he commits
are piteous in their fumbling
and shallow daring.

Surely he's still beautiful, wandering
beneath the distant gaping hole left
by the missing moon into which his sporadic
baying is inevitably sucked away to silence.
In this time, his moonless eyes, moving
randomly here and there, sometimes
turning backwards into his head,
are blind to all but the moonless.

He can only breathe in the weak
and floating evening webs of broken
constellations, can only lick the withered
black marrow from the night's skinny
ribs, can only read his own vague

intuition of possible scripture, a past
union, a past breach and break.

This landscape of lack exists within,
exactly like the reality shaping
his loping form. Even if the black
bowl of his hollow heart should crack
with sorrow at midnight, there could
never be any moonlight shining
from within to illuminate the unique
pattern of his grief.

In the consistency of his privation,
as he ceases his shambling to pause
inside the space of this absence,
as he reveals, by so being, everything
he cannot possess, I know and understand
his pining, for I am the lost and shattered
moon over which his missing shadow
once passed.

MILLENNIUM MAP OF THE UNIVERSE
(FROM THE NATIONAL GEOGRAPHIC SOCIETY)

It's a beautiful heaven, shining aqua
arrangements on black, scattered
chips of pure turquoise, gold, sterling
white, ruby sand, dimmer clouds
of glowing stellar dust, beads
like snow, like irregular pearls.

Last week, I thought this heaven was
god's body burning, as in the burning
bush never consumed, sudden flarings
of the omnipresence, the coal tips
of god's open hand, the brilliance of god's
streaming hair, the essence of grace
in flames, the idea of creation illuminated.
I believed each form of light and darkness
in that combustion was the glorious
art of god's body on fire, the only
possible origin of such art. Maybe god's
body remains invisible until it ignites
into its beginning. I could almost detect
the incense rising from such transfiguration.

But yesterday I believed it was music,
the circling and spiraling of sound
in a pattern of light, a design I might
begin to perceive, each note, each count
and measure of the concert-in-progress
being visible, constellations of chords,
geysers of scales, the bell-like lyricism
of overlapping revolutions and orbits, deep
silent pauses of vacancy, as we might
expect, among the swells and trills,
the cacophony of timpani, the zinking
of tight strings. Yesterday this seemed
a reasonable thought, a pleasing
thought. It seemed possible.

Today, I see it is just signal numbers,
static and spate: the sun, 25,000 light-
years from the center of "our galactic

realm" around which we travel once
every 200 million years, you understand.
I don't resist the calculated mass of "our
supercluster." I don't deny those 100
trillion suns of our suns among which
we pass, turning over and over day
after night after day. The last "outpost"
in our cluster, before a desert cosmic
void begins, is named Virgo. I stop there
for rest and provisions, to water the horses,
pour oats in their trough, to cradle my child.

I wish I could sing like electrons
on a wheel. I wish I could burn
like god.

THE STARS BENEATH MY FEET

Not the burrowing star-nosed
mole or the earth roots of the star
thistle or the yellow star flowers
of star grass, not the fallen webs
and empty egg sacs of star-bellied
spiders, not blood stars or winged
sea stars tight on their tidal rock
bottoms, and I don't mean either
the lighted star-tips of the lantern
fish and anglerfish drifting
miles deep at the ocean's end
of their forever good night.

I mean those actual stars filling
the skies directly below me with ignited
hubs and knotted assemblies combusting
into the waves of their own momentum,
the same stars in kind as the ones
above—gaseous blue clusters of clouds
expelling hot superstellars, fusing
galaxy upon galaxy of old histories
and reverberations. Those stars.

Were the earth made of glass,
any of us could look down now and see
them speeding away deeper into their vast
eras of math and glory existing immediately
beneath us where we stand suspended.

Even while marsh rains slowly
fill the hoofprints of passing
deer, even while flocks of lark
and longspur fly across the evening
with accordion motions of fracture
and union, even while you, fragranced
with sleep, draw me close or send me out,
stars and myriads of stars possess
their places, surrounding us as if
their facts bore us upward from below,
sheltered us in matrices of invisible
canopies above, as if they graced us
with a balance manifest in their far
numbers extending away equally
on our left and on our right.
They are the designated ancestors
of our eyes created in the lasting

moments of their own dead light.
They keep us on all sides bound safe
within their spheres and apart
from that great dire and naught
existing beyond the measurable
edges of their established dominions.

––––––––––

Just to Say It

All of those will stir and rise
from the night of the sea floor,
gather themselves to the surface
and breathe, sun in the sun once more,
stretched and dozing on placid beaches.

Others will move backward,
drawing themselves up out
of their own dispersed smoke
and cold ashes to stand entire.

Those wasted and vanished
will rouse to bread, fruit and chocolate,
cheese and eggs, jugs of cider,
pitchers of cream, drink and feast
without hurry, satiated.

Far sleeping infants will wake
in the laps of their living
mothers, wrap up in their lost
and disintegrated, loved blankets,
lullabied, found and made whole.

Song of the World Becoming

Deep field dust will congeal
to many who will remember
and speak again their several
names. Coal bog and granite
strata will open their eyes and see.
Mountaintop and chasm fossils
will mend their broken facets,
sail their fins and winds, stitch
and bind and contrive. Ice
skeletons will turn to viable
bone and stone become blood,
and all those uncounted
will be distinguished, all those
unheard will be attended,
all those disassembled will be
coherent, and this is true
and it will be.

VIII

The Known Unknown

Some unknowns we can identify—
the untraversed knife-rare ravines
and gorges, the unmapped inner-salt
canyons of an iceberg mountain extending
downward beneath the brief blue spear
of its crag visible above the polar sea.

There are unnamed species
of rainforest beetles undiscovered,
and, though I myself have never seen them
and therefore cannot truthfully
be said to know them, I believe
in the cosmos of roots composing
subterranean forests of aspen
and pine beneath the forest
where I walk.

None of us will ever know
how a crystal of honeysuckle honey
feels on the tongue of the digger bee.
We will never collect the flowers
of the field daylilies mowed under
in their buds, nor realize any god
whose divinity is left unproclaimed.

There is something a little rapturous
in contemplating the unheard portion
of the phoebe's call, the portion

that might exist beyond this evening's
call were the phoebe to push a measure
further into another realm of itself.
And despite always remaining unknown,
it might be pleasurable to imagine
the sound of Plato's voice, the touch
of Mary's hand, or how it might be
to kiss the blind eyes of Homer, the living
lips of Arthur the King.

The unknown yet known also is vast,
residing from the beginning in the acumen
of the fingertips, the discernment
of the eye, inherent to the unspoken
canon of careful footsteps.

Yet, though I worship it, this
is most fearful to me, being nothing
more than the look of its letters,
the sound of its words: the unknown
unknown.

The Form of That Which Is Sought

It could fill and take the shape
of the multiple spaces in the pauses
and sliding shrills of a coyote's
long yodel, or it might match
in measure the pieces of the jagged
sky crossed once and split twice
by the screeching tin bells

of two green hummingbirds fighting
in flight. Perhaps, standing alone
in a field of winter grasses,
my back to the gorged and robust
moon, it assumes the configuration
of all the vacancies not silver-
white with light.

Maybe its structure is like the quick
erratic descent and collapse
of the licks of black that allow
the leaping of flames at night,
or maybe it is the shape fitting
exactly the circle sizes created
inside the atom by its theory.
Its form might be the one difference
between the plump red–gold pulp
of a nectarine and the hard wrinkle
of the pit of its living heart,
or it might possess the form
of the one similarity held in common
by a grey-speckled longhorn grazing
in rain and a splintered crack
spreading in the glass of an Arctic
iceberg and the final lingering
chord of a requiem mass.

If it could just be put in the mouth,
then one might know it by the tongue,
feeling all the edges and folds,
the dimensions and horizons
of the shuddering bittersweet shape
of its word. Or, how about this:

it is like love in total darkness,
its form moment by moment becoming itself
and tangible through the gentleness
and finesse upon which the blind
will always depend.

SELF-RECOGNITION OF THE OBSERVER AS MOMENTARY CESSATION OF PROCESS

1.
Surrounded by great thunder-floods
and rending storms, a small face,
wrinkled as a peach pit, is seen
for an instant in the sky, wild hair
and bountiful beard the whipping
manes of rainclouds and winds.
A split-second reflection of stillness
and pause, it disappears at once
into the wide tangle of the fracas
covering the heavens.

2.
Within the family portrait, a circle
of painted mirror above the mantle
reveals the artist at work both within
and beyond the frame and reveals
as well the window behind the artist,
outside which paned glass a moon
cat with round yellow mirrors
for eyes sits looking back through
the moment when we first perceive

the center and the score
of the before and the after.

3.
From a train traveling
through a midnight countryside,
one might glimpse on a distant
hill a hut, scarcely detectable
in its passing speed. Inside,
a tailor, by lantern-light
at his machine, bends over a single
stitch, then vanishes into the unseen
needle and wheel of the proceeding
history of his work.

4.
A cliff swallow soaring above the river
stops mid-sky, not hovering, but ceasing
all movement—negative-beat, negative-
breath—a bird-conjunction of the recognized
everywhere, before descending again
into the rage and vacuum of the rock
canyon below.

ARCHETYPE

I do not move through time. I move
through rain. When rain falls
straight down on mossy brick walks
or the bodies of lounging seals
or continuously at a slant into the rush

of gorges or the open mouths of desert
birds, that isn't at all the way time
moves, is it? Rain is not time,
and I know it is rain I move within.

Or snow, as one in its infusion,
even at midair, is more an ever-present
covering of sky and land than a future
or a passing. Walking through this frozen
ruggled weave of white, it's obvious
I live in forest snow, not time.

Time can't happen all at once
in random multidimensional features
like the swirling rise and shifting,
overlaying orbits of wing bones and cries
that happen when the egrets leave
their lakeside roost. My place
has always been the surrounding sounds
of wetland peepers and crows, the silence
of sun-sprung pods and buds among tree
lattices and their shadows crossing
themselves, departing and doubling back.
This is nothing like the strictly
linear place of time.

Wind can come from all directions,
simultaneously down from invisible
black portals and tunnels in the night
and dark and up from caverns of cool
earth, bringing with it wet rock
fragrances, sullen bat and moth mold
and must. Wind has no marked beginning,

no signal ending. It can be slashed
by switchgrasses and spurge nettles
into a million slits and figments
that have no specific designations,
as moments and seconds and instants do.
The south wind newly warm once came
round and round through my hair, cupped
my face, lifted my blouse, and left.
Time has never been so charmingly
caressive. And I say it is the realm
of wind without time where I exist.

Poor hopeless fool.

IX

VERGES

The line of the great blue heron's wing
in flight glides at the very seam
between a soaring angel's blue clavicle
and the blue bottomless canyon of the sky.
And the margin of each balancing leaf
of the bur oak almost gives way too,
falling into the disappearance
of the summer morning, teetering
on the vanishing curve of itself.

The gathering webs inside the warbler's
egg are shaking on the precipice
of breath, wavering on the threshold
of dust.

With pink riffled umbrella
in one hand, the clown in shiny leotards
steps each rope step slowly before the other,
genius toe against heel against foolish
toe, almost plunging, almost lifting.
His one wit is desperate for the hold
and ladder at the end, his one prayer mad
with passion for the fall mid-way.

Never quite possessing ecstasy, never
fully possessed by peace—by now I should know
vertigo. I should be relaxed with dizziness,
at ease with reeling, skilled along narrow

borders and the steep peripheries
of breaking walls. I have an intimacy
with the claws and desperations of bristlecones,
old saviors, old spoilers, not exactly rock,
not precisely wave, rimming on crumbling
cliff paths above a sea gorge.

My mouth around the fruit, my teeth
pressed against its tight skin
not yet broken—its fragrance is a yearning,
its swelling sugar wine still a wish
just beyond the tongue. What is the name
for this: on the verge of redemption?
on the brink of loss?

Once Upon a Time, When I Was Almost Dead with Fear and Doubt

I cavorted with my harp. I recovered her
first from the closet, dusted and polished
the curves and flowers of her finely
molded architecture, tuned and tightened
her most subtle nuances. I twirled her
gracefully round and round on her one toe,
bending her toward the ground until
we almost kissed and then raising her again
in a swirl, as if from the dead, plucking
her many little tones all the while.

Me in my patent leather slippers,
she in fake furs and feathers wrapped

about her slender neck, I danced her
out across the flat grey surface
of the sea, farther and farther, never
looking down, as one is advised,
keeping my eyes steadily on the narrow
rim of distant earth beyond. I nearly
swooned, strumming and strumming
her many little teases and woebegones
in time to the waves. Such whispers,
such rocking hushes and sighs.

Landing on the opposite shore,
we had our picture made, she nestling
on my breast, me aglow, my arms
around her golden body. She hummed,
off and on, little snatches of senseless
tunes, engaging various keys and octaves
with the winds on the cliffs above that sea-
side village. Together all the moonless night,
I held her up to the heavens. I brought
her close. I sang to her, plinking
the many little silver scales and stars
I saw shining between the strings
of her soul. She was a-shimmer,
a perfect trembling array. I listened.

And with the morning, in short,
I returned recovered, stashed her away
again in the same closet where I keep
the painted, wooden horse on wheels,
the paper kite with yellow wings,
my mask of the moon, the top that spins
and wobbles and falls and spins.

ALMANAC

When Jesus the Christ was born,
it was the anniversary of the day
the last living dinosaur crumpled,
fell to the ground like a giant
sequoia, died in its bones,
and ceased.

On the day Jesus the Messiah
was born, the grand river-sea,
Rio Amazonas, nearly white, as usual,
with light-reflecting particles
of suspended clay, flowed along
steadily toward its confluence
with the Rio Negro.

The crater rocks lay
just as we see them tonight
on the moonlight side of the moon,
when the King of Kings first
came to be. But the Leonid shower
of two hundred thousand meteors
was traveling still centuries
from earth, and Krakatau loomed
serene, benign, without murder,
in the southern sea.

At the same hour the infant Jesus
of Nazareth first drew breath,
Great China went forth in imperial
parade and regalia, a wagon of bronze
chimes rolling and ringing like sun

on a river in full morning, and a lone
zither, played in the countryside,
was tapped by the left finger
of the solitary musician, and so sounded
"the echo of an empty valley."

On the night of the day the Savior
was born, a mother Marie, her first infant
daughter stillborn, died alone in childbirth
in a dark stable on the other side
of another realm of another plane.

On the day of the first Christmas,
sea elephant cows lolled in fat harems
among snorting bulls guarding
their western sandy beaches, and cannibals
blessed and ate in the land of tinkerbirds,
pottos, bush pigs, and drongos, and a caracal
on the desert carefully licked clean
the crevices of each of her bloody claws,
and unnamed winds ravaged the rock-
ice pinnacles of the Himalayas,

and the presentiment of illusory union
moves closer and moves farther away
and passes through from the center onward.

SONG OF THE OCEANS OF THE WORLD BECOMING

The song of the oceans
of the world becoming is always
among us. It rises over and over
from the oceans of the grasslands,
rippling like shifting waves of orange
autumn sorrel, green May barley.
It ascends in immediacy
from the oceans of the forest floor,
spreads through a flotsam of mosses,
ferns, vine maple, pine accretions;
thus it is permeated by branches,
staubs, leaves, thorny seeds, shingled
bark, which become, in truth,
the momentary architecture
of its carriage and meter.

Smelling slightly of salt, wet weed,
and sea sand, down comes this song
again and again like a tidal blue
surf of the skies, down from the floating
black depth of the stars. It swirls
like channeled winds flooding rock
caverns, like lolling swells of winter
in a whiteout. It engulfs with daylight,
spilling around and throughout
a solar deluge of summer.

The song of the world becoming
in its expanse and bottomless height
can nonetheless gather wholly
into one molecule on the tip of one

tentacle of an anemone attached
to the rim of a low-tide rock,
and briefly balance there. It is complete
and prophetic in a gesture of light
off the neon needle of a damselfly
vanishing and reappearing above
warm mud and water rushes.

The song of the oceans of migrating
caribou, flocking bats, goldfinches,
of swarming honey bees, swarming
suns and stellar dusts, travels
beautifully with all the masses
of its expanding cosmic horizons.
Present in circular motions to the outer
edges of the known universe evolving,
it is ancient, it is partial.

So the song is becoming as the world
becomes, and it can never leave us;
for we are the notice in its passages,
and we are the divining in its composition,
and we practice in death the immortality
of its nature forever.

X

Watching the Ancestral Prayers
of Venerable Others

Lena Higgins, 92, breastless,
blind, chewing her gums by the window,
is old, but the Great Comet of 1843

is much older than that. Dry land
tortoises with their elephantine
feet are often very old, but giant

sequoias of the western Sierras
are generations older than that.
The first prayer rattle, made

on the savannah of seeds and bones
strung together, is old, but the first
winged cockroach to appear on earth

is hundreds of millions of years
older than that. A flowering plant
fossil or a mollusk fossil in limy

shale is old. Stony meteorites buried
beneath polar ice are older than that,
and death itself is very, very

ancient, but life is certainly older
than death. Shadows and silhouettes
created by primordial sea storms

erupting in crests high above
one another occurred eons ago,
but the sun and its flaring eruptions

existed long before they did. Light
from the most distant known quasar
seen at this moment tonight is old

(should light be said to exist
in time), but the moment witnessed
just previous is older than that.

The compact, pea-drop power
of the initial, beginning nothing
is surely oldest, but then the intention,

with its integrity, must have come
before and thus is obviously
older than that. Amen.

BEFORE THE BEGINNING: MAYBE GOD AND A SILK FLOWER CONCUBINE PERHAPS

The white sky is exactly the same white
stone as the white marble of the transparent
earth, and the moon with its clear white
swallow makes of its belly of rock neither
absence nor presence.

The stars are not syllables yet enunciated
by his potential white tongue, its vestigial
lick a line that might break eventually,

a horizon curving enough to pronounce
at last, my love.

The locked and frigid porcelain barrens
and hollows of the descending black plain
are a pattern of gardens only to any single
blind eye blinking, just as a possible stroke
of worm, deaf with whiteness, might hear
a lace bud of silk meridians spinning
and unraveling simultaneously on the vacuous
beds of the placeless firmament.

An atheist might believe in the seductive
motion turning beneath the transparent gown
covering invisibly the nonexistent bones
and petals of no other. Thus the holy blossom,
spread like the snow impression of a missing
angel, doubts the deep-looped vacancy
of her own being into which god, in creation,
must assuredly come.

Is it possible there might be silver seeds
placed deep between those legs opening
like a parting of fog to reveal the plunging salt
of a frothy sea? But god digresses, dreaming
himself a ghost, with neither clamor nor ecstasy,
into inertia, his name being farther
than ever from time.

Static on the unendurably boring white
sheet of his own plane, he must think hard
toward that focus of conception when he can rise
shuddering, descending and erupting into the beauty

and fragrance of their own making together—
those flowering orange-scarlet layers and sun-
shocking blue heavens of, suddenly, one another.

———————

IN ORDER TO BE

Some, like the netted roots of water
willows with their sessile leaves,
sink down deliberately for mud-soil,
spread and waver up for day. Others,
like seed shrimps, scavenge, feeling
and sucking along the oily leaf muck
of pond bottoms. Still others, like lug
worms and gem anemones, wait,
stationary, securing particles, crusts
and crumbles of sea bread washed
and currented among them.

There is this way as well: a fur-fondle
of rodent, detected below the wild
celery and frogbit, is targeted, snatched
and taloned up; and this way: a flint-
sparking spectacle of gills and scales
is beaked below water, lifted twisting
to the sky, gulleted down whole.

By each of these means, being declares
and declares itself, and also by plucking
and mulling the nectar and pulp of berry
and peach, by winding sugary green
stems around the tongue, by searching,

slooping, licking the syrup from hollow
honey trees, by plunging nose first
into the sun-sap of lily billows.

Maybe god too, with the same skills,
the same need, stalks, pounces,
swallows whole the silver-sun
curves and chords of praise on winter
mornings; brings down in thrashings
through fathoms of evening all bounding
and leaping incantations and *Glorias;*
craves, savors, tongues, licks deep
inside the waxes and combs of every
nectared prayer and swelling *Hosanna;*
pursues and gathers in all flurries
and rookeries of crying anthems
on the wing; requires each, secures each,
feeds clear to the core, and thus becomes
and thus avows and thus proclaims.

———————

THE BACKGROUND BEYOND THE BACKGROUND

On an autumn afternoon, perhaps selecting
apples from a crate or examining pickled beets
and onions in a jar, or watching two honeybees
at one red clover, we stand unaware
before a background of behest and sanctity.

Or floating down a river through elm
and cottonwood shadows, past sandbar
willows and lines of turtles on sunning logs,

over underwater thickets, bottom beds
of leaf roughage and mud, we are, all the while,
made finely distinct upon a more distant
background of singularity.

Anywhere we turn, this background
stays, a domain for mortal and immortal,
for crystal grids, for shifting furls of smoke,
for structure and fallibility, for each nexus
of sword and cross.

Atop a barn roof, a glossy green-tailed
rooster with auburn feathers lifts his wings
against a backdrop of dawn. Is it the passing
moment of occupied event or the passing fact
of barnyard morning that creates the impression
of presence before this silk of elusive
light behind light?

Like a clear horizon at the edge of a wide
field, the background beyond the background
of sky reveals most explicitly the figures
of those that come before it—elephant
or ostrich or seed-heavy grasses, saint,
sow, runt or sire, summer lightning,
blowing ice. It achieves us all.

Far, far beyond those far mountains of stone
and cavern against which I am outlined now
there is another background—translucent,
stolid, eloquent, still.

THE EXPECTATIONS OF LIGHT (1981)

I

IN ORDER TO PERCEIVE

At first you see nothing. The experience is similar
To opening your eyes wide as white marbles
Inside the deepest cave, beneath tons of limestone,
Or being awake in a dark room, your head
Under a heavy blanket.

Then someone suggests there is a single candle
Wavering far off in one corner, flickering red.
You think you see it
As someone else draws your attention to the sharp
Beaming wing tips, the white end of the beak,
The obvious three points of the wild goose overhead
And the seven-starred poinsettia to the west, the bright
Cluster at its belly.

You are able to recognize, when you are shown,
The sparks flying from the mane of the black stallion,
The lightning of his hooves as he rears,
And in the background a thick forest spreading
To the east, each leaf a distinct pinprick of light.

Then you begin to notice things for yourself,
A line of torches curving along a black valley,
A sparkling flower, no bigger than a snowflake,
Shining by itself in the northwest coordinate.
It is you who discovers the particular flash
Of each tooth inside the bear's open mouth and the miners
With their lighted helmets rising in a row.

How clear and explicit, you tell someone with confidence,
That ship, each separate gleaming line of its rigging,
The glowing dots of the oars, the radiating
Eyes of the figure on the prow, the corners
Of each sail lit.

Soon there is no hesitation to the breadth
Of your discoveries. Until one night during the long
Intensity of your observation, you look so perfectly
That you finally see yourself, off in the distance
Among the glittering hounds and hunters, beside the white
Shadows of the swans. There are points of fire
At your fingertips, a brilliance at the junctures
Of your bones. You watch yourself floating,
Your heels in their orbits, your hair spreading
Like a phosphorescent cloud, as you rise slowly,
A skeleton of glass beads, above the black desert,
Over the lanterned hillsides and on out through the hollow
Stretching directly overhead.

CONTAINMENT

Across the surface of the egg, couched
In the marsh weeds, a fragile
Break appears, releasing
Light for the first time.

Hung in the top of the still sycamore,
The cradle has no name
Until the wind and the sky against which it functions
Allow it to become itself.

The moon, completely full
And self-contained, is held in its place
By the black circular muscle of the night
And by that power alone.

Cracked from its base
To the break at the top of its head,
The cradle no longer depends
On the containment of the sky.
The egg, by holding night tightly
In one place long enough, has allowed
It to assume a different name.
Strung up in the sycamore, the moon
Is completely broken, the pieces
Of its shell having spilled its shadow
For the first time.

––––––––––

DWARF

There is a dwarf in my ancestry.
He gleams from behind my grandmother's stories,
Peeping through the shadowy legs of a grandfather's uncle.
Crouching beside potted palms in the parlor,
Eyes gauging above fanned fronds,
He is a toadish coquette.
He stares,
A lizard who has seen us first,
Steadily.
A statue with eyes assaying,
His vertical pupils shine against grey stone.

Abashed adult with no stature,
He hurries with a twisted gait,
Clicking on nights when love is quiet,
Popping up, a clown out of a coffin,
Putting hesitancy in the laughing chatter
Of maternal blood,
Poking his tilted head around the lattices
Of prospective marriages.
He giggles within the blurred faces
Of my unborn children,
In the restive fears of my own beginning.

He is
The one thing common to all my aunts.

OLD WOMEN

I live with old women,
Grandaunts, maternal great cousins,
Aged mothers of my mother.
They crowd to my house,
Still in their skirts,
Spectacled and black creped,
Mumbling to their hands.
Their white hair is as thin and dry as desert grass.
The loose skin on their upper arms
Hangs like a pale silk purse.
Their milk-blue eyes were once brown.

Sitting with me at dinner,
Wizened old leather sticks,

They eat with deliberation,
Jutting their lower lips to catch their spoons,
Dripping tea on their bosoms.
They study the tilt of a fork,
The glint of the butter on peas.

Always before me, moving down hallways,
They inch out of doorways into my path,
Shuffling with legs bent like weak candles,
So slow the room at the end is a strange city.
There is no way around.

In our chairs at night,
I watch them nodding, snoring the gurgle of the old,
Jaws open on their chests.
They jerk awake and wonder who I am.

One by one they bring their deaths—
The spasms and failures,
The slow drowning of lying prone,
The plug of phlegm corked in the throat,
The string pulled too tightly
Down the left side of the cranium,
Drawing the wrist, wedding band and all,
To the chest permanently.

My hands are on their elbows.
I have watched all their steps.

Second-Story Ballroom

Think how the soldiers took down every mirror
In the second-story ballroom, how they left
The bare walls standing as if they had their hands
Between their knees. Think how they carried
Those plates of glass down the stairs,
The heavy gilt frames holding candles
In gold roses half-opened. They took them
To the forest behind the house,
Propped them against the trees and began
Their target practice. Every shot hitting
Right between the eyes meant the forehead cracked
Open perfectly with a blinding light, fell apart
In slivers of silver jangling like bells
Against the earth.

Think then of all the dancers dancing
Past the darkened windows of the second-story ballroom.
Picture their dusty satins, their shadowy brocades.
Listen to the hush and swish of their movements
Down the length of the hall,
Across the blank corridors, round
And round back again.

The Reincarnated

Before our common ancestor knew itself,
It was many things. For one millennium it washed
Back and forth on the bottom of the sea. The bowling
Of the surf, it rolled lathers of sand ahead of it

And caught the green jelly of tiny creatures in its girth.
It sang salt and never kept its brow dry.

Between the time of redwoods and the peaks
Of the Kofa Range, it was mist on the desert.
It clung to the backs of beetles swung to windward
Of the dunes. It dipped down stems of dead weeds
To mouse pits and snake caverns, to live roots waiting.
It drifted in drops and became moisture seeping
To every crack in the sand.

Before our ancestor recognized itself, it was the quiet
Of the gorge rising slowly in pale blue smoke.
It surrounded and shaped itself to everything
It passed—leaf fungus, butt of rock, fur jackal.
Inside of us today is a hollow space left
For the wide bird holding in white above the firs.

Our ancestor has been polar ice and the camel's nostril,
The dorsal fin of transparent fish. Like the flying fox
And the porpoise, it has moved in darkness by sound alone.
It has lived in mold underground with every one of its fingers
Cut off. It has come back each time, adding to itself,
Recalling everything it has been before.

Shatter of primal moss, remnant of lizard hair, clay
Hooves and extinct thumbprints;
Reader, try hard to remember.

SUPPOSE YOUR FATHER WAS A REDBIRD

Suppose his body was the meticulous layering
Of graduated down which you studied early,
Rows of feathers increasing in size to the hard-splayed
Wine-gloss tips of his outer edges.

Suppose, before you could speak, you watched
The slow spread of his wing over and over,
The appearance of that invisible appendage,
The unfolding transformation of his body to the airborne.
And you followed his departure again and again,
Learning to distinguish the red microbe of his being
Far into the line of the horizon.

Then today you might be the only one able to see
The breast of a single red bloom
Five miles away across an open field.
The modification of your eye might have enabled you
To spot a red moth hanging on an oak branch
In the exact center of the Aurorean Forest.
And you could define for us, "hearing red in the air,"
As you predict the day pollen from the poppy
Will blow in from the valley.

Naturally you would picture your faith arranged
In filamented principles moving from pink
To crimson at the final quill. And the red tremble
Of your dream you might explain as the shimmer
Of his back lost over the sea at dawn.
Your sudden visions you might interpret as the uncreasing
Of heaven, the bones of the sky spread,
The conceptualized wing of the mind untangling.

Imagine the intensity of your revelation
The night the entire body of a star turns red
And you watch it as it rushes in flames
Across the black, down into the hills.

If your father was a redbird,
Then you would be obligated to try to understand
What it is you recognize in the sun
As you study it again this evening
Pulling itself and the sky in dark red
Over the edge of the earth.

WITHOUT VIOLENCE

That cat who comes during sleep, quiet
On his cushioned claws, without violence,
Who enters the house with a low warm rattle
In his throat; that cat who has been said
To crawl into a baby's crib without brushing
The bars, to knit his paws on the pale
Flannel of the infant's nightdress, to settle
In sleep chin to chin with the dear one
And softly steal the child's breath
Without malice, as easily as pulling
A silk scarf completely through a gold ring;

The same cat who has been known to nudge
Through castle doors, to part tent flaps,
To creep to the breasts of brave men,
Ease between their blankets, to stretch
Full length on the satin bodices of lovely

Women, to nuzzle their cheeks with his great
Feline mane; it was that cat who leaped last night
Through the west window of father's bedroom.
Who chose to knead his night's rest on my father's
Shoulder, who slept well, breathing deeply,
Leaving just before dawn to saunter toward
The north, his magnificent tail and rump
Swaying with a listless and gorgeous grace.

COMING OF AGE

It begins with the bones.
They must be light, delicate
As tea leaves, intricate as white wires
Glowing like glass threads,
A structure of thin hollow shells showing
The moon on full nights with no shadow.

Barely covered with pale silver skin,
They must extend from the shoulder blades
To points far beyond the furthest extension
Of the middle finger stretched outward. Tipping
And angular, free of movement,
They will develop muscles in time.

Remaining weightless as frost,
Unfractured, they must be covered completely
With silk sorrels and strings, as easy to the breeze
As tassels on a willow, fine as cobweb,
Layered like the first fronds
Of the lattice fern uncurling.

Almost invisible then, one night, without sound,
Without touching anyone, they will remember
How to rise, how to open wide like two tall gates
Swinging apart, how to lift up, taking into themselves
More hollow stars, more thick knots of space
Than they can ever encompass.

———————

FOR STEPHEN DRAWING BIRDS

They catch your eye early, those rising black
Out of the water oaks at dusk or those skimming
The grey lakes at dawn. You know you must learn
Them by name, calling the redstart, pointing out
The towhee, the slate-colored junco. You begin
To trace their drummings through the forest, the click
Of their matings in the rocks, and grow accustomed
To waiting, sketchbook in hand, for the mottled
Vireo to nurse at the fruit tree, the woodcock to rise
To the spring willow bait. You are patient
With the snow goose appearing at the bottom of the reeds
And the thrasher untangling itself from the hedgerow.
What luck, the day you find a whole cliff of gannets,
Their pale yellow heads as smooth as eggs, their eyelids
And nostrils distinctly blue.

Matching pencil to feather, you begin to take them
One by one—the marbled owl pulling at the skull
Of the lemming, the dusky tanager in the afternoon
Snipping at dragonflies. How well you execute
Their postures, the wings of the overland dove spread

Like a Japanese fan, the jackdaw frozen
At the moment of his descent into the locust.

It grows easier and easier. Soon the cedar shrike stops
On his own and waits for you, gripped to the fence post.
The grosbeak rests all day on the limb by your page,
And when you picture the rare azure-throated swallow,
He suddenly materializes under the eaves, preparing
His mudball. In the evening before the fire,
As you remember the *Réunion* solitaire, the giant auk,
They appear in the room, roosting on the ginger jars
Above the mantelpiece. You even wake one morning
To discover that the lark bunting has been nesting
Under your knuckles just as you dreamed he was.
There is a definite stir of preening among your papers.

Tonight, a strange chukal hen has flown to the cornice
Above your window. The invisible grey-green thimble bird
Is slowly coming into sight by your glass, and perched
On the bedpost, an unmarked polar hawk is watching
With his stern golden eye over the entire length of your quilt.

STRUCK SEVEN TIMES

He knows them all—ball lightning twice,
One dancing a full minute over his desk;
Two years later, the forked straddling the lawn
From his shoulder to the gate. In August of '65
The beaded bounced across the field like a stone
Over water, right into the window from which he watched.
Knocked out for three days, he was blind
For a month. He has been gripped since by the ribbon,

The streaked, the relative of St. Elmo's fire.

He grows weak now at the sight of melted lead, ill
At the odor of singed meat. He can't remember
The meaning of "accident." Jesus, in the morning
He believes in the finger of God, at night
In the rapier of Baal. He retraces his thoughts
Prior to each encounter, looking for clues. He studies
The similarities of sins current at the time,
The direction of his feet, the inclination of his head.
Who knows what might be attracted by the power
Of certain wishes?

Working nightly, he discovers that the sum of the dates
Of his confrontations equals his age times
The possible year of his death. Gradually he develops
An affinity for weather balloons. He blesses cats.
Lightning rods become a fetish, the spiraled,
The spiked, the pre–Civil War. He begins to fantasize
On the evolution of their designs.

He learns to make friends with electro-physicists,
Drawn to the terminology of ampere upheaval, stroke
Currents. He wills his body to the Franklin Institute
For the Study of Magnetic Disturbances in Human Form,
Becomes convinced that the chemical make-up of his blood
Is the inverse replica of cumulous vapor. He almost soars
Being bound in the rhetoric of blinding discharges,
The shock of flashing impacts recalled.
Even his dreams are totally dominated by Kansas,
Thunderheads, the third-story turret of an isolated farm.

It's his own fault now. His entire future
Depends on the eighth.

WATCHING DREAMS

From the case notes of Adelaide Monroe, author of The Intrigues of the Unconscious

What happens when you begin your journal,
Keeping it on the table by the bed, each dream
Immediately transferred to the page?
The dream-mind, aware of being studied, never forgets
The pencil and pad in the shadow to the far left.
Pleased at its reception, for instance, it might be encouraged
To repeat the mastiff of last week, enlarging
Its feet, chaining it for diversion to the cellar door.
And the frogs lining the road you walked in your dream
Last night must be embellished by the scrutiny
They receive this morning.

Suppose a dream, causing its own termination,
Wakes you at 3:12 A.M., and you record the room
In which you were anxiously selecting clothing
With your mother. You describe the nature and color
Of the garments, the depth of the closet, but forget
To mention the sense of thunder outside,
Which was crucial. This faulty account must influence
Subsequent dreams.

Assured of an attentive audience, the dream
Might be tempted to play tricks, might be capable
Of wit. Suppose the dream is subtle enough
To portray itself being watched. The dream becomes
The flower in the dream, alone in a mowed field
Meticulously fondled. The dream becomes the dead father
In the dream to whom one looks for signs.
Suppose the dream, aware of the hidden observer, learns

To say what it knows the dreamer wishes to hear—
"This is God speaking."The conscious mind
Can claim innocence.

Watching the journal with its one eye,
The dream knows its own inventiveness
And never forgets who it is it entertains.

———————

THE CARETAKERS

They prepare the way for morning. Naked
And completely grey, they sweep
The walks using brooms without bristles.
For them alone, all the dust of the desert
Lies down in one silk face flat beneath the moon.

They carry eggs like candles cupped in their hands
From one nest to another.They untangle the fur
Of the willow, straighten the necks of flowers,
Suck the honey of their stamens, the horns
Of their groins upward. How their tongues
Influence the funnels of leaves.

Searching among jack mice and tree tarsiers, fish
And marmosets, they pinch shut the eyes
Of those who have died without warning and pull
Shadows to cover the clearing where the sexton beetle
Works.They thrum on hollow trunks as if their fingers
Had no joints.

Watching over the bodies of those sleeping
Like stones in a field, they tuck at their toes,

Measure their breathing with their own glass eyes,
Push the cold bowl of pain under the bed.

They are the ones who whisper over metal accidents
Refined definitions of failure.

Near the end, their arms begin to stretch
Twice as long as their bodies upward. Their faces lengthen
With the twist of peeled cypress until the cups
Of their cheekbones glow and their mouths become split
Ovals among the trees disappearing without a sound
Into the overall sky exactly their color.

THE RITES OF PASSAGE

The inner cell of each frog egg laid today
In these still open waters is surrounded
By melanin pigment, by a jelly capsule
Acting as cushion to the falling of the surf,
As buffer to the loud crow-calling
Coming from the cleared forests to the north.

At 77 degrees the single cell cleaves in 90 minutes,
Then cleaves again and in five hours forms the hollow
Ball of the blastula. In the dark, 18 hours later,
Even as a shuffle in the grass moves the shadows
On the shore and the stripes of the moon on the sand
Disappear and the sounds of the heron jerk
Across the lake, the growing blastula turns itself
Inside out unassisted and becomes a gut.

What is the source of the tension instigating next
The rudimentary tail and gills, the cobweb of veins?

92

What is the impetus slowly directing the hard-core
Current right up the scale to that one definite moment
When a fold of cells quivers suddenly for the first time
And someone says loudly "heart," born, beating steadily,
Bearing now in the white water of the moon
The instantaneous distinction of being liable to death?

Above me, the full moon, round and floating deep
In its capsule of sky, never trembles.
In ten thousand years it will never involute
Its white frozen blastula to form a gut,
Will never by a heart be called born.

Think of that part of me wishing tonight to remember
The split-second edge before the beginning,
To remember by a sudden white involution of sight,
By a vision of tension folding itself
Inside clear open waters, by imitating a manipulation
Of cells in a moment of distinction, wishing to remember
The entire language made during that crossing.

II

How to Stay Safe in the City

It is best to make this rule:
Keep your door of hard hickory barred,
No exceptions.

If you should hear the bell sound twice,
Go to the keyhole and listen. Heavy breathing
Means two or more people taller than you
Are waiting. Stay quiet.

If the knocker sounds, it is the pretentious
Lady in purple, wanting your skin color, the amount
Of change in your pockets.
Ignore her.

Anyone who calls through your lock announcing
His mission too loudly is a person
In robes, clearly fictitious. If you come face to face
With him, you will be accosted.
Don't answer.

Be careful, careful. A loud insistent
Rapping with bare knuckles means someone needs
Assistance badly. He will be ugly, humpbacked
And reeking. If you allow it, he will fall
On your neck and remain there.
Leave the door shut.

Let no one on the other side see your face.
Peer from behind curtains, through BB-sized slots,

Cracks by the casement. Gauge your callers
With mirrors and shadows but stay hidden.
This is to your advantage.

Beware of dwarves and pygmies, monks,
Spacemen, young girls with flowers and candles,
Animals that come alone.

On windy nights push a chair against the knob.
The clawing and scratching, the whispering
Of the hinges, the shifting of the door
On its axis are the sounds of those
Who have been fed without milk, bearing you no kinship.
They bring with them their boney cats, bare branches,
Birds without feet. Stay alert, they will be there
Until morning.

After a sudden heavy knocking
Should you hear nothing but the shuffle of boots,
The clanking of tools, quickly turn off every light
In the house. Start backing down your hallway
As quietly as you can toward that secret door
In the corner under your bed,
At which you must begin to tap
Softly, softly.

HOW YOU CAME

It's a wonder how you came
Clear across a city,
Jumping the roofs of marble towers

Like stepping stones,
Weaving under metal girders,
Tripping up orange steel,
Bolts as big as sausages.

Like a bully goat over bridges,
Ignoring dark trolls and their gleaming spikes,
You were brave,
In the black beneath concrete viaducts,
Their undersides pinned with the brushwork of birds
And dripping the green of last week's water.

Past a thousand, thousand wooden doors,
You circled the rooms of glass buildings,
Skirted cement walls,
Walking sideways just above rivers.

You balanced like dusk,
Even moss couldn't cause a stumble.

Without pebbles or string,
Without magnets or stars,
Without even my line
Blue on white paper,
You came,
Found your way at last,
Turning, like a branch bent quick in the wind,
The latch at my very window.

The Question of Affection

We don't know yet what it means to be touched,
To be the recipient of caresses, what the ear
Learns of itself when its lines are followed
By the finger of somebody else.

We know the spine of the infant can expand,
The neck grow sturdy, the shoulder blades facile
By fondling alone. The acuity of the eye is increased,
The lung capacity doubled by random nuzzles
To the ribs.

But we don't understand what the mind perceives
When the thigh's length is fixed by the dawdling
Of the lover's hand, when the girth of the waist
Is defined by the arms of a child.

An affectionate ear on the belly must alter
The conception of the earth pressing itself against the sky.
An elbow bent across the chest must anticipate
Early light angled over the lake. The curl of the pea
Can be understood as one hand caught carefully inside another.

Cores and cylinders, warm boundaries and disappearing curves,
What is it we realize when these interruptions of space
Are identified with love in the touch of somebody else?

I must remember now what it was I recognized
In the sky outside the window last night
As I felt the line of my shoulder drawn
In the trace of your lips.

Being Defined

This room and the wind outside
Create the facts of each other tonight—
The wind identified by the interferences
Of the eaves, the walls known
By what they separate.

This light, dim beneath its brass shade,
Is repeated in the curve of your glass,
Defined again in your eyes, becomes
The ghost of itself on the rise of your cheek.
You give the light these places to exist.

And by the line of your neck, my finger
Becomes an aspect of caress.
By the boundaries of your forehead, my hand
Becomes a trace of gentleness.

What I am now
Is only she who binds spaces for you.
And your breath, the softest motion
Against my ear, will never understand itself
In any other terms.

Seduced by Ear Alone

Someone should explain how it happens, starting
With the dull stimulation of anvil and stirrups,
The established frequency of shifting air molecules
Initiated by your voice, entering my ear.

The mind, having learned how, can find the single silk
Strand of your breath anywhere, latch on and remember.

But not actually touching the body at all,
How do words alone ease the strictures of the palms,
Alter the tendency of the thighs, cause
The eyes to experience visions? I can see clearly
The stark white sliver of passion running a mile deep
In your whisper.

Maybe the ease of your voice suggests
The bliss of some previous state—sleeping
In a deep crevice at the top of a mountain, the eyes
Sealed tight, or being fed by motion in warm water
At the edge of the sea. By the twist of leaves
In a forest of poplars, I understand how light is fractioned
And born again in the aspects of your words.
I listen like an eddy in deep water turning easily
From one existence to another. I want now
To be covered by you.

And alone on any night, if the wind in the trees
Should sound by accident like the timbre of your voice,
I can be fooled for an instant, feeling suddenly in the dark
Estimable and saved.

———————

HEARING THE UNEXPECTED

Hearing is not an instinct. Deaf children, cured,
Must be taught to hear. Beginning with the smallest
Silver bell, the brain is instructed on the isolation

Of ringing, the counter clunk of the wooden block.
The mind must be led to single out and name the rush
Of wild ducks slapping across the lake, wind rubbing
Backward on the trees, the teacher's voice
Saying, "These are your hands clapping."

The tremble of the inner ear is constant. The selection
By the brain is taught. "That is the mucous slide
Of the worm through sand. Those are spindle shells
Knocking in the surf."

What becomes then of sounds that enter
The ear without names—the whine
Of the moon muffled in clouds, the high-pitched
Terror of the earth turning into night?
This evening, the hissing and sizzling
Of the inflexible social vectors bound to this group
Have been completely missed.

We must practice fine distinctions.
"Hear the sloving of evening's soft sheet
Over the hills. Hear the hard ranchet
Of the wish abandoned. That is the sking
Of the roof's edge against the sky."

Listen. Listen. This is crucial.
In time the ear may even be capable of hearing
Its own function.

THE FIRST NORTHER

1.

Arriving all evening, turning up the bellies
Of oak leaves, parting the edges
Of cotton hulls and spikelet shafts, it comes,
Having swept first over deserts
Of black tundra, having brushed the flanks
Of the musk ox, descended into the dark
Bubbles of the pipits' lungs and out again.
It has been slack in the wings
Of the snowy owl, static in the webs
Of a thousand firs, but it comes now
Pressing particles of down
And whale smoke, penetrating windows
With spirits of cedar, frost
From the lemming's mouth.

2.

Aware of its presence, what will happen to us then
If we choose to leave this room together,
If we walk out among the trees maintaining
Their broken intentions against the wind
And stop beside the wall, feeling the hiss
Of Arctic lichen in our sweaters, the rush
Of frozen grasses in our hands?
You and I, tasting the same air that touched
The eye of the caribou in migration,
Taking into our lungs the same molecules
That reckoned their motion over icy plains
By darkness alone? Surrounded
And utterly possessed, how will you speak
To me then? How will I ever reply?

ACHIEVING PERSPECTIVE

Straight up away from this road,
Away from the fitted particles of frost
Coating the hull of each chick pea,
And the stiff archer bug making its way
In the morning dark, toe hair by toe hair,
Up the stem of the trillium,
Straight up through the sky above this road right now,
The galaxies of the Cygnus A cluster
Are colliding with each other in a massive swarm
Of interpenetrating and exploding catastrophes.
I try to remember that.

And even in the gold and purple pretense
Of evening, I make myself remember
That it would take 40,000 years full of gathering
Into leaf and dropping, full of pulp splitting
And the hard wrinkling of seed, of the rising up
Of wood fibers and the disintegration of forests,
Of this lake disappearing completely in the bodies
Of toad slush and duckweed rock,
40,000 years and the fastest thing we own,
To reach the one star nearest to us.

And when you speak to me like this,
I try to remember that the wood and cement walls
Of this room are being swept away now,
Molecule by molecule, in a slow and steady wind,
And nothing at all separates our bodies
From the vast emptiness expanding, and I know
We are sitting in our chairs
Discoursing in the middle of the blackness of space.

And when you look at me
I try to recall that at this moment
Somewhere millions of miles beyond the dimness
Of the sun, the comet Biela, speeding
In its rocks and ices, is just beginning to enter
The widest arc of its elliptical turn.

ON YOUR IMMINENT DEPARTURE: CONSIDERING THE RELATIVE IMPORTANCE OF VARIOUS MOTIONS

Which is more important, the motion of the wind
Forcing every top-heavy reed along the shore
To precisely the same height, or the manipulations
Of the moon moving the white lines of our window slowly
Across the wall of this room?

Or your hand in motion across my back, suggesting
The scarcely noticeable rising of the lake,
The possible empty sky deepening without interruption
In this bed moving relative to the moon
Twenty-five miles away from two minutes ago?

Consider the various subtleties becoming singular
In the eleven motions of our bodies
Pinpointed together here on the night-facing side
Of the earth tilted in summer angle toward the sun
Consistently dragged by the galaxy further out
Into no known direction whatever.

The mind is the only object
That can ever return to this same spot exactly
Over and over.

Beside the calm of the pine trees brushing
Against each other in the dark, how important
Is the hard twist of my refusal to believe in your departure,
You going away alone, westward at one speed
Over forests moving eastward at another, above clouds
Creating southward-flowing shadows touching
Everything left below? Inside this room, how irreversible
Is the steady speed of the inevitable, keeping up,
Always keeping up with us?

Picture the motion of my voice rising now
To ask you this question, leaving itself forever afterward
Motionless in mid-air?

TRYING MAGIC

Do you think if I looked at him hard and said
Over and over to the back of his head, "Don't be hurt,"
It would make a difference? Some people believe
In chants, the effects of memorable sound repeated.
They speak of a resonating power building inward
Under the breastbone, pressing outward simultaneously,
Gathering momentum in the form of circles radiating
Until they reach something somewhere that can make a difference.

Knowing that lead remains in ashes, I could write
In pencil, "Remember how definitely his attitude
Can be injured. Just remember that." And I could burn
The message in the light of the last sun of the equinox,
Leave the ashes in a jar at a spot designated
For those having influence.

Suppose I present him to the sky.
Suppose for three nights in a row I think of him
Spread naked against the stars. And I follow
Every line of his body with my eyes, from one foot
Up the thigh, the striations of the belly,
Throat, head, down the other side, filling in
The triangle of the groin, over and over
Thinking, "Shielded, shielded." Would it make a difference,
Like immersing him in a beneficent river,
Every pore protected?

I can believe in the energy of wishing.
How the body must engender electricity for the speech,
The chemistry of concentration in the pitch of the voice.
I could make someone notice if I sent this with great force
Sparkling into the atmosphere on a windless night—
"I *wish* him not to be hurt again."

Then shouldn't some bold angel somewhere hear
And help us?

Hiring the Man Who Builds Fires for a Living

He comes when I ask him, during the last half hour
Of evening, begins with his earthen circles,
His rings of rock. Infuriating swagger,
He carries about him the distinct odor of mitigating humus.

But he knows his business. He disappears again and again
Into the trees, taken as if the forest knew him personally,
And comes back always from another direction, his arms

Full of branches having fallen themselves
From great heights without wings nights ago.

When the trees are not totally black, not yet fully entrenched
In the grey sky, imagine how he kneels down
And bends close, how he proceeds with the arrangement.
What is it he believes about this altar? He lays
Each stick religiously as if it had grown
Toward this place from the beginning. What is he whispering
To those dried-up leaves as if they had souls?
There's a blessing here he definitely finds amusing.

I can never see at this point what it is he moves
With his hands or how he concentrates on molding
The invisible as if he could manipulate prophecy, shape
The promise to fit the gift to come. Perfect sculptor,
He knows his element thoroughly.

Watching the deep blue curtains as they fall constantly now
Among the dark trees, I admit
He knows with his breath how to make flame live.

And in the midst of it all, what can I think of a man
Who has created in this black forest tonight
A popping circus of blue-gold brilliance plummeting
With such acrobatic radiance that I laugh out loud myself?
Well, I hired him on faith. He was obliged to be
More than I expected.

CROCODILE GOD

Sand-warm, his toes,
His bronze calves swell like the bellies
Of round golden fish.
Movements under his skin are flashing little fins,
The ripples of silk tails.
He is oiled for beauty.

From two fingers he dangles trinkets,
A ringed cross snapped from dark river silt
On a bright morning, his two-footed cane
Dredged from the bodies of snails and eels.
He has rooted the bottoms of unknown swamps.

Sandalless,
He may swagger in his grand bodice,
Displaying mosaic wrist bands, biceps bracelets.
His sash relaxes navel high on his slender hips.
The plated collar around his throat is more than a napkin.

But it is his head,
Green as moss, bumpy as bark,
And the corners of his smile, the scaley cheeks;
It is the tilt of his long toad-spotted snout,
The exposure of numerous teeth in his cold pink smirk,
The slit-eyes (he never wonders)
And the hiss of his breath,
Smelling of salt clams, old backbones,
That cause us to
Love him.

The Viewpoint of the Unbelievable

Suppose I believe this couch is a boat
And I am stretched out asleep at sea.
Suppose I believe I hear in this room the current
Sucking at the sides, and I feel through the tremor
Of the boat the grebe and his soft sudden
Tricking of the waves, the slip of the silver
He lifts up dripping into the sun.

Suppose I believe I am buoyant three miles above
Giant tubular worms shifting in their warm-water
Beds below. And I accept everything that hangs
Suspended beneath me—the long translucent curtains
Of jelly fish strings, the coil of the eel turning
In mid-water, in every direction the claws of crabs
Askew in the coral, and, passing in my shadow,
The furled silk of the manta ray.

And through my eyelids I can see the amoeba
Of the sun stretching in the reflection of the sea,
Like an explosion, the green neon streak of the gull shrieking.
In gusts of grey, I recognize the occasional brush stroke
Of the wind. Suppose, even beside this wall,
I believe in the continuous deep dart and stream
Of the turned fin gliding below, the glazed
Golden eye disappearing downward.

Then, if you should call to me from the other room,
And I should rise, step off without hesitation, I know
Someone watching from the shore a long way off
Will bear witness to how I moved from the boat without fear
And walked on waves.

HOW THE MOON BECOMES ITSELF

Think how it is altered
By what I hold in my hands when I see it.
Fingering the sharp spikes
Of a sweet-gum ball, it becomes covered
With glass thorns and glows with enmity.
Or pressing a leaf between my palms,
A sudden network of grey veins traces
Across its mountains, and it hangs
Thin and tenuous against the sky.

If I touch the fuzz of the billie's
Cocoon, it goes unfocused with fur.
The moon is so totally dependent.
With one finger, the pocks
Of the orange rind become its craters.
A white fruit, how simple to consume
It by mouth, to chew it
And spit silver seeds.

In gloves, I call it the diviner of snow,
The seer of ice. Last December,
As I stood at the door watching you leave,
It was that hard knob that will never turn.

Gripping the sides of the boat tonight
It is the essential illumination
In the throats of all fish, the way
By which water flames. And as I lie
On the hillside, my hands flat to the sheet,
It is only a cushion against which I see myself spread.

Holding your face between my hands then,
The moon appearing on your right,
As you bend to my neck, the moon
Shifting to your left, it is that coin
Definitely shining lucky side up.

III

ILLUMINATION

Having blown out the only candle
In the unlit room, we still thought
We could see through the dark a string
Of smoke rising from the snuffed wick.

The raccoon, fascinated by reflection,
Is unable to light his den
With his gathered bits of metal,
His scraps of foiled glass.

Standing under the yellow poplar at noon,
She cares nothing for the tree,
Being interested only in the way light
Moves across its turning leaves.

If we study a mirror in a black cave
Long enough, the absence of light
Will be made clearly visible.
Sitting on a high branch in the cloudy night,
Can the raccoon see what expectations
Light has led him to understand?
When the last leaf of the yellow poplar
Has been blown away,
Will the eye of the girl remembering
Be the only body left there for light?

THE BRAIN CREATES ITSELF

A thread of tissues takes shape
As I first comprehend the red rock crossed twice
By the fringe-toed lizard at dusk.
A unique chain of cells becomes actual
As I identify the man beneath the silver beech
And his influence on the nesting kiwi bird.

A new vein of reactions must arise
With my discovery of the dark star
On the rim of Sirius. A split-second network
Must be brought into being as I find the African
Dung beetle's egg buried in the elephant bolus.
And for each unacknowledged aspect of the purple
Spikenard beside the marsh-elder-to-be, for each unrecognized
Function of the ogre-faced stick spider at dawn,
A potential neuron is absent in the frontal lobe.

Imagine the molecular structure I create
As I contemplate the Galapagos dragon
At the bottom of the ocean stopping his heart
At will, dying for three minutes motionless
In the suck and draw of the sea. Imagine,
When I study his rapid zigzag swagger to the surface,
How a permanent line like silver makes its way
From the inner base of my skull to the top of my head.

And as I look at your face, following the contours
From your forehead to your chin, coming back again
To your eyes, I can almost picture the wide cranial
Web developing as my definite affection
For these particulars.

How the Body in Motion Affects the Mind

Consider the mind
As it perceives the hands rising
To grasp the tree branch, each finger
Tightening on the limb and the effort
Of the arms pulling the body upward.
What pattern of interpretation synthesized
From that event
Must establish itself in the neocortex?

We know there are precise configurations
Forced on the brain by the phenomena
Of the hand clenched, by the tucking in
Of the thumb, by the sight of the foot
Flexed on the ground and pushing backward.
How do these configurations influence the study
Of duty or manipulate the definition
Of power? The mind, initiating the motion,
Must be altered itself
By the concepts contained in the accomplishment.

I could almost diagram on this paper
The structure of interactions implanted
In the neuronic fibers by the runner's
Leap across the dry gully. Who can say for certain
That structure has nothing to do
With the control of grief?
Think how the mind has no choice
But to accommodate itself to the restrained
Pressure of the fingertips tracing
The lover's spine. The subtlety

Of that motion must turn back
To modify the source of itself.

We are bound by the theorem of sockets and joints,
Totally united with contraction and release.
The idea of truth cannot be separated
From the action of the hand releasing
The stone at the precise apogee of the arm's motion
Or from the spine's flexibility easing
Through a wooden fence. The notion
Of the vast will not ignore the arm swinging
In motion from the shoulder or the fingers
Clasped together in alternation.

And when the infant, for the first time,
Turns his body over completely, think
What an enormous revelation in the brain
Must be forced, at that moment, to right itself.

THE MAN HIDDEN BEHIND THE DRAPES

When I entered the room and turned on the lights,
There were his feet bare beneath the edge
Of the draperies, his tendons flexed, the bony
Diamonds of his ankles shadowed. If I'd seen
His face I might have laughed.

Remember the naked feet of Christ seen so often,
Washed, kissed, dried in women's hair,
Or crossed and bleeding, pinioned
Like butterfly wings?

When I opened the door,
There were his feet below the drapes, as quiet
As if they lounged beneath a fine robe. Headlights
Moving slowly up the drive at this point
Would have fully exposed his nude body in the window,
His buttocks tensed, his face turned toward the glare
For that moment, then disappearing again into the darkness.

An artist might have pictured snow on the lawn
And a moon and a child looking out from the house
Across the way, watching the figure behind the glass,
The white panes across his back, his hands reaching
For the parting in the curtains.

When I entered the room the light spread first
In a rectangle straight across the floor to his feet,
His toes squeezing under in a crippled kind of gripping.
Someone watching from the end of the hall behind me
Would have seen my body framed in the light of the doorway
And beyond me the wall of the drapes.

Understand the particular axis at which he stood
In the vision of each different beholder, the multiple
Coordinates of hour and position and place coinciding
With the grids of light and sound and preceding
Interpretations. Consider that indeterminable effect
Of his being on the eye of the one unaware of his existence.

There is a house three blocks away that has no man
Behind the drapes. There is a house on a high sea wall
That has two men and no window. There is a house
That does not speak this language and consequently
Tells us nothing.

Almost laughing, my hand still on the door,
I stood watching his feet, and had there been an old woman
Living in the attic, then looking down through a chink in the ceiling
She would have seen in two dimensions, the knuckles of his toes,
The top of my head.

HOW THE FIELD, WITHOUT BEING TOUCHED, CAN BE ALTERED

Think of the field that surrounds
The woman in blue walking on the path.
Notice how each hair of each grain head
Beside her comes definitely into view
Against the dark relief of her jacket,
Then fades out of focus again as she passes.
Observe the expanse of her shadow
As it falters over the wheat to her east,
Turning the stalks momentarily black, taking the sun
Completely out of itself down to the earth.

Understand how the field changes.
Consider the crippled man and the aspects
Of his interactions, how his resolute
Preoccupation with stones and rain-ruts
Creates a new and distinct fear
Out of the terrain. A locust knocking
Against his arm produces an awkwardness
Right there among the weeds
Where it didn't exist before.

And the birds, rising now
From the hedgerow, make eight black
Changes of motion over the grasses.
How do their cries alter the concept
Of the dust pillars teetering on the pistils
Of the coneflowers? The house on the far side
Of the field, seen only when the wheat bends,
Provides justification for pronouncing the field,
On a windless day, obstructive.

Take note of how anonymity can come and go
In this field. The color of the burnished
Acres and the split tassel on the near stalks
Will not be named by the boor passing through.
The mouse cave will receive no identity,
And the seed of the moth
Will not be announced by the wicked.
But the fastidious will remember
The spittle bug and its location.

And we, being nowhere near the field now,
Alter it also by endowing it with the faith
Which enables us to believe, after all,
In its existence.

The Zoo: How the Captured Animal Maintains His Power

Notice how the elephant house
Accommodates its creature,
The inner wall built to withstand

The leaning of the great bulk, the post
Buried deep to survive the rub
Of the haunch. The elephant establishes
His place by demanding that the force
Of each foot
Be of prime consideration.
He must be the subject of investigation,
Being the center
Around which the zoo master must function,
The reason for the zoo master's existence at all.

An animal must prevail to insure
The survival of his prison.
The round-domed ceiling of the hippo's
Building must emulate his girth,
Leaving room for the guttural
Groans of his digestion, the expansion
Of his pig river breath.
And merely by his presence, the deer
Determines the height of his wire fence,
The dimensions of its woven pattern.

Isn't the success of the zoo based
On the master's ability to assess
The character of the cheetah's paw,
The clever teeth of the wild horse,
The shoulder muscles of the brown bear
At bay? Dependent on perceiving
Ultimate lizardry, he must divine the quirks
Of the iguana, the antipathies of the anole.

Observe how each animal causes his environment
To duplicate the ancient veldt or the primitive

Rain forest, the Arctic Circle at dusk.
The essence of alligator will bring forth
The murky pool, the persistent odor
Of fish bone and water gut.

Remember, not only must the roof
Of the great ape's domain be structured to withstand
The vibrations of his screeching, but the beams
Must also be bolstered against the pressure
Of the jungle tree which will take root by itself,
Spread, push upward to fit exactly
The black fingered grip enduring there,
The long arms waiting.

CONCEPTS AND THEIR BODIES
(THE BOY IN THE FIELD ALONE)

Staring at the mud turtle's eye
Long enough, he sees *concentricity* there
For the first time, as if it possessed
Pupil and iris and oracular lid,
As if it grew, forcing its own gene of circularity.
The concept is definitely
The cellular arrangement of sight.

The five amber grasses maintaining their seedheads
In the breeze against the sky
Have borne *latitude* from the beginning,
Secure *civility* like leaves in their folds.
He discovers *persistence* in the mouth
Of the caterpillar in the same way

As he discovers clear syrup
On the broken end of the dayflower,
Exactly as he comes accidentally upon
The mud crown of the crawfish.

The spotted length of the bullfrog leaping
Lakeward just before the footstep
Is not bullfrog, spread and sailing,
But the body of *initiative* with white glossy belly.
Departure is the wing let loose
By the dandelion, and it does possess
A sparse down and will not be thought of,
Even years later, even in the station
At midnight among the confusing lights,
As separate from that white twist
Of filament drifting.

Nothing is sharp enough to disengage
The butterfly's path from *erraticism*.

And *freedom* is this September field
Covered this far by tree shadows
Through which this child chooses to run
Until he chooses to stop,
And it will be so hereafter.

————

WHAT THE BODY MEANS TO BELIEF

Belief in the evil of the sun, we know,
Without doubt, affects the complexion,
Causing a paling of the pigment, a fading

Of the hue. Shut away, avoiding windows,
The demeanor grows ashen. The daylight view
Of the face is thus depressed, giving good reason
For a siding with night.

And that one who is convinced of a return
By sea, who watches from the slippery cliffs
Above the bay, learns to see the ocean well,
Detecting on the furthest rim every surge
That is not wave, every rising corner
That is not brine or fin. Even on the blank side
Of the horizon, he can distinguish the approach
Of the man-made. His stance becomes gradually
Bent at an angle into the wind, easing his balance.
There is medical evidence of salt immunity
In his eyes, of a definite modification of calcium
Along the spine.

And the eyesight of the necromancer, as a result
Of his belief in the candle and its powers,
Becomes capable of isolating the split-second flutter
Of the flame. The physician notes a swelling
Of the optic buds, an increased number of cells devoted
To sporadic flashes. And having faith in bodily
Extremities, the nerves at his outer perimeters
Grow agitated with practice, clever at detecting
The slightest stir. He locates a moth merely
By feeling the disturbance of air about its wings.
In his scalp, he can count the concentration
Of electrical charge at the ends of his hair.

Will you believe that a sincere belief in the beneficent
Relaxes the muscles at the corners of the lips,

Precipitates a minute lapse in the strictures
Of the rib cage? That this allows for an expansion
Of the capillaries enabling them to carry
More oxygen to the frontal lobe, thus greatly increasing
The capacity for love, causing the chin
To tilt upward, the hands to turn naturally out?

Understand that a total belief in this poem
Will cause a subtle squint of perception
In the left eyelid, a permanent twist
In the analytic gyrus of the outer brain.

AN ACT OF CONVICTION

From the case notes of Dr. Charles Atlon, Resident Drama
Psychiatrist, Liverpool School of the Dramatic Arts

That person who makes a deliberate decision to pretend
Madness, to act out the part with conviction,
In time becomes insane. Such is the global influence
Of the brain on itself. The pronunciation of each word
Is not without its effects, as he studies his role, learning
What is to be expected of one practicing the unpredictable.

He begins his performance, leaving fragments of notes
Where they will be found easily, raving letters
Torn to make sense in pieces. He has a stroke
Of genius—to sidle across the lawn with his nose
Held high, pretending to be led by the odor
Of wing-berries over the wall. Tricks of this sort
Make him laugh. He memorizes his act like a dancer.

In time he becomes a master at the semblance
Of misinterpretation, mixing the nitwit with the pea tom,
Disturbing the boundaries of body and place. He practices
Transferring his awareness from behind his face
To the pink primrose vase on the étagère. He can't resist
Believing in the words of his own fabrications
When they are spoken out loud.

He becomes more and more proficient. In the midst
Of company, he stares out the window at a broad
Expanse of snow, contemplating the vacancies of calling
Oneself insane. He adopts the gestures of madness
So perfectly that he finds himself by habit
Curled beneath the kitchen table, considering the state
Of the sane who pretends himself mad. He resists
Every effort to break down his talents.

When the performance is over—unrestrained sanity,
Madness acquainted with itself—who can blame him?
What else can the brain know of itself
Except through its own words?

HANDLING DESPAIR

*The following is an account of a study made by wiring various
sections of a musician's brain for monitoring by a computer with
color graphics. The study was made as the musician performed with
his symphony orchestra.*

During the pianissimo beginning, the area of his brain
Controlling thumb and forefinger appears on the computer screen
Agitated in purple and shifting in heat. There is visible

Chemical interchange alternating in tones of brown
On the portion of the frontal lobe transferring
The printed symbol to muscular fact.

Well into the passage adagio, his brain clearly identifies
The falling mouthpiece of a trumpeter which appears
On the screen as a red flash barely encroaching
Upon the steady perception in blue of the conductor's baton
Lying in the same mode as the purple regulatory
Line of his pulse.

During the marche grande, the activity in the ivory
Parietal lobe is his sudden vision of a satin sash
Lying across his wife's lap. This vision hardly affects
His contribution to the orchestral crescendo in violet
Or the clear gold stimulation of the switch to G minor
Which occurs simultaneously with the grey ease of sweat
Clocked by the brain to materialize at this temperature
Along his brow.

The sense of taut strings under his fingertips, the recognition
Of the pressure of the wooden chair against his buttocks,
Are both located in right-angle graphics just beyond
The black-and-white checkered symbol of his wife's legs
Crossing again in silk which takes precedence
Over the electrical impulse generated by a reptile-like
Dissatisfaction below the limbic area.

It is found that the composition of his unrecalled
Memories appears as the layering of a rose coiled
In light, and a shimmer above the left ear suggests
That his brain is holding in an unknown location
The knowledge that Tchaikovsky has been dead for 87 years.

Beside the pulsing orange control of his breath,
The green streaks of his eye movements and the black
Dormancy of the unacknowledged, the mathematics of his mother
Standing at the top of the wooden steps in recollection
Emerges as he begins the staggering points
Of his pizzicato into the finale.

During the last screening, his brain appears
In the indescribable colors of itself,
Displaying the clear sense he possesses now of rising
Above the stage, over the heads of the musicians, relinquishing
His instrument, to play by mind alone.

At the conclusion, there is definite concern
As to how the validity of this study might be affected
By the musician's own perusal of the results tomorrow.

DETERMINING LOCATION

A man, hunched beside a wall, looks south
Through the morning haze toward a ragged field.
On the sun-side of his foot, a locust stutters
Then smooths its way to silence.

The man is thinking of a woman reading
In her study at night. He sees firelight
Moving on the walls like gold moths out of focus.
The window panes are blank
As black onyx. He knows snow
Is falling outside.

Two snipe quibble in the marsh
Behind the wall. The fire hisses.
The field grows mellifluous in the heavy sun.

The man imagines the woman shifting her legs,
Continuing to read of a walkway disappearing
Through a forest of beeches. The branches
Are soft, barely sketched in early green.
A girl is running down the walk, her red
Sweater spreading like a cape behind her.
From the top of a tree a bird rises, reflecting
In his eye a rush-filled pond
And the blue rim of sky it encircles.

In the field, the woman raises her eyes,
Scarcely hearing the tick of snow, and considers
The pond whose only place is the eye of the bird.
How important are the coordinates of the winter night
In which she exists this morning?
Is it possible for the snipe to find
The beeches which are just beyond the wall?
In the study, there is only one direction
For the girl to run. The man opens his hands
To the forest whose page he has forgotten.

Heading east across the field, a truck approaches,
Carrying a small boy who believes
The side mirror contains grey-gowned figures
That rise and fall in the billowing dust.

THE DETERMINATIONS OF THE SCENE

Consider one born in the desert,
How he must see his sorrow rise
In the semblance of the yucca spreading
Its thorn-covered leaves in every direction,
Pricking clear to the ends
Of his fingers. He recognizes it
And deals with it thus. He learns to ponder
Like the reptile, in a posed quiet
Of the mind, to move on the barest
Essentials, to solve problems
Like the twisted mesquite sustaining itself.
He puts edges to the nouns of his statements,
Copying the distinct lines of the canyon in shadow,
And establishes cool niches out of the sun
In every part of his dogma. He understands
His ecstasy in terms of fluidity, high spring water
In motion through the arroyo.

That one born in the forest, growing up
With canopies, must seek to secure coverings
For all of his theories. He blesses trees
And boulders, the solid and barely altered.
He is biased in terms of stable growth vertically.
And doesn't he picture his thoughts springing
From moss and decay, from the white sponge
Of fungus and porous toadstools blending?
He is shaped by the fecund and the damp,
His fertile identifications with humus
And the aroma of rain on the deepening
Forest floor. Seeing the sky only in pieces

Of light, his widest definition must be modeled
After the clearing hemmed in by trees.

And consider the child raised near the sea, impinged
Upon constantly by the surf rising in swells,
Breaking itself to permanent particles of mist
Over the cliffs. Did you really think
The constant commotion of all that fury
Would mean nothing in the formation of the vocabulary
That he chooses to assign to God?
The surge, the explosion must constitute
The underlying dominion unacknowledged
In his approach to the cosmos.

And we mustn't forget to inquire:
Against what kinds of threats must the psyche
Of the Arctic child protect itself in sleep?

———————

BEING OF THIS STATE

In the entire night sky, in all of the inverted
Slipped-back-upon-itself almost total emptiness
With its occasional faint clusters of pinprick
Fluctuations, there is not one single
Star grateful for its own light.

And on the stalk of blossoming confusion
Outside my door, barrelheads of camelia fistfuls,
There is not one petal that esteems
The ivory ellipse of its own outer edge
Or the molecules of its own scent escaping.

Who can detect a joy of beholding in the golden
Pipe fish filtering among the golden coral
Or in the blue-bred musk ox with its shaggy frost?
Which one among the tattered fungi remembers
The favor of the damp, the gift of decay?

Along the beach the Arctic terns rush forward
Up to their bellies in salt foam and shell-
Shag rolling, but not one is able to bless first
The mole crab it snips up and swallows.

Inside the network of the clearing, among the scritching
And skeetering, the thuz and the tremulous ching,
There is not one insect able to recognize the sound
Of its own beatification. Clinging to the weeds

In the middle of that broad field spread wide
And pressed against the open night, neither those insects,
Nor the hissing grasses, nor the ash-covered moon
Can ever contemplate the importance
Of the invention of praise.

––––––––––––

SUPPOSITION

Suppose the molecular changes taking place
In the mind during the act of praise
Resulted in an emanation rising into space.
Suppose that emanation went forth
In the configuration of its occasion:
For instance, the design of rain pocks

On the lake's surface or the blue depths
Of the canyon with its horizontal cedars stunted.

Suppose praise had physical properties
And actually endured? What if the pattern
Of its disturbances rose beyond the atmosphere,
Becoming a permanent outline implanted in the cosmos—
The sound of the celebratory banjo or horn
Lodging near the third star of Orion's belt;
Or to the east of the Pleiades, an atomic
Disarrangement of the words,
"How particular, the pod-eyed hermit crab
And his prickly orange legs"?

Suppose benevolent praise,
Coming into being by our will,
Had a separate existence, its purple or azure light
Gathering in the upper reaches, affecting
The aura of morning haze over autumn fields,
Or causing a perturbation in the mode of an asteroid.
What if praise and its emanations
Were necessary catalysts to the harmonious
Expansion of the void? Suppose, for the prosperous
Welfare of the universe, there were an element
Of need involved.

————

How the Scene Influences Occasions

The quarrel occurring between two people standing
Under a winter oak is bound
To be regimented by the pattern of branches

Surrounding it. How can it take shape
Except inside the tangled lines
Of those black branches against the sky?
And who could think the creak and snap
Of the freezing tree would have no effect
On the choice of its syntax? The pauses forced
By the gusting wind must also render the quarrel episodic.

The mad man's curse shouted over the meadow
Rises without obstacle, expands
Over the grasses, taking in the energy
Of the unicorn beetle and the lizard worm.
It can even attach itself in its grandiosity
To the birds circling overhead.
But the same curse shouted from the cliff
Above the sea loses itself immediately,
Unrecognized and downed in mist.

Imagine how the love song sung among the roots
And bugs of high weeds is altered by the activities
Around it, as if insects burrowed in its sounds,
As if spores and vines curled through its lapses.
Think of the difference in the same song sung
On the planks of an empty shack, speared
By dusty light and rescued by a single spider.

We know how the quality of night snow
Lightens the lullaby, does not interrupt
The prayer, demures to the blessing,
How it enhances the bonfire set
Beside the frozen lake. The speech of the dullard then
Must be improved by thunder rattling
The casements, by rain in profusion on the glass.

We will never say a grief remains the same
In the velvet parlor as it exists by the lake
In utter stillness or expresses itself
On the road driven past ditches of spring flowers.

Being aware of these facts,
We must remember when the poem is read
To be on the west side of the mountain,
To have our backs to a red sky, to read
From the page held high in black silhouette
Beside a full pine.

THE SUCCESS OF THE HUNT

> *There was a white hart that lived in that forest, and if anyone*
> *killed it, he would be hanged. . . .*
> —MY ÁNTONIA

He was sighted once in a clearing at dusk, the gold
Grass up to his shoulders and he standing like a pillar
Of salt staring back; seen again from a high ledge,
A motionless dot of white curled like a bloom
In the green below; surprised along a lake shore
At night, taken for an irregular reflection
Of the moon on the surf.

Some looked only for his red eyes, believing
The body could be too easily hidden
By the translucent green of lighted leaves,
That it could sink blue below the water
Or become boundless against the snow, almost invisible,
That it was not white at night.

Some who followed what was presumed to be his trail
Found the purple toadflax said to grow only
From his hoof marks, and some became engulfed
By cecropia moths thought to spring from his urine.
Others testified to the impassable white cliffs
Alleged to be an accumulated battery of his shadows.

Those who lost their way were forced to rediscover
The edible buds of the winter spruce and to use
The fronds of the cycas for warmth, to repeat again
To themselves the directional details of moss,
And part the pampas grasses clear to the earth,
To smell their way east.

But those who followed farthest with the most detail,
Who actually saw the water rising in his hoof prints
And touched the trees still moist where their bark
Had been stripped, those who recognized at the last moment
The prongs of his antlers disappearing over the edge
Of their vision, they were the ones who learned to tell
By the imbalance of their feet on the earth where it was
He slept at night and by their own vertigo how it was he rose
To nip the dogwood twigs above his head. They learned to smell
His odor in their bedclothes and to waken suddenly at night
To the silence of his haunches rubbing on the ash.
Even now they can find the spot where he walked
From the water dripping and trace on their palms
The path of his winter migration. They can isolate
From any direction the eight lighted points
Of his antlers imprinted in the night sky.
And these, who were methodical with the most success,
Always meant to do more than murder.

IV

A GIANT HAS SWALLOWED THE EARTH

What will it do for him, to have internalized
The many slender stems of riverlets and funnels,
The blunt toes of the pinecone fallen, to have ingested
Lakes in gold slabs at dawn and the peaked branches
Of the fir under snow? He has taken into himself
The mist of the hazel nut, the white hairs of the moth,
And the mole's velvet snout. He remembers, by inner
Voice alone, fogs over frozen grey marshes, fine
Salt on the blunt of the cliff.

What will it mean to him to perceive things
First from within—the mushroom's fold, the martin's
Tongue, the spotted orange of the wallaby's ear,
To become the object himself before he comprehends it,
Putting into perfect concept without experience
The din of the green gully in spring mosses?

And when he stretches on his bed and closes his eyes,
What patterns will appear to him naturally—the schematic
Tracings of the Vanessa butterfly in migration, tacks
And red strings marking the path of each mouse
In the field, nucleic chromosomes aligning their cylinders
In purple before their separation? The wind must settle
All that it carries behind his face and rise again
In his vision like morning.

A giant has swallowed the earth,
And when he sleeps now, o when he sleeps,
How his eyelids murmur, how we envy his dream.

THE SIGNIFICANCE OF LOCATION

The cat has the chance to make the sunlight
Beautiful, to stop it and turn it immediately
Into black fur and motion, to take it
As shifting branch and brown feather
Into the back of the brain forever.

The cardinal has flown the sun in red
Through the oak forest to the lawn.
The finch has caught it in yellow
And taken it among the thorns. By the spider
It has been bound tightly and tied
In an eight-stringed knot.

The sun has been intercepted in its one
Basic state and changed to a million varieties
Of green stick and tassel. It has been broken
Into pieces by glass rings, by mist
Over the river. Its heat
Has been given the board fence for body,
The desert rock for fact. On winter hills
It has been laid down in white like a martyr.

This afternoon we could spread gold scarves
Clear across the field and say in truth,
"Sun you are silk."

Imagine the sun totally isolated,
Its brightness shot in continuous streaks straight out
Into the black, never arrested,
Never once being made light.

Someone should take note
Of how the earth has saved the sun from oblivion.

COUNTING WHAT THE CACTUS CONTAINS

Elf owl, cactus wren, fruit flies incubating
In the only womb they'll ever recognize.
Shadow for the sand rat, spines
And barbary ribs clenched with green wax.
Seven thousand thorns, each a water slide,
A wooden tongue licking the air dry.

Inside, early morning mist captured intact,
The taste of drizzle sucked
And sunsplit. Whistle
Of the red-tailed hawk at midnight, rush
Of the leaf-nosed bat, the soft slip
Of fog easing through sand held in tandem.

Counting, the vertigo of its attitudes
Across the evening; in the wood of its latticed bones—
The eye sockets of every saint of thirst;
In the gullet of each night-blooming flower—the crucifix
Of the arid.

In its core, a monastery of cells, a brotherhood
Of electrons, a column of expanding darkness
Where matter migrates and sparks whorl,
And travel has no direction, where distance
Bends backward over itself and the ascension
Of Venus, the stability of Polaris, are crucial.

The cactus, containing
Whatever can be said to be there,
Plus the measurable tremble of its association
With all those who have been counting.

MAKING A HISTORY

The glutinous snail
In silvery motion
Has rubbed his neck
Against his mate's, covered
Her side-slatted orifice
With his own. The newt,
Jumping suddenly forward underwater,
Has twisted and dropped
His pocket of sperm. And in the field
The fritillary, frenzied for orange,
Has skittered straight up and hovered.

The chortle of the Siamese fighting fish
Held upside down by her mate
Has subsided. The dragon fish
Has chewed the tail of his lover,
And the frigate has been swollen
Three times, burgeoning in red.
Bison have risen from their dirt clouds
Blowing. Antlers have entangled, caribou
Collided, cockerels have caught hold,
And the crack of the mountain sheep meeting
Has broken over the arroyo, and the bowerbirds
Have howled and the fruit bats screamed,
And the wild pigs have lain down
In punctuated barking, and the zigzag cocking
Of the stickleback has widened, and alligators
Have spit and strumped, thrashing
In the crumpled reeds. Storks have bent backward
Rooting at heaven with their long beaks banging,

And the alley cat, in guttural moaning,
Has finally been released, bleeding
At the neck, and everyone
Has something to remember.

———————

FINDING THE FIRE LINE

Storks precede grass fires
On the Serengeti, snapping up small
Fleeing reptiles.

If I state a location—
In the middle of the Mojave Desert at dusk,
In the core of the cathedral cactus,
Bound by the fragrance of dark milk—
I have partially described whatever must be there.

Gordon read aloud, "Wounded soldiers
In long grey coats came to the house all night,
And I gave the first one my bed."

Gordon doesn't know whether smoke on the Serengeti
Is grass partially read aloud or the dark
Fragrance of whatever the storks have predicted.
Will lizards fleeing the fire line
Find whatever must be totally defined
In the center of the beak's bed?
By describing the wounds preceding them,
Those who move toward the middle
Of the long grey dusk can be located.

PORTRAIT

This is a picture of you
Reading this poem. Concentrate
On the finite movement
Of your eyes as they travel
At this moment across
The page, your fingers
Maintaining the stability
Of the sheet. Focus on the particular
Fall of your hair, the scent
Of your hands, the placement of your
Feet now as they acknowledge
Their name.

Simultaneously with these words, be aware
Of your tongue against
Your teeth, the aura
Of heat at your neckline
And wrists, the sense
Of your breath inside its own hollows.

Imagine yourself
Ten feet away and look back
At your body positioned
Here with this book. Picture
The perspective, the attitude
Of your shoulders and hips,
The bend of your head as you
Read of yourself.

Watch how you turn back as you
Remember the sounds surrounding you now,

As you recall the odors
Of wood fibers in this place
Or the lack of them.

And take note of this part
Of your portrait—the actual
Mechanism by which you are perceiving
The picture, the fixed
Expression on your face as you
Arrange these words at this moment
Into their proper circles, as you
Straighten out the aspects
Of the page, the linguistics of the sight
And color of light on the paper.

This is the printed
Form of you watching
Yourself now as you consider
Your person. This portrait is
Finished when you raise
Your eyes.

SEEING THE GLORY

Whatever enters the eye—shade of ash leaf,
Torn web dangling, movement of ice
Over the canyon edge—enters only
As the light of itself.
It travels through the clear jelly
Of the vitreo, turning once like the roll
Of a fish in deep water, causing a shimmer
In that thimbleful of cells waiting,

Then proceeds as a quiver on a dark purple thread
To pass from life into recognition.

The trick is to perceive glory
When its light enters the eye,
To recognize its penetration of the lens
Whether it comes like the sudden crack
Of glass shot or the needle in the center
Of the hailstone, whether it appears like the slow
Parting of fog by steady trees or the flashing
Of piranha at their prey.

How easily it could go unnoticed
Existing unseen as that line initiating
The distinction of all things.
It must be called by name
Whether it dives with triple wings of gold
Before the optic nerve or presses itself
In black fins against the retina
Or rises in its inversion like a fish
Breaking into sky.

Watching on this hillside tonight,
I want to know how to see
And bear witness.

————

ON THE EXISTENCE OF THE SOUL

How confident I am it is there. Don't I bring it,
As if it were enclosed in a fine leather case,
To particular places solely for its own sake?
Haven't I set it down before the variegated canyon

And the undeviating bald salt dome?
Don't I feed it on ivory calcium and ruffled
Shell bellies, shore boulders, on the sight
Of the petrel motionless over the sea, its splayed
Feet hanging? Don't I make sure it apprehends
The invisibly fine spray more than once?

I have seen that it takes in every detail
I can manage concerning the garden wall and its borders.
I have listed for it the comings and goings
Of one hundred species of insects explicitly described.
I have named the chartreuse stripe
And the fimbriated antenna, the bulbed thorax
And the multiple eye. I have sketched
The brilliant wings of the trumpet vine and invented
New vocabularies describing the interchanges between rocks
And their crevices, between the holly lip
And its concept of itself.

And if not for its sake, why would I go
Out into the night alone and stare deliberately
Straight up into 15 billion years ago and more?

I have cherished it. I have named it.
By my own solicitations
I have proof of its presence.

SYNTHESIZING THE WORD

The speckled wood butterfly guards his spot of light
On the forest floor. He rests in that circle of sun
Like a powdery flower against the earth, sounding
Its fragrances. He flies in a spiral upward

Against usurpers, settles again on everything good
That he can distinguish. I am trying to find
Your name. I am trying to remember.

In the field after dark, everything has a sound,
The damp gathering under the weeds, the shift
Of the comb-footed spider, the edges of the trees
Against the night. I am aware of what moves across the tops
Of the grasses and keeps on going. I attend to the pauses
Of the grape-skin peepers, the pine crickets. I am trying
To recall your name. I am watching.

The wild wheat, evening-brown and counting, rises
And bends in the ditches by the road. The other side
Of its existence is here in these words. The hair
Of each seed-head, the invisible crack in each sheath,
The wind taking form among the stalks, all have been here
On this page waiting for themselves from the beginning.
I will put together your name. I am adding.

Reminiscence of barn owls and tit-toms, filaments of jackanapes
And iris bands, auras of glassed-in candlelight and unbroken
Spans of snow, the underwater worm slides along the body
Of the Choctaw reed, feeling its presence. I am
Next to where you are. I will use my fingertips. I will use
My belly. I will study long enough to remember your name.

———————

THE LITERARY MAN

He isn't a curiosity, merely an object
Of study. If he reads these words, "the castle
On the hill," he sees immediately the block

Fortress, the greystone turrets, wooden gate.
Each detail is as real as the paper he holds—
The mossy foundation, the weed-filled grasses.

Show him this grouping of letters: "Red poppies
And purple iris grow by the crumbling wall." He has
No trouble. Or: "All night long he kept his hand
On her thigh." It might just as well have happened.

This is not so remarkable. We shouldn't be amazed.
But he told me yesterday that if your name
Were spelled differently you wouldn't be the same.
And today on the beach he saw—entirely present there ˙
And as recognizable as the spread of their wings—
The word "gulls" at the same instant as he saw the birds.
"Flight" and "swoop" appeared with their maneuvers,
And printed in among them as if a plane trailed
A banner, "S-C-R-E-E! S-C-R-E-E!"

He says he would be blind, wouldn't recognize
This fruit on my table at all, if he didn't
See "apple" at the same moment, and the fruit
Responds by becoming so nearly "apple" that the name
Is tighter to it than its own stretched and grown-on
Red skin. He says you could cut it in half and the two
"p's" would be split down the middle staring back at you.

Elm becomes different merely by becoming "elm,"
And he challenges you to identify the tree outside your window
Right now without seeing, in that fraction of a second
When you know that you know it, the word that is its name.

By Hearing the Same Story Over and Over

Some things can be established and then forgotten,
For instance—the general area above is always occupied
By sky; the overall sense of the forest never depends
On a particular tree; light is itself only up to the perimeters
Of darkness.

One is left then to concentrate on details.
You might not have realized before how the sun
Never clears the haze from the meadow until the pine trees
Draw their shadows into their trunks at noon,
And the connection between the dry southwestern wind
And the toad caches dug in on the northeastern slopes
Might seem suddenly obvious on the sixth reading.
The violet butterfly keeping pace with the dry leaf shuffle
Of the villain all the way through the forest
Must have been here unseen all along.

Learning to know the story by heart, you might wonder
How events are altered by being anticipated.
What happens to the momentum of the rock scheduled
To crash by surprise down the hillside
When its fall is seen in expectation five minutes before
It begins to move? And how does it affect the clear air
Over the valley when you can smell smoke
From the Indians' fire two days before their camp
Comes into existence? There is no doubt, you come,
By these means, to believe in endings before they happen.

Occasionally you embellish the story yourself.
Your wish on the 20th reading for a clear lake hidden
In reflective black beneath the ledge where the hero

Waits, means it is there, complete with surface beetles
And shore decay, in somebody's eyes for a moment.
And your desire to be the one who rides with the lawman
This time through the thick poplars means you might discover,
Without its being written, that branches can slap hard
While still remaining stationary. Your growing love
Of the hero's aspect in boots must draw his body,
As if he breathed, nearer to actuality.

On the 100th reading after you have seen once more
How the hero binds the wrists of the villain
And have noticed for the first time the ingenuity
Of that knot and after you have said to yourself
As they disappear into the town, "termination,"
Then when you turn back to start at the beginning again
It might occur to you to ask why the sky must always
Occupy the same general area above. You might be struck
By the singular notion that the overall sense of the forest
Must always depend on every particular tree. And light,
You know by the details of your own anticipated embellishments,
Can be itself only by never accepting the perimeters
Of any darkness.

—————

ALL THE ELEMENTS OF THE SCENE

In the upper right-hand corner of this scene is a copse
Of cottonwood *(Populus deltoides)*. Each leaf
Like a silver dollar twists on its flattened stalk.
And parallel to the edge of this scene runs
A line of forest, thin dwarf oak, scrub vine,

The smoketree. Leaning to the left of that, a field
Of flat grasses sways, heavy with thorny seeds. Blue
Toadflax and bee balm bend in the wind toward
The bare rim of the pond in the foreground, its lazy
Wash surfaced with baweedle bug, the raised eyes
Of the leopard frog *(Rana pipiens)*. Pickerelweeds
Make hostage of the dragonfly, the nesting mud tortoise.

Here am I in this scene too, my shadow wrinkling
On the water of the pond, my footprints making pools
Along the bank. And all that I say, each word
That I give to this scene is part of the scene. The act
Of each thing identified being linked to its name
Becomes an object itself here. The bumblebee hovers
Near the bitter orange of the mallow weed. That sentence
And this one too are elements of the scene.

This poem, as real as the carp sliding in green
At the bottom of the pond, is the only object
Within the scene capable of discussing both itself
And the scene. The moist, rotting log sinks
Into earth. The pink toothwort sprouts beside it.
The poem of this scene has 34 lines.

And see, reader, you are here also, watching
As the poem speaks to you, as it points out that you
Were present at the very first word. The fact of your
Cognizance here is established as you read this sentence.

Take note of the existence of the words in this scene
As they tell you—the pond is purple; the sun is blocked
In branches below the oak; there are shadows
On this poem; night things are stirring.

The Expectations of Light   147

THAT SONG

I will use the cormorant on his rope at night diving
Into the sea, and the fire on the prow, and the fish
Like ribbons sliding toward the green light in the dark.

I will remember the baneberry and the bladderwort
And keep the white crone under the bosackle tree
And the translucent figs and the candelabra burning alone
In the middle of the plains, and the twig girdler,
And the lizard of Christ running over the waves.

I will take the egg bubble on the flute
Of the elm and the ministries of the predacious
Caul beetle, the spit of the iris, the red juice shot
From the eye of the horny toad, and I will use
The irreducible knot wound by the hazel scrub
And the bog myrtle still tangling, and the sea horse
With his delicate horn, the flywheel of his maneuvering.

I will remember exactly each tab folded down
In the sin book of Sister Alleece and each prayer
Hanging in its painted cylinder above the door
And the desert goat at noon facing
The sun to survive.

I will include the brindled bandicoot and the barnacle
Goose and the new birds hatching from mussels
Under the sea and the migrating wildebeests humming
Like organs, moaning like men.

The sand swimmers alive under the Gobi plateau,
The cactus wren in her nest of thorns and the herald

Of the tarantula wasp and each yellow needle
In the spring field rising, everything will be there,
And nothing will be wasted.

THE LITERARY ADVENTURE

At the exact moment that you begin to read this, a wasp
In the Kalahari Desert appears at the top
Of a large sand hill. Understand how she stops,
Spotting her prey, the crystal sand spider. Alerted,
The spider turns to fight, rising up on his white legs, striking
With rapid blows the blue-black body of the wasp
As she darts forward. He retreats,
Forms an eight-spoked cartwheel and spins
Wildly down the sand.

As you read these lines, she follows quickly,
Catches him on his back by his crystal legs
And straddles his body. The needle of her poison
Tube sinks slowly into the golden raisin
Of his abdomen. She remains poised until he rests.

If you continue, she begins to burrow, throwing
Sand with a fine whisking of her feet. There is a clatter
And dry careening of small rocks and gravel as she kicks
The refuse behind her.

Proceeding down the page: she drags
His heavy body to her tunnel, stuffs it
With the pins of her legs deep into the hole.

His feet draw together at the top like a stringed
Purse. His mandibles, his multiple eyes are frozen.

When you conceive the oval of this word, she
Places her egg like a glistening snowdrop
On the spider's pulsing frame, climbs out,
Turns backward, fills the hole to the top.

Look at this stanza. In the orange sun
She is combing the dust from her double wings.

As you finish this sentence to the end, she hurries away,
Head lowered, the practiced wires of her body
Disappearing with the alacrity of the very small,
Over the edge of the broad evening dune.

NASA Takes a 63-Year-Old Poet to the First Space Station

Finally ready, they come for him at dawn.
Touching each elbow, they surround him carefully
Like a porcelain vase. They have a car waiting.
He needs no special suit, his gabardine pants,
Flannel shirt, khaki tie. They are pleased
With his fingertips, the creases in his shoes.

Into the gleaming shuttlecraft, they lead him
To his room. All of his walls are wide
Circular windows facing forward, his ceiling,
A skylight. He settles on pillows
In his high-domed cubicle of glass.

The rise is perfect, silent, without tremor.
He is carried up through the early grey
Fog of the eastern seaboard, out over
The earth, an enormous belly of blue.
Far ahead he sees the massive construct floating,
The pristine exactness of its white metal, silver
Girders, wired columns of crosses
And mirrored wheels turning slowly.

As he watches, sped forward into the cloudless
And the snow-silent, into the blue-black hollow,
Into the dust-free, spit-and-polished starlight
Of the nethermost,
They hand him his pencil and pad.

THE FEAR OF FALLING

It comes from the tree apes, this instinct
To grasp, to fill the hollow of the hand
And fasten. Emerging from the womb,
How each must have clawed, grabbing before breathing,
Its mother's hairy knee, the slip of her rump.
Imagine the weak, the unimpressed, dropping
Through leaves like stones to the ground below.

The mind has become itself inside the panic
Of bodies falling with fingers spread useless.
How many times in the jerk of sleep
Has the last hand-hold been seen
Disappearing upward like a small bird sucked into space?

Bound to the clenching habit of the fingers, united
With the compulsion of the hands to grasp, the mind
Perceives in terms of possession, recognizing
Its lack from the beginning—the black fur
Of the void, the bowl of the wide belly, the dark
Of that great invented thigh out of reach.

The first need of the brain is to curl
The conceptual knuckles and tighten.
And whether it is on each warm-water crack
At the bottom of the sea or on every maneuver
Of the swamp muskrat or around the grey spiral
Details of forgiveness, the grip of the brain
Is determined not to be negligible.

Here in the wind at the top of these branches
We recognize
The persistent need to take hold of something
Known to be sure-footed.

CAPTURING THE SCENE

With pen and ink, the artist takes care
To be explicit, each board of the covered bridge
Elucidated, each shingle of the roof. The columns
Of the termites and the holes of the borers to be,
He remembers. He is deliberate to denote those specifics
He understands, filling in the blank with the pause
Of the dragonfly, the scratch of the myrtle weed.
He watches to maintain in his lines exactly
That tedious balance between the river in motion

And the river itself. Like wires, he coordinates
The trees and their affinity for disorder.

How skillfully he locates the woodthrush clearing
The last field beyond the hills, and the worn rocks
Along the bank, each with its own specific hump
Against space. He acknowledges the sunken
And the sucked away, the shadows on the far left
Bearing witness to objects still outside the scene.

And notice how he achieves that incandescence of ink
Around the seed pod. He knows that the scream of the jay,
The odor of the sun-dried wood is entirely in his stroke.
Without making a single mark, he executes the heavens.

And hasn't he understood from the beginning where he must never
Look directly—into the dark hedgerow on the opposite bank,
Among the crossed sticks of the rushes and the spaces between,
How he must not stare steadily at the long fall
Of the sky below the horizon or probe too deeply that area
Lying between the ink and its line on the paper? He knows
There is that which he must draw blindfolded or not at all.
And before he can give to the scene its final name,
He must first identify every facet of its multiplicity
In detail; he must then turn away his face completely
And remember more.

THE TATTOOED LADY IN THE GARDEN (1986)

I

The Pieces of Heaven

No one alone could detail that falling—the immediate
Sharpening and blunting of particle and plane,
The loosening, the congealing of axis
And field, the simultaneous opening and closing
Composing the first hardening of moment when heaven first broke
From wholeness into infinity.

No one alone could follow the falling
Of all those pieces gusting in tattered
Layers of mirage like night rain over a rocky hill,
Pieces cartwheeling like the red-banded leg
Of the locust, rolling like elk antlers dropping
After winter, spiraling slowly like a fossil of squid
Twisting to the bottom of the sea, pieces lying toppled
Like bison knees on a prairie, like trees of fern
In a primeval forest.

And no one could remember the rising
Of all those pieces in that moment, pieces shining
Like cottonwood dust floating wing-side up
Across the bottomland, rising like a woman easily
Lifting to meet her love, like the breasting,
The disappearing surge and scattering crest of fire
Or sea blown against rock, bannered like the quills
Of lionfish in their sway, like the whippling stripe
Of the canebrake rattler under leaves.

Who can envision all of heaven trembling
With the everlasting motion of its own shattering
Into the piece called honor and the piece
Called terror and the piece called death and the piece
Tracing the piece called compassion all the way back
To its source in that initial crimp of potential particle
Becoming the inside and outside called matter and space?

And no one alone can describe entirely
This single piece of heaven partially naming its own falling
Or the guesswork forming the piece
That is heaven's original breaking, the imagined
Piece that is its new and eventual union.

ANGEL OF THE ATOM

Actual but nonexistent, she is a crease
Of light spinning to a hair-sliver
Of silver in the tip of the needle pointing north.
She is the invisible clutching and releasing
Of the fundamental particles of all summer affirmations,
The length in the flickering wave initiating
The spermatozoa of princes and newts.

Nodding and nodding, she rocks slowly, a real illusion
Buried in the ultimate distinction of the swaying gonad
Of the cottonwood seed. She closes her eyes and creates time
By her steady trembling inside the winter shudder
Of an elm twig filled with eggs.

And she floats above the pond with the silent drift
Of indistinguishable trillions, weaving and flocking,
Rising through the reeds like fog. What a joy
To turn completely once in the sky with dawn, to change,
By that turning, the spread of the sun from coral to gold.

Chanting to herself as she circles in the expanse
Of her disappearing orbits, she is the syllabic movement
Of the cricket's leg, the voweling burr of the bullfrog's
Throat, the still hollow echo of the bottomless cave
Of spring filled with stars. More than herself,
She is both sound and breeze caught in the upper branches
Of the birches constituting the mountain forest she composes.

And when she folds her transparent wings like a soft
Skin of morning around her knees and arms and sleeps,
She dreams of the reality of the vision
Of multiple energy existing inside her dream
Of the nucleus soaring into night.

A measurable body sustaining the immeasurable,
She presses herself continually upward
Through the inner walls of crotch and spine,
Filling breath and vein, hearing the sound of her own name
Spoken by the voice she becomes in the brain.
She meets herself continually as heaven in the eye.
And I know that what I can never perceive is simply
That instant of darkness she imagines she holds tightly forever
Inside the perfect clasp of her shining hands.

SECOND WITNESS

The only function of the red-cupped fruit
Hanging from the red stem of the sassafras
Is to reveal the same shiny blue orb of berry
Existing in me.

The only purpose of the row of hemlocks blowing
On the rocky ridge is to give form to the crossed lines
And clicking twigs, the needle-leaf matrix
Of evergreen motion I have always possessed.

Vega and the ring nebula and the dust
Of the Pleiades have made clear by themselves
The constellations inherent to my eyes.

What is it I don't know of myself
From never having seen a crimson chat at its feeding
Or the dunnart carrying its young? It must be imperative
That I watch the entire hardening of the bud
Of the clove, that I witness the flying fish breaking
Into sky through the sun-smooth surface of the sea.

I ask the winter wren nesting in the clogged roots
Of the fallen oak to remember the multitoned song
Of itself in my ears, and I ask the short-snouted
Silver twig weevil to be particular and the fishhook
Cactus to be tenacious. I thank the distinct edges
Of the six-spined spider crab for their peculiarities
And praise the freshwater eel for its graces. I urge
The final entanglement of blade and light to keep
Its secrecy, and I beg the white-tailed kite this afternoon,
For my sake, to be keen-eyed, to soar well, to be quick
To make me known.

MAINTAINING THE INDISTINGUISHABLE

Sonia and Cecil are surprised to learn
That the large, snow-covered objects dotting
The beach across the lake are not stones
Or pieces of broken ice washed ashore,
But whooper swans, waiting through the storm, drawn-in
And pressed close to the earth, their heads out of sight
Beneath their wings, their bodies gradually
Becoming indistinguishable from the snowdrifts
Building on the beach.

Gordon, sitting by the fire inside, likes to imagine
The white snow slowly covering the white swans, snow so light
Its only recognizable touch is cold, and the invisible
Black spaces caught inside the crystals
Of each white flake. And he likes to imagine the thick
White feathers beneath the snow, feathers so soft
A blind man might miss their touch, and the dark
Spaces caught deep inside the down of each soft barb.
And beneath the feathers, he likes to imagine the swans
So real their most definite touch is the shudder
Of the invisible spaces of light caught inside their black eyes,
Spaces almost indistinguishable from the blind
Crystals caught against the windows looking out
On the white cavity of the storm.

Felicia is excited by this discovery
And has convinced Albert to join her in fashioning
Swans of snow all along the lakefront before the house.
Afterward they will curl up on the shore,
Put their faces under their arms and wait in the falling snow
Until Sonia tells them they are indistinguishable

From the snow-swans they have created on the beach,
Which are indistinguishable from the swanlike drifts
Spanning the snowy shore, which are indistinguishable
From the whooper swans waiting across the dark lake,
Sleeping inside the falling black spaces caught
Inside the touch of white caught inside their eyes.
Felicia and Albert, curled inside the black cavity
Of sleep inside the swans they have invented inside themselves,
Are also able to maintain such spaces.

Gordon is certain that all swanlike figures
Are completely indistinguishable from the white shudder
Of words caught in the act of creating
Their most peculiar distinctions.

———————

THE DOCTRINE

Someone might think there is a tiny human fetus
Alive and curled inside each bristled germ
Of the bottlebrush grass in the field this afternoon.
Someone might imagine those infants inside their clear shells
Deep beyond the plumules of the brown seeds
Of the sow thistle, at the bottom of the frostlike
Blooms of the black haw. And someone might picture
Each one perfectly contained, drifting inside a coral
And white light of its own, shining in its nurturing oils,
The rich purple cord buoyant over knees and heels,
Across the buttocks, latched to the belly buried
Inside each white spore of every violet larkspur.

And someone might think those tiny unborn children fill
The sea, tumbling in their soft crystal cases, their thumbs
At their mouths, encompassed by seaweed, sucking
With the filefish and sargassum crabs, secure
Inside the cave of the cuttlefish, inside the ovaries
Of the dragonet, rising with the spittle of the archerfish;
That they are the first whisper heard on shore
By the boneless tadpole of the spadefoot toad, the first shudder
Felt in the wet paper wings of the darner fly; that they hang
In midair in the colored silk sac of the marbled spider,
Mingling with the claws and fangs, the spinnerets
Of the fetal araneus.

And someone might think they can be seen scattered far away
Across a black heaven, embryos of breathing light,
That they are the point pulsing in the core of every star
Caught like candles in mantles of glass, that they float
Inside the cells inside the cells of their own eyes,
That they see themselves turning slowly and perfectly
Inside their own hearts, the only center inside the center
Around which they turn in the sky and in the earth
And in the sea, and someone might even *believe*
A thing like that.

THE FAULTY REALIZATION OF THE HOARY PUCCOON

Felicia's uncle is insane. Completely aware
Of being caught in an unfinished expression of his own,
He believes he is the hoary puccoon. He believes
He grows in grey, nearly stalkless leaves
Among the rocky borders of the grasslands to the north

Which he watches all day from his window.
He has relinquished his fingers and his feet. The soup
Drips from his mouth. He doesn't know his tongue.
He lies, a scatter of blossoms spreading as orange
Corolla with five flaring lobes almost immobile
Under the sky, across the dry, dusty borders
Of his velvet settee.

At dusk he grows violent, fearful
Of his approaching blindness, the gradual advancement
Of his own destruction. At midnight, still staring
From the window in despair, he can see no way at all
To exist.

How can the actual white-haired, five-inch stems
Of the hoary puccoon be expected to bear the weight
Of a witness such as this? Even if they wanted,
The four barely emerging nutlets aiming toward August
Could never be made to accommodate such an expansion.

If he could just decide to leave the field
As the hoary puccoon and enter the realization
In the eyes of the man who watches from the window;
If he could just see himself leaving the field,
Moving as bright orange flowers through the air
Into the bright orange flowers of his retina;
If he could just rise and leave the field
As the branches of narrow articulated leaves and unite
With the identical, sun-flecked leaves inside
His voice, then he might remember once again
What it is he still has to say.

Felicia has been told that it will never do to speak
To the rooted, wind-blown, stalwart, orange-filled

Hoary puccoon of the field.
He knows better than to hear, realizing,
As terminal cluster of tubular flowers,
He has already said everything
He can ever know to say.

DUALITY

Sonia says a single perfect tree lives inside her,
That the more she tries the more distinctly she can see it,
As if it stood alone on a hill against a light sky,
All the tangled details of its barks and girders and tapering
Twig crosses revealing themselves clearly. She says
She can examine the impetus in the brown, folded nubs
Of its new leaves if she wishes. She says the tree
Is stationary and multitudinous in her chest, untouched
And skeletal, almost like metal, in its network against the sky.

And Sonia told Gordon the tree fills her body
Without pressure, its roots becoming one with her veins
And arteries. She can feel the small limber tips
Of its branches constantly in the palms of her hands.
She can detect, in her breath, the invention of its shifting
Attitude toward changing light. Anyone trained to look
With a scalpel could find its hardwood beginning in her brain.

Sonia says she wills the existence of the tree
By giving it a name, she wills the reality
Of the tree by giving it the location of her own body.

Sonia almost believes that the tree, created by the mind
But united with the body, can give the flesh eternity.

Gordon, laughing, calls it the Tree of Life.

Her Delight

After Psalms 1:2, 3

The tupelo, the blackgum and the poplar,
The overcup oak and the water hickory stand
Along the riverbank being eternal law all day.
They have risen, transforming soil, yielding
To each other, spreading and bending in easy-sun
Contortions, just as their branches decreed they must
During their rising.

Their shadows cast shadow-law this evening
In the long narrow bars of steady black they make
Over the river, being the permanent mathematical
Matrixes they invent relative to the height
Of their ascending trunks.

And the law taking in the soft moisture
Of slow, pervading rivers underground
Is called root. And the root consistently sorting
Ion and mineral by the describable properties
Of its gated skin is called law.

The plum-shaped fruit of the tupelo
Is the rule defining the conformity
To which it shapes itself. The orange berry

Of the possumhaw creates the sugary orange law
Of the sun by which it makes its reality.
Every flattened pit and dark blue drupe and paper-skin
Seed obeys perfectly the commandment it fashions
By becoming itself.

The trees only write the eternal law
Of whatever they have written—the accomplishment
Of the blackgum ordaining autumn red
In the simultaneous commandment of its scarlet leaves;
The accomplishment of the hickory branching
Its leaf in naked, thin-veined everlasting statutes
Of yellow across the sky.

And the woman standing this evening beneath the river trees,
Watching them rise by fissured bark, by husked and hardened
Fruit held high above the water, watching the long bodies
Of their shadows lying unmoved across the current,
She is the easy law that states she must become,
In the hazy, leaf-encroached columns of the evening sun,
Her meditation in this delight.

RAISING THE EYES THAT HIGH

It always happens, looking up to the tops
Of the sycamores still white and yellow with sunlight
Above the dark river bottom, or bending back to see
The wind, heard first as a caravan of paper horses
In the upper branches of the pines, or following
The flurried lightning bug to where it disappears
Above the parsley haw then catches on again

Even higher, raising the eyes that high,
The body begins to feel again something of significance.

Maybe it's the result of some predisposition
We've inherited from the trees, something in the genes
Promoting a belief in the importance of ascension
Or reaffirming the 70-million-year-old conviction
That stretching one leaf higher might be enough
To finally discover the sky. There's a feeling
In the body of a conviction like that.

Maybe the act of tilting the head backward
To search the sky for Mizar or Draco
Merely flexes the spinal cord at the neck,
Thus doubling the strength of every impulse
Passing there, or maybe sight is actually deepened
When blood flows backward from the eyes,
Or maybe more oxygen, helped by gravity
To the frontal lobe, expands the normal boundaries
Of the perceived heavens.

It might be something as simple as that.
But it's certain, watching the pale-pearl angle
Of the early evening moon, or following the five
Black cowbirds reel across the greying clouds,
Or tracing the easy drift of a cottonwood seed
Slowly rising directly overhead, it's certain,
There's bound to be something new again of power
Astir in the body.

Love Song

It's all right, together with me tonight,
How your whole body trembles exactly like the locust
Establishing its dry-cymbal quivering
Even in the farthest branch-tip leaves
Of the tree in which it screams.

Lying next to me, it's all right how similar
You become to the red deer in its agitated pacing
On the open plains by the sea, in its sidling
Haunch against haunch, in the final mastery
Of its mounting.

And it's all right, in those moments,
How you possess the same single-minded madness
Of the opened wood poppy circling and circling,
The same wild strength of its golden eye.

It's true. You're no better
Than the determined boar snorgling and rooting,
No better than the ridiculous, ruffled drumming
Of the prairie chicken, no better
Than the explosion of the milkweed pod
Spilling the white furl of the moon deep
In the midnight field. You're completely
Indistinguishable from the enraged sand myrtle
Absurd in its scarlet spread on the rocky bluffs.

But it's all right. Don't you know
This is precisely what I seek, mad myself
To envelope every last drupe and pearl-dropped ovule,
Every nip and cry and needle-fine boring, every drooping,
Spore-rich tassel of oak flower, all the whistling,

Wing-beating, heavy-tipped matings of an entire prairie
Of grasses, every wafted, moaning seed hook
You can possibly manage to bring to me,
That this is exactly what I contrive to take into my arms
With you, again and again.

———————

THE HUMMINGBIRD: A SEDUCTION

If I were a female hummingbird perched still
And quiet on an upper myrtle branch
In the spring afternoon and if you were a male
Alone in the whole heavens before me, having parted
Yourself, for me, from cedar top and honeysuckle stem
And earth down, your body hovering in midair
Far away from jewelweed, thistle and bee balm;

And if I watched how you fell, plummeting before me,
And how you rose again and fell, with such mastery
That I believed for a moment *you* were the sky
And the red-marked bird diving inside your circumference
Was just the physical revelation of the light's
Most perfect desire;

And if I saw your sweeping and sucking
Performance of swirling egg and semen in the air,
The weaving, twisting vision of red petal
And nectar and soaring rump, the rush of your wing
In its grand confusion of arcing and splitting
Created completely out of nothing just for me,

Then when you came down to me, I would call you
My own spinning bloom of ruby sage, my funneling
Storm of sunlit sperm and pollen, my only breathless
Piece of scarlet sky, and I would bless the base
Of each of your feathers and touch the tine
Of string muscles binding your wings and taste
The odor of your glistening oils and hunt
The honey in your crimson flare
And I would take you and take you and take you
Deep into any kind of nest you ever wanted.

THE POWER OF TOADS

The oak toad and the red-spotted toad love their love
In a spring rain, calling and calling, breeding
Through a stormy evening clasped atop their mates.
Who wouldn't sing—anticipating the belly pressed hard
Against a female's spine in the steady rain
Below writhing skies, the safe moist jelly effluence
Of a final exaltation?

There might be some toads who actually believe
That the loin-shaking thunder of the banks, the evening
Filled with damp, the warm softening mud and rising
Riverlets are the facts of their own persistent
Performance. Maybe they think that when they sing
They sing more than songs, creating rain and mist
By their voices, initiating the union of water and dusk,
Females materializing on the banks shaped perfectly
By their calls.

And some toads may be convinced they have forced
The heavens to twist and moan by the continual expansion
Of their lung sacs pushing against the dusk.
And some might believe the splitting light,
The soaring grey they see above them are nothing
But a vision of the longing in their groins,
A fertile spring heaven caught in its entirety
At the pit of the gut.

And they might be right.
Who knows whether these broken heavens
Could exist tonight separate from trills and toad ringings?
Maybe the particles of this rain descending on the pond
Are nothing but the visual manifestation of whistles
And cascading love clicks in the shore grasses.
Raindrops-finding-earth and coitus could very well
Be known here as one.

We could investigate the causal relationship
Between rainstorm and love-by-pondside if we wished.
We could lie down in the grasses by the water's edge
And watch to see exactly how the heavens were moved,
Thinking hard of thunder, imagining all the courses
That slow, clean waters might take across our bodies,
Believing completely in the rolling and pressing power
Of heavens and thighs. And in the end we might be glad,
Even if all we discovered for certain was the slick, sweet
Promise of good love beneath dark skies inside warm rains.

BETRAYAL: THE REFLECTION OF THE CATTAIL

The black lines of the cattail reeds sway in grace
Before the purple sky. On the stalk above the thick
Brown fruits of the velvet female, I can see the shriveled
Spike of the expended male making slow and crooked
Slices through the early stars.

A single long leaf bends and bows above the lake,
Its narrow tip barely tracing the surface of the water
With the breeze. It moves, making random trails exactly
Like an unfaithful lover makes, tracing with her finger
The features of her only love.

The single arch of a cattail leaf can rest lightly
Like an arm across the glowing belly of a softly falling sun,
And it can bend over the clear water of the lake,
Steady and gentle and graceful as a faithful lover
Bent above the face of his only love.

The slender grasses of the cattail twist now
And turn in a sudden breeze against the purple sky
Like lovers locking their legs at the ankles, like lovers
Turning their thighs once in a sudden locking,
Like lovers opening once to unlock and expose
The sudden gleaming surface of a dark red sun.

In the earth the cattail spreads
And widens its roots and the bases of its reeds.
It presses down and holds on hard as if it believed
The shore was its only faithful lover.
And when the loon cries and when the king rail calls,
The tangled reeds of the cattail stiffen imperceptibly
And move their shining edges among the stars

As if they screamed themselves. And when the loon rises
And when the king rail soars, the reeds shudder
Like tangled lovers feeling the slicing edges
Of a million stars escaping from their bodies to the sky.

The cattail knows how to bear the staunchest grace
Beside the lake, just as if it didn't realize
It was being carried, along with us, across the vast
Deceptive light of forgiveness this evening, through darkness
Into darkness.

———————

AT THE BREAK OF SPRING

Caddisfly larvae, living in clear-water
Streams, construct tiny protective cases
Around themselves with bits of bark,
Grass and pieces of pink gravel in mosaics.

Little temples, Felicia calls them.

Albert loves temples and knows a man who lives
Beside one, the northern wall of his cottage
Being the temple itself. He can imitate perfectly
The running of twelve-tone bells announcing birth or death.

Gordon wants to study the pattern of clear
Running water covering caddisfly larvae in sunlight
And compare it to the pattern of running bells announcing
Death in the clear morning as seen from below.

Felicia thinks caddisfly larvae can forgive any sin
Because they live inside temples underwater
Continually in a state of baptism.

Christ called the body a temple.

Cecil loves bodies and thinks Sonia's is a mosaic,
Dark and unseen, lit as if by light underwater.
To completely cover Sonia himself
Is a baptism of sin Cecil is afraid to perform.

Felicia likes to believe the morning sky
Is a temple immersed in light and, by running
Across the open lawn to the arbor house, she herself might
Become the twelve-tone sounding of its multiple bells.

Sonia, walking beside the stream after dark, thinks
Any temple continually immersed in the light
Of its own birth and death has earned the right to call sin
A baptism of performance, clearly forgivable.

THE POSSIBLE SALVATION OF CONTINUOUS MOTION

Adapted from a love letter written by E. Lotter (1872–1930)

If we could be taken alone together in a driverless
Sleigh pulled by horses with blinders over endless
Uninhabited acres of snow; if the particles
Of our transgression could be left behind us
Scattered across the woodlands and frozen lakes
Like pieces of light scattered over the flashing snow;

If the initiation and accomplishment of our act
In that sleigh could be separated by miles
Of forest—the careful parting begun
Under the ice-covered cedars, the widening and entering
Accomplished in swirls of frost racing along the hills,
The removal and revelation coming beside the seesaw shifting
Of grassheads rustling in the snowy ditches; all the elements
Of our interaction left in a thousand different places—
Thigh against thigh with the drowsy owlets in the trees
Overhead, your face caught for an instant above mine
In one eye of the snow hare;

If the horses could go fast enough across the ice
So that no one would ever be able to say, "Sin
Was committed *here,*" our sin being as diffuse
As broken bells sounding in molecules of ringing
Clear across the countryside;

And under the blanket beside you in the sleigh,
If I could watch the night above the flying heads
Of the horses, if I could see our love exploded
Like stars cast in a black sky over the glassy plains
So that nothing, not even the mind of an angel,
Could ever reassemble that deed;

Well, I would go with you right now,
Dearest, immediately, while the horses
Are still biting and strapping in their reins.

THE DELIGHT OF BEING LOST

There are times when one might wish to be nothing
But the plain crease and budded nipple
Of a breast, nothing but the manner in the lay
Of an arm across a pillow or the pressure of hips
And shoulders on a sheet. Sometimes there is a desire
To draw down into the dull turn of the inner knee, dumb
And isolated from the cognizant details of any summer night,
To be chin and crotch solely as the unrecorded, passing
Moments of themselves, to have no name or place but breath.

If wished enough, it might be possible to sink away completely,
To leave the persistent presence of pine trees
Brushing against the eaves, loons circling the lake,
Making an issue of direction; to sink away, remaining
Awake inside the oblivion deep within a naked thigh,
To open the eyes inside the blindness of a wrist, hearing
Nothing but the deafness in the curve of the neck.

It would seem a perfect joy to me tonight
To lie still in this darkness, to deny everything
But the rise in the line of ankle or spine, ignoring
The angles of walls establishing definable spaces,
Ignoring the clear, moon-shadow signals of specific
Circumstance, to recognize no reality but the universal
Anonymity of a particular body which might then be stroked
And kissed and fondled and worshipped without ever knowing
Or caring to ask by whom or where or how it was given
Such pleasure.

An Experiment of Faith

Gordon thinks doubt is the hallmark of our species
Since it brings about inquiry, faith, bravery
And the desire for verification.

Watching the candelabra at dinner, Felicia asked
If flame itself ever had a shadow.

Cecil doubts that flame casts a shadow,
But Sonia will attempt to verify his position
By an experiment to be conducted with three candles
And a torch in the white parlor after dark.
She has named the event, "An Enquiry into the Doubtful
Properties of the Shadow of Light."

Albert is not brave enough to doubt
That his finger held above the flame
Will eventually show a shadow of pain.

Gordon finds it possible to doubt the existence
Of the snow-covered forest just outside the east window
But possesses enough faith to say with certainty
It is the moon again tonight that makes the shadow
Of the branch across the silk drapes.

Though doubting that he will be brave enough
To touch Sonia's breast in the dark tonight
And possibly create thereby a shadow of light,
Cecil allows himself to daydream a verification
Of his faith in its silky warm existence.

Gordon asked Albert to verify the bravery

Of his attempt to prove that absolute faith
Is a prerequisite to doubt, since the existence
Of doubt itself can never be doubted.

A Daydream of Light

We could sit together in the courtyard
Before the fountain during the next full moon.
We could sit on the stone bench facing west,
Our backs to the moon, and watch our shadows
Lying side by side on the white walk. We could spread
Our legs to the metallic light and see the confusion
In our hands bound up together with darkness and the moon.
We could talk, not of light, but of the facets of light
Manifesting themselves impulsively in the falling water,
The moon broken and re-created instantaneously over and over.

Or we could sit facing the moon to the east,
Taking it between us as something hard and sure
Held in common, discussing the origins of rocks
Shining in the sky, altering everything exposed below.
What should I imagine then, recognizing its light
On your face, tasting its light on your forehead, touching
Its light in your hair?

Or we could sit on the bench to the north,
Buried by the overhanging sycamore,
The moon showing sideways from the left.
We could wonder if light was the first surface
Imprinted with fact or if black was the first

Underlying background necessary for illumination.
We could wonder if the tiny weightless blackbirds
Hovering over our bodies were leaf shadows
Or merely random blankness lying between splashes fallen
From the moon. We could wonder how the dark shadow
From a passing cloud could be the lightest
Indication across our eyes of our recognition of the moon.

Or we could lie down together where there are no shadows at all,
In the open clearing of the courtyard, the moon
At its apex directly overhead, or lie down together
Where there are no shadows at all, in the total blackness
Of the alcove facing north. We could wonder, at the end,
What can happen to light, what can happen to darkness,
When there is no space for either left between us.

We must ask if this daydream is light broken
And re-created instantaneously or simply an impulsive
Shadow passing across the light in our eyes,
Finding no space left for its realization.

II

THE DEFINITION OF TIME

In the same moment
That Kioka's great-great-grandfather died,
11,000 particles of frost dissolved into dew
On the blades of the woodrush,
And three water lily leaf beetles paused
Anticipating light making movements
Of their bodies in the weeds.

And in that same moment an earthworm
Swallowed a single red spore down its slimmest
Vein, and the chimney crayfish shoveled a whisker farther
Through slick pond-bottom silt, and one slow
Slice of aster separated its purple segment
From the bud.

Simultaneously the mossy granite along the ridge shifted
Two grains on its five-mile fault, and the hooves
Of ewe and pony, damp in the low-field fog,
Shook with that shift. The early hawk on the post
Blinked a drop of mist from its eye, and the black tern
With a cry flew straight up, remembering the marsh
By scent alone over the sandy hills.

And in that instant the field, carried
Without consent through the dark, held
Its sedges steady for the first turn
Into the full orange sun, and each tense sliver
Of pine on the mountains far to the east

Shone hot already in a white noon,
And in the dark night-sea far behind the field and forest,
The head of a single shark sperm pierced
An ovum and became blood.

The twelfth ring of the tallest redwood
Hardened its circle, and the first lick of the hatching
Goatweed butterfly was made tongue. And Kioka
And his ancestors call the infinite and continuous
Record they make of this moment, "The Book
Of the Beginning and the Chronicle of the End."

————————

The Possible Suffering of a God during Creation

It might be continuous—the despair he experiences
Over the imperfection of the unfinished, the weaving
Body of the imprisoned moonfish, for instance,
Whose invisible arms in the mid-waters of the deep sea
Are not yet free, or the velvet-blue vervain
Whose grainy tongue will not move to speak, or the ear
Of the spitting spider still oblivious to sound.

It might be pervasive—the anguish he feels
Over the falling away of everything that the duration
Of the creation must, of necessity, demand, maybe feeling
The break of each and every russet-headed grass
Collapsing under winter ice or feeling the split
Of each dried and brittle yellow wing of the sycamore
As it falls from the branch. Maybe he winces
At each particle-by-particle disintegration of the limestone

Ledge into the crevasse and the resulting compulsion
Of the crevasse to rise grain by grain, obliterating itself.

And maybe he suffers from the suffering
Inherent to the transitory, feeling grief himself
For the grief of shattered beaches, disembodied bones
And claws, twisted squid, piles of ripped and tangled,
Uprooted turtles and rock crabs and Jonah crabs,
Sand bugs, seaweed and kelp.

How can he stand to comprehend the hard, pitiful
Unrelenting cycles of coitus, ovipositors, sperm and zygotes,
The repeated unions and dissolutions over and over,
The constant tenacious burying and covering and hiding
And nesting, the furious nurturing of eggs, the bright
Breaking-forth and the inevitable cold blowing-away?

Think of the million million dried stems of decaying
Dragonflies, the thousand thousand leathery cavities
Of old toads, the mounds of cows' teeth, the tufts
Of torn fur, the contorted eyes, the broken feet, the rank
Bloated odors, the fecund brown-haired mildews
That are the residue of his process. How can he tolerate knowing
There is nothing else here on earth as bright and salty
As blood spilled in the open?

Maybe he wakes periodically at night,
Wiping away the tears he doesn't know
He has cried in his sleep, not having had time yet to tell
Himself precisely how it is he must mourn, not having had time yet
To elicit from his creation its invention
Of his own solace.

The Tattooed Lady in the Garden   183

THE POSSIBLE ADVANTAGES OF
THE EXPENDABLE MULTITUDES

There could be a quirk in the conception of time.
For instance, the brief slide of a single herring
In the sights of an ocean bird might be measured,
At the last moment, in a slow motion of milliseconds,
Each fin spread like a fan of transparent bones
Breaking gradually through the green sea, a long
And complete absorption in that one final movement
Of body and wave together. It could be lengthened
To last a lifetime.

Or maybe there is a strange particulate vision
Only possible in a colony of microscopic copepod
Swaying in and out of the sand eel's range, swallowed
Simultaneously by the thousands. Who knows
What the unseen see? There might be a sense
Of broadcast, a fulfillment of scattering felt
Among the barnacle larva, never achieved
By the predatory shag at the top of the chain.
And the meadow vole crouched immediately below
The barred owl must experience a sudden and unusual
Hard hold on the potential.

Death coming in numbers among the small and uncountable
Might be altered in its aspects. An invaded nest
Of tadpoles might perceive itself as an array of points
Lit briefly in a sparkling pattern of extinction
Along the shore. An endless variety of split-second
Scenes might be caught and held visible in the separate eyes
Of each sea turtle penned on the beach. Death,
Functioning in a thousand specific places at once,

Always completing the magnitude of its obligations,
Has never been properly recognized for its ingenuity.

We must consider the possibility
That from the viewpoint of a cluster of flagellates
We might simply appear to be possessed
By an awkward notion of longevity, a peculiar bias
For dying alone.

THE VERIFICATION OF VULNERABILITY: BOG TURTLE

Guarded by horned beak and nails, surrounded
By mahogany carapace molded in tiles
Like beveled wood, hidden within the hingeless
Plastron, beneath twelve, yellow-splotched
Black scutes, buried below the inner lungs
And breast, harbored in the far reaches
Of the living heart, there it exists,
As it must, that particle of vulnerability,
As definite in its place as if it were a brief glint
Of steel, buried inside the body of the bog turtle.

And it is carried in that body daily, like a pinpoint
Of diamond in a dark pouch, through marshy fields
And sunlit seepages, and it is borne in that body,
Like a crystal of salt-light locked in a case
Of night, borne through snail-ridden reeds and pungent
Cow pastures in spring. It is cushioned and bound
By folds of velvet, by flesh and the muscle
Of dreams, during sleep on a weedy tussock all afternoon.
It is divided and bequeathed again in June, protected

By thick sap, by yolk meal and forage inside its egg
Encompassed by the walls of shell and nest.

Maybe I can imagine the sole intention present
In the steady movement of turtle breath filled
With the odor of worms this morning, stirring
Clover moisture at the roots. Maybe I can understand
How the body has taken form solely
Around the possibility of its own death,
How the entire body of the bog turtle
Cherishes and maintains and verifies the existence
Of its own crucial point of vulnerability exactly
As if that point were the only distinct,
Dimensionless instant of eternity ever realized.
And maybe I can guess what it is we own,
If, in fact, it is true: the proof of possession
Is the possibility of loss.

———————

The Limitations of Death

No form of its own at all, less than a wraith,
It is bound forever to the living, totally
Dependent on viable bone, on the breath
Of the oxpecker and the buffalo, on the sustaining
Will of black-billed cuckoo and threaded bittium,
On the success of potential rooting in rhubarb
And bluebonnet seed, for its future.

Nonexistent without the continuous rise
Of bittersweet sapling and loblolly bay, lost,
Doomed, doomed without the prevailing heart

Of the basswood, the heart of the holding madtom,
The heartfelt knot of the chicory, it has no place at all
Except the upward thrust of the aphid, the spreading lips
Of the hawthorn bloom.

So obviously dependent on the continual well-being
Of the living, death must always admit, for the sake
Of its own reality, must always testify to the enduring
Glory of its victims and, even in the performance
Of its only act, must continue to praise the proceeding
Diligence of the nursery web spider, the pure structure
Of the muskrat's cave, the focus of the cleaner shrimp
Nibbling carefully at the flank of the angelfish
Far below the sea and the angelfish and the shining
Flank itself, for the predominating ascendancy
They consistently maintain.

JUSTIFICATION OF THE HORNED LIZARD

I don't know why the horned lizard wants to live.
It's so ugly—short prickly horns and scowling
Eyes, lipless smile forced forever by bone,
Hideous scaly hollow where its nose should be.

I don't know what the horned lizard has to live for,
Skittering over the sun-irritated sand, scraping
The hot dusty brambles. It never sees anything but gravel
And grit, thorns and stickery insects, the towering
Creosote bush, the ocotillo and its whiplike
Branches, the severe edges of the Spanish dagger.
Even shade is either barren rock or barb.

The horned lizard will never know
A lush thing in its life. It will never see the flower
Of the water-filled lobelia bent over a clear
Shallow creek. It will never know moss floating
In waves in the current by the bank or the blue-blown
Fronds of the water clover. It will never have a smooth
Glistening belly of white like the bullfrog or a dew-heavy
Trill like the mating toad. It will never slip easily
Through mud like the skink or squat in the dank humus
At the bottom of a decaying forest in daytime.
It will never be free of dust. The only drink it will ever know
Is in the body of a bug.

And the horned lizard possesses nothing noble—
Embarrassing tail, warty hide covered with sharp dirty
Scales. No touch to its body, even from its own kind,
Could ever be delicate or caressing.

I don't know why the horned lizard wants to live.
Yet threatened, it burrows frantically into the sand
With a surprisingly determined fury of forehead, limbs
And ribs. Pursued, it even fights for itself, almost rising up,
Posturing on its bowed legs, propelling blood out of its eyes
In tight straight streams shot directly at the source
Of its possible extinction. It fights for itself,
Almost rising up, as if the performance of that act,
The posture, the propulsion of the blood itself,
Were justification enough and the only reason needed.

EULOGY FOR A HERMIT CRAB

You were consistently brave
On these surf-drenched rocks, in and out of their salty
Slough holes around which the entire expanse
Of the glinting grey sea and the single spotlight
Of the sun went spinning and spinning and spinning
In a tangle of blinding spume and spray
And pistol-shot collisions your whole life long.
You stayed. Even with the wet icy wind of the moon
Circling your silver case night after night after night
You were here.

And by the gritty orange curve of your claws,
By the soft, wormlike grip
Of your hinter body, by the unrelieved wonder
Of your black-pea eyes, by the mystified swing
And swing and swing of your touching antennae,
You maintained your name meticulously, you kept
Your name intact exactly, day after day after day.
No one could say you were less than perfect
In the hermitage of your crabness.

Now, beside the racing, incomprehensible racket
Of the sea stretching its great girth forever
Back and forth between this direction and another,
Please let the words of this proper praise I speak
Become the identical and proper sound
Of my mourning.

Trinity

I wish something slow and gentle and good
Would happen to me, a patient and prolonged
Kind of happiness coming in the same way evening
Comes to a wide-branched sycamore standing
In an empty field; each branch, not succumbing,
Not taken, but feeling its entire existence
A willing revolution of cells; even asleep,
Feeling a decision of gold spreading
Over its ragged bark and motionless knots of seed,
Over every naked, vulnerable juncture; each leaf
Becoming a lavender shell, a stem-deep line
Of violet turning slowly and carefully to possess exactly
The pale and patient color of the sky coming.

I wish something that slow and that patient
Would come to me, maybe like the happiness
Growing when the lover's hand, easy on the thigh
Or easy on the breast, moves like late light moves
Over the branches of a sycamore, causing
A slow revolution of decision in the body;
Even asleep, feeling the spread of hazy coral
And ivory-grey rising through the legs and spine
To alter the belief behind the eyes; feeling the slow
Turn of wave after wave of acquiescence moving
From the inner throat to the radiance of a gold belly
To a bone center of purple; an easy, slow-turning
Happiness of possession like that, prolonged.

I wish something that gentle and that careful
And that patient would come to me. Death

Might be that way if one knew how to wait for it,
If death came easily and slowly,
If death were good.

———————

THE ART OF BECOMING

The morning, passing through narrowing and widening
Parabolas of orange and spotted sunlight on the lawn,
Moving in shifting gold-grey shawls of silk lying low,
Thinning and rising through stalks of steeplebush
And bedstraw, through the first start of the first finch
Streaking past the vacancy in the sky where the last
White stone of star was last seen, can only be defined
In the constant change of itself.

The particular leaf, pushing its several green molecules
Outward to a hard edge of photosynthesis, microscopic
In its building and bumping continuously
From one moment to the next, only becomes magnolia
In this prolonged act of its dying.

Realization itself is the changing destruction
And process of cells failing and rising constantly
In their creation of thought. If every white glint
On the surface of the holly, every clenching hair
In the amber center of spirea, every sleight of insect
Wing and cactus spire, the creviced tricks
Of fern segment and sunfish blade were halted right now,
In this moment, one instant caught perfectly and lasting forever,
Then "now" would be the only and final statement of this work.

Immortality must only exist in the sound
Of these words recognizing, through the circling and faltering
Of oak peaks, through the knot of midnight tightening
And loosening, through star streams inventing destination
By the fact of their direction, in the sound of these words
Recognizing their need to pray over and over and over
For the continuing procedure of their own decay.

———————

THE GOD OF ORNITHOLOGY

Observed feathers are his pride—the iridescent purple
And blue-grey gloss, the perfect sheen of barb and shaft
Upon vane and hook, the scarlet-gold cacophony.

The snatching and jerking of moss
And rootlets, seaweed and fishbones,
The binding and stitching of straw and tendrils,
The knotting of cobwebs, the twig-tucking and plotting
Of mud, the quick-needled winding and twisting
Of plant down, bark strips and snake skins
Are the supposed mechanisms of his contemplations.

He is the expanded listing of perching birds,
Seed birds, carrion birds and shore birds,
The naming of stall and slot, major pectoral
And minor pectoral. He remembers by the delineation
Of the bones of the Ichthyornis and the Hesperornis.
He feels his own skeleton by the detailed classification
Of bee eaters and goatsuckers, mousebirds, swifts,
Rollers and their allies. The identification of the eye orbit

Of the thrush establishes the field of vision
By which he is able to perceive his own image.

And when the bank swallows are seen soaring upward
He opens his arms wide. And when the pied-billed grebe
Is acknowledged gliding along the surface of the lake,
He breathes deeply. By the recognized spread
Of each pale grey primary feather of the harrier's wing
He achieves dexterity.

Understand how the identification of the rattle
Of the wren is his listening, how the noted tremulo
Of the dove is his acuity, how the recognized shrieks
And quocks and stutterings and trills, the prolonged whistles
Of the grackles provide the means he needs to invent
The compassion that is essential to their survival.

The consideration of the movement of space
Within the scattering of blackbirds molding the sky
Above the field, the consideration of the body
Of the gull forming the ocean fog through which it flies,
The consideration of the gannets constituting the reality
Of the cliff on which they nest, the consideration
Of the fan-shaped descent of every bird verifying
The exact point at which the earth begins, all become
The crisscrossing pattern of his identity maintained
As the only possible medium in which these activities may occur.

Remember how he waits, as if he were settling in the dark
Evening rocks beside the sea, as if he were brooding
Among the tall marsh grasses, as if he were quiet
In the tops of the black jungle trees. Remember how he waits,
Dependent for his creation on the continued discovery
Of every physical manifestation he nurtures.

The Creation of the Inaudible

Maybe no one can distinguish which voice
Is god's voice sounding in a summer dusk
Because he calls with the same rising frequency,
The same rasp and rattling rustle the cicadas use
As they cling to the high leaves in the glowing
Dust of the oaks.

His exclamations might blend so precisely with the final
Crises of the swallows settling before dark
That no one will ever be able to say with certainty,
"That last long cry winging over the rooftop
Came from god."

Breathy and low, the vibrations of his nightly
Incantations could easily be masked by the scarcely
Audible hush of the lakeline dealing with the rocky shore,
And when a thousand dry sheaths of rushes and thistles
Stiffen and shiver in an autumn wind, anyone can imagine
How quickly and irretrievably his whisper might be lost.

Someone far away must be saying right now:
The only unique sound of his being
Is the spoken postulation of his unheard presence.

For even if he found the perfect chant this morning
And even if he played the perfect strings to accompany it,
Still, no one could be expected to know,
Because the blind click beetle flipping in midair,
And the slider turtle easing through the black iris bog,
And two savannah pines shedding dawn in staccato pieces
Of falling sun are already engaged in performing
The very same arrangement themselves.

TRANSFORMATION

When the honeysuckle vine blooming beside the barn
First became the white and yellow tangle of her eye,
And the mouse snake passing beneath the dry grasses
Became the long steady hush of her ear, and the spring hill
Was transformed into the rise of her bare feet climbing in April.

When the afternoon between the canyon walls
Became the echoing shout of her voice, and the line
Of orange-stone sun, appearing through a crevice
Of granite, shone as the exact hour of her solstice;
When the cold January wind turned to the flesh
Of her stinging fingertips, and the birds flying
Over the rice beds became the seven crows of her count;

When the dawning sun was the beginning rim
Of light showing over the eastern edge of her sight,
And the earth became, for the only time in its history,
The place of her shadow, and the possibilities
Lying far away between the stars were suddenly
The unwitnessed boundaries of her heart . . .

Felicia was born.

FILLING IN SPACES

Watching through the east window this afternoon
Sonia knows there are no empty spaces left
Inside that winter frame. All the lines
Of the field have been filled perfectly with pieces

Of fitted snow, and the field allows no room behind it
As it leans tightly against the crowded blue cedars
On the hillsides. The stream gully has risen slowly
Out of itself, through its own vacancy, becoming one
And identical with field-white.

And in the only spot where a black branch of crooked
Garden ash might exist drawing across the blue hills
And heaven, a bare branch of crooked garden ash exists.
And in the only seams where sky might press
Between blades of icy pine, the sky has penetrated
In needles of grey. Any fallen oak leaf frozen in ice
Can only force the curved edge of its icy hollow
Into the evening by finding the place where evening
Has already discovered its own curl of hollow cold.

Sonia is confident that all spaces are filled
This afternoon, that there is no room left in the window
For anything else, until she sees Albert moving
Across the white field far away, a small but definite
Crack coming between heaven and snow, until she watches
His approaching body as it widens and enlarges
The vacant space it creates by itself in the dusk,
Until she recognizes the real emptiness of his open arms
As he runs toward the window, kicking up spirals of snow
That strike the glass void existing right before Sonia's vision
Just barely beginning now to be filled.

Exposing the Future with Conviction

Grunion have convictions. Coming up out of the sea
Without a doubt, they clear the moon's surface of wave
And saltwater completely. They are scarcely able to breathe
In that unhindered light. Even in their silver
Strait jackets they have believed from the beginning
In this particular tide, this particular black beach.
They have seen, before it ever occurred, the glycerin
Eye burning on dry land. How else could they come
With so much certainty?

Think of one egg left behind, buried like a drop
Of oil in the dark sand. Even before the eye in that egg
Is a black dot, even before the heart is a red grain
Sunk in its tiny bubble, every detail of the first high tide
Of next summer and the summer beyond that
Is waiting, caught and held tight inside. Imagine
The whole heaven of the full moon a year from now,
And the black wind over the sea-to-come and the salt air
Cupped in the conch-not-yet-crystallized,
All held in their entireties inside that jelly shell.

What if there were an instrument small enough to locate
And expose all the elements of the future spawnings
Contained in a single grunion gene?
Then from here we could watch next year's moon dripping clear,
Changing its white focus, and we could examine
The sea birds not yet born waiting on the bluffs
Along the bay and hear the sounds of the potential crabs
Scratching in their caves. From already having seen,
We could believe in the hard pull of the new children's
Children's children up that beach.

And what if the speck of a grunion egg just beginning
Should be planted inside the embryo heart of our next child born?
Then wouldn't he know from the start how he was to rise
Like silver fruit in a swollen tide, how he was to start up
And break through elements? Wouldn't he know in his lungs,
Before it happened, the sudden changing dimension
Of his own breath? Wouldn't he understand how he was bound
To decide to head straight for what he already knew was coming,
And couldn't he tell us everything we need to know
About convictions like that?

LINEAGE

Before the day when Kioka was converted,
Proclaiming himself a born Indian, he knew nothing
About coupsticks or calumets or pinto ponies
Or his own bare legs below breechcloths or famine
On a prairie in dry, waist-high grasses or nightmares
Behind eyes frozen shut with sleet. Before that day,
He had never seen or touched the angel of the abyss
Or the enemy of the abyss.

It was only after Kioka became a perfect Indian
That his elderly mother grew gradually obsessed
With clay pottery and reeds, appearing on summer days
In her lace peignoir at dawn, gathering mud
In hand-woven baskets by the river bottom. It was then
That his sister amazed everyone by creating,
On the croquet courts, a multicolored sand painting
Of sun gods and fire gods by heart.

And after Kioka had been a perfect Indian
For fifty moons, his father's physician found
Strains of red corpuscles from Fleet Deer, Warrior Girl
And Cocotyl in samples of the family's blood.
And, in an old painted gourd filled with raw chocolate
And hammered silver jewelry, his uncle discovered
A portrait, never seen before, of his great-paternal-aunt
Dressed in green quetzal feathers with her hair dyed blue.

Now Kioka's brother can call wolves or wild turkeys
With a weird tremolo, and they come. His first cousin
Can perform ritual music on shell trumpet, clay whistle
Or two-toned drums. And the relative who ridiculed Kioka,
Making gestures behind his back, was visited twice
By night stranglers smelling of bear grease and piñon nuts.
Afterward, when he could speak again, he gave
Seven sincere prayers for the spirits of Serpent Woman
And Rain-God-with-Jaguar-Teeth.

Kioka, having no permanent abode and having reinterpreted
His sense of direction, rarely sees his family
And will not attest personally to these phenomena.
But the oldest white-winged hawk in the canyon, circling
The sacred place where the graves of Kioka's ancestors
Have now come to be, cries the names of his six fathers
Day after day into the rock-walled sky.
And everyone who hears it knows it to be so.

INTERMEDIARY

For John A. and Arthur

This is what I ask: that if they must be taken
They be taken like the threads of the cotton grass
Are taken by the summer wind, excited and dizzy
And safe, flying inside their own seeds;
And if they must be lost that they be lost
Like leaves of the water starwort
Are lost, submerged and rising over and over
In the slow-rooted current by the bank.

I ask that they always be found
With the same sure and easy touch
The early morning stillness uses to find itself
In needles of dew on each hyssop in the ditch.

And may they see everything the boatman bug,
Shining inside its bubble of air, sees
Through silver skin in the pond-bottom mud,
And may they be obliged in the same way the orb snail,
Sucking on sedges in shallow water, is obliged.
And may they be promised everything a single blade
Of sweet flag, kept by the grip of the elmid
On its stem, kept by the surrounding call
Of the cinnamon teal, kept by its line
In the marsh-filled sky, is promised.

Out loud, in public and in writing, I ask again
That solace come to them like sun comes
To the egg of the longspur, penetrating the shell,
Settling warmth inside the potential heart
And beginnings of bone. And I ask that they remember

Their grace in the same way the fetal bird remembers light
Inside the blackness of its gathering skull inside
The cave of its egg.

And with the same attention a streamer of ice
Moving with the moon commands, with the same decision
The grassland plovers declare as they rise
From the hayfields into the evening sky,
I ask that these pleas of mine arrest the notice
Of all those angels already possessing a lasting love
For fine and dauntless boys like mine.

If a Son Asks

Luke 11:11

I would bring him hatchetfish, goatfish
And albacore. I would bring shad with the finest
Silver-sloughing scales, the gristled stems
Of broad-nosed cat, fat orange salmon filled
With eggs and slick sturgeon round with oily roe,
The rich milt of mackerel, tarpon still turning,
Their grey gills revealing the inner movements
Of the prairie rose, and the intent of the sea caught
In the clear salty syrup of the yellow-fin's eye,
And each transparent scale of the carp showing
Its circling rings as a still lake shows time
By a single drop of rain.

If a son asks, I would bring
The invisible fish in the treetops and the way

It uses sunlight for water and the way it shapes
The air between branches and the way it holds itself
Against the rushing current of the wind.

And if he asks, the fish keeping the bracing structure
Of cobwebs in its bones, the fanning of bracken
Fronds in its veins, keeping the sliding sky of summer
For a pale blue flank, the black tail-ripple of night
In its quick forward swerve; the fish stroking
In darkness behind the eyes, if he asks, treading
Like sleep, the one that can take fathers and swallow
Mothers and consume sons, making a world of its belly
As it sounds, sounding deep, the backwash of space
Roaring and cresting over its rolling descent, I would give
That fish in its entirety to a son who asks
And kiss him as he takes it and hold him,
And hold him while he eats.

THE BIRTH SONG AND THE DEATH SONG

One of them moves like a continuum of stars rising
Out of the lake on the east, making, by its crossing,
A void to cross above poplar and chain fern,
Night-threading teal and a nebula of carp.
And one of them moves like a season of stars
Sinking into the reeds and water lilies
Of the lake on the west, making, by its passing,
An interval to pass far below mud-laden roots
Of arum, the bright undersides of wheel snails,
Hydra and yellow-budded lotus.

One turns itself inside out, exposing
Its tender intimacies to every rush
And hook and spire of mayhem and mercy.
And the other one gathers into itself continually,
Surrounding every spicule and template
Of pity and quickening and atrocity
With its most private solicitudes.

And the first one releases suddenly
Like a spider dropping and swinging free
In the evening light between branchtop and earth.
And the last one accepts release instantaneously
Like a moment of evening light becoming
The floating liberty of a spider's fall
Between branchtop and earth.

The finer one is the opening deep
In the flower of the purple pleatleaf leading
From the disorder of eternity to an upright
Petal of blue cobwebbed in morning sun.
And the greater one is the tight
Closing of a single seed of pleatleaf
Fastening around the certain infinity
Of its only place in the field.

And one is like strong wooden arms spread wide
And sailing, and the other is like the steady
Bracing bones of a rising kite, by which means
Both *do* support and endure at once
The soaring tension of the paper soul
As it spirals and spins—sunside,
Earthside—across the open spaces of the sky.

The Tattooed Lady in the Garden

III

LITTLE FUGUE

Felicia and Albert, running through the thin grasses
In the mown field this afternoon, are attempting
To keep up with the red-tailed hawk's shadow
As it glides across the pond and the meadow.

Cecil can also see the red-tailed hawk
In the sky in the pond as he dangles his feet
In the water, his toes startling the basking killifish.

The curious killifish rise slowly now to suck
At Cecil's toes in the same way the hawk soars upward
Toward the basking sun, its winged shadow becoming a small
Black fish swimming through the slender grasses.

Cecil sees the killifish as flashing slips of light
Darting through the feathers of the hawk as it glides
Across the blue water of the heavens at his feet.

Albert thinks Felicia's laughter soaring
Over the meadow is like slips of light
Flashing off the fins of little killifish.

Felicia can imagine slips of sun darting like killifish
In the sky between her legs as she runs after the wings
Of the red-tailed hawk over the mown meadow.

Cecil can see the red-tailed hawk growing smaller
And smaller, circling his feet, disappearing finally

Into the black mouth of a single killifish gliding
At the bottom of the pond.

The killifish, simultaneously swallowed like a slip of sun
By the shadow of the hawk, can be seen as itself once again
Inside Felicia's laughter.

Felicia, catching up and stepping on the shadow
Of the hawk, has finally seen the black wings of her feet.

When Sonia calls from the porch, telling everyone
That the magician has arrived for the party, all the sounds
Of finned light passing like laughter over the stubbled sun
Are swallowed by Albert's announcement
That this is the end of the game.

———————

PARLOR GAME ON A SNOWY WINTER NIGHT

Albert, standing at the window, began by saying,
"False china eggs in a chicken's nest stimulate
The hen to lay eggs that are real,
And they also occasionally fool weasels."

"Telling the truth to a chicken then"
Replied Sonia, "must be considered a grievous sin,
And deception, in this case, an extraordinary virtue."

"Chickens, brooding on china eggs as well as real ones,"
Said Cecil, rubbing his chin, "might regard glass eggs
As admirably false, but a weasel nosing the nest
Would consider glass eggs a malevolent tomfoolery
And the devil's own droppings."

"A weasel, testing the reality of eggs,
Must find glass and albumen
Equally easy to identify," continued Albert.

"China eggs, whether warm or not," said Felicia,
Mocking herself in the mirror, "at least consistently maintain
Their existence as false eggs."

"Perhaps the true egg, unable to maintain its reality
For long, is actually a weak imitation
Of the eternal nature of the glass egg," said Albert,
Drawing his initials on the frost windowpane.

"Someone must investigate how the real image
Of a false egg in the chicken's true eye causes the cells
Of a potential egg to become an actuality," said Gordon,
Laying his book on the table.

"Can we agree then that the false china egg,
A deceptive but actual instigator,
Is the first true beginning of the chicken yard?"
Asked Sonia, filling in the last line of the game sheet.

Albert, rushing outdoors to discover
What the dogs had cornered in the brush beside the barn,
Found a weasel in the snow
With bloody yolk on its whiskers and a broken tooth.

OBSERVING THE QUESTIONS OF A GREY SKY

What we observe is not nature itself but nature exposed to our method of questioning.
    —WERNER HEISENBERG

Who would suppose that one sky by itself
Could contain so many colors called grey—
Blue grey, beige grey, toad grey, and broken grey,
Birch grey, severe grey, and barely perceived,
Sable grey at mid-heart, and never perceived but postulated,
The lavender grey of flowers found in winter moss
Beneath juniper trees? To the north a lateral column
Of soldier grey rises like smoke, forced without wind
To its own statuesque devices. Low in the south
An illusion of grey covers the sun.

And the sky above possesses the same multiple greys
As the sky in the lake below. Which sky is it then
That moves backward through the flight of five black birds
Skimming the tundra grey surfaces? And which sky holds
The five black shadows with wings in its clouds?
If the birds should soar, in which direction
Would they fall? If the birds should dive,
Into which clouds would they disappear?

Does the grey body of the wooden shed beside the lake
Find an aspect of itself in the slivered grey
Of the eleventh layer of cloud above? Does the loon
Learn something new of its breast matched perfectly
In color with the knife grey edge of the sky
Against which it floats? Does the meadow vole
Become forever related to cumulus vapor
By being its identical brother in grey this afternoon?

What if the brown grey grasses of the field
Are simply the limited vision of the sky making seeds?

Where is the grey parting of the sky
Made by the bow of the boat moving across the lake?
And in this wide expanse, who can find the grey shoulder
Of father's coat or the grey separation of your footsteps
On the path or the grey ring of the rock thrown in anger
Into the sky? Must the entire history of grey descend
Forever beyond the bottom of the lake or can it disappear
Diagonally into the dark line of the circular horizon?
Remember how the motion of grey can come suddenly like rain
Breaking the sky into overlapping circles in the lake below.

Any question occasioned by the grey sky this evening
Must be part of the sky and a metallic grey itself,
Easily observed in the mirror of grey
Found in a reflective eye.

FINDING THE TATTOOED LADY IN THE GARDEN

Circus runaway, tattooed from head to toe in yellow
Petals and grape buds, rigid bark and dust-streaked
Patterns of summer, she lives naked among the hedges
And bordered paths of the garden. She hardly
Has boundaries there, so definite is her place.

Sometimes the golden flesh of the butterfly,
Quiet and needled in the spot of sun on her shoulder,
Can be seen and sometimes the wide blue wing
Of her raised hand before the maple and sometimes

The crisscrossed thicket, honeysuckle and fireweed,
Of her face. As she poses perfectly, her legs apart,
Some people can find the gentian-smooth meadow-skin showing
Through the distant hickory groves painted up her thighs
And the warm white windows of open sky appearing
Among the rose blossoms and vines of her breasts.

Shadow upon tattooed shadow upon real shadow,
She is there in the petaled skin of the iris
And the actual violet scents overlapping
At the bend of her arm, beneath and beyond
The initial act announcing the stems
Of the afternoon leafed and spread
In spires of green along her ribs, the bronze
Lizard basking at her navel.

Some call her searched-for presence the being
Of being, the essential garden of the garden.
And some call the continuing postulation
Of her location the only underlying structure,
The single form of flux, the final proof
And presence of crafted synonymy.
And whether the shadows of the sweetgum branches
Above her shift in the breeze across her breasts
Or whether she herself sways slightly
Beneath the still star-shaped leaves of the quiet
Forest overhead or whether the sweetgum shadows
Tattooed on her torso swell and linger
As the branches above are stirred by her breath,
The images possessed by the seekers are one
And the same when they know them as such.

And in the dark of late evening,
Isn't it beautiful the way they watch for her
To turn slowly, displaying the constellations
Penned in light among the black leaves
And blossoms of her back, the North Star
In its only coordinates shining at the base
Of her neck, the way they study the first glowing
Rim of the moon rising by its own shape
From the silvered curve of her brilliant hip?

THE COMPASSION OF THE IRIS

Compassion, if it could be seen, might look
Like an early blossom of iris,
Something like an uplands flower on a wooded
Morning, five purple suns visible on its petals
As five points of a shallow dawn.

If compassion appeared as an iris
It would be possible to trace the actual outline
Of its arched and crested edges, to describe
The crucial motivation coming at the juncture
Of its yellow-ridged sepals, to examine
The significance in the structure of white veins
Covering its calyx, to discover, by touch,
The hidden meat of the bulb from which the origin
Of its concept must first have arisen.

And maybe the benevolence inherent to ordinary
Purple-streaked flowers could be understood
As they cover, without intrusion, the lowest rim

Of evening, when they draw their violet lines
As carefully as dusk draws time above the dusty floor
Of the pine barrens. Corms and stems,
Lobes and basal clusters might be
Recognized as the subtlest, most crucial
Tenderness of the soil.

And it might be possible to imagine how the bond
Creating the central fact of compassion is exactly
The same fact binding a gene of violet
In the ovary of the iris, how compassion
Possesses the same grip on its own form
As the perfumed rhizome maintains
On the tight molecule of its scent.

And what astonishing union is it that takes place
On the day when compassion is offered as a gift
In the form of spring iris gathered from the field?

One might wonder if the iris
Should be studied meticulously in order to reveal
The intricacies of compassion,
Or whether one should act compassionately
In order to fully perceive the peculiarities
Of that extraordinary blue-violet flower.

REACHING THE AUDIENCE

From the introduction to The First Book of Iridaceae

We will start with a single blue dwarf iris
Appearing as a purple dot on a hairstreak
Butterfly seen in a distant pine barrens and proceed
Until we end with a single point of purple spiraling
Like an invisible wing in the center of the flower
Making fact.

We will investigate a stand of blue flags crimsoned
By the last sun still showing over the smoky edges
Of the ravine and illustrate in sequence the glazing
Of those iris by the wet gold of an early dawn.

We will survey a five-mile field of purple iris
Holding bristle-legged insects under the tips
Of their stamens and measure the violet essence
Gathered at the bases of their wings and devote
One section to a molecule of iris fragrance
Preserved and corked in a slender glass.

There will be a composition replicating the motion
Of the iris rolling sun continually over its rills
And another for the stillness of the iris sucking ivory
Moonlight through its hollows making ivory roots.

There will be photographs in series of the eyes
Of a woman studying the sepals of an iris
In a lavender vase and a seven-page account of the crested
Iris burning at midnight in the shape of its flame
And six oriental paintings of purple petals torn apart
And scattered over snow beneath birches and a poem

Tracing a bouquet of blue iris tied together like balloons
Floating across the highest arc of a spring heaven.

There will be an analysis of the word of the iris
In the breath of the dumb and an investigation
Of the touch of the iris in the fingertips of the blind
And a description of the iris-shaped spaces existing
In the forest before the forest became itself
And a delineation of those same blade-thin spaces
Still existing after the forest has been lost again.

It is the sole purpose of these volumes-in-progress
To ensure that anyone stopped anywhere in any perspective
Or anyone caught forever in any crease of time or anyone
Left inside the locked and folded bud of any dream
Will be able to recognize something on these pages
And remember.

—————

DISCOVERING YOUR SUBJECT

Painting a picture of the same shrimp boat
Every day of your life might not be so boring.
For a while you could paint only in the mornings,
Each one different, the boat gold in the new sun
On your left, or the boat in predawn fog condensing
Mist. You might have to wait years, rising early
Over and over, to catch that one winter morning when frost
Becomes a boat. You could attempt to capture
The fragile potential inherent in that event.

You might want to depict the easy half-circle
Movements of the boat's shadows crossing over themselves

Through the day. You could examine every line
At every moment—the tangle of nets caught
In the orange turning of evening, the drape of the ropes
Over the rising moon.

You could spend considerable time just concentrating
On boat and birds—Boat with Birds Perched on Bow,
Boat with Birds Overhead, Shadows of Birds Covering
Hull and Deck, or Boat the Size of a Bird,
Bird in the Heart of the Boat, Boat with Wings,
Boat in Flight. Any endeavor pursued long enough
Assumes a momentum and direction all its own.

Or you might decide to lie down one day behind a clump
Of marsh rosemary on the beach, to see the boat embedded
In the blades of the saltwort or show how strangely
The stalk of the clotbur can rise higher than the mast.
Boat Caught like a Flower in the Crotch of the Sand Verbena.

After picturing the boat among stars, after discovering
The boat as revealed by rain, you might try painting
The boat in the eye of the gull or the boat in the eye
Of the sun or the boat in the eye of a storm
Or the eye trapped in the window of the boat.
You could begin a series of self-portraits—The Boat
In the Eye of the Remorseful Painter, The Boat in the Eye
Of the Blissful Painter, The Boat in the Eye of the Blind Painter,
The Boat in the Lazy Painter Forgetting His Eye.

Finally one day when the boat's lines are drawn in completely,
It will begin to move away, gradually changing its size,
Enlarging the ocean, requiring less sky, and suddenly it might seem
That you are the one moving. You are the one altering space,
Gliding easily over rough surfaces toward the mark

Between the ocean and the sky. You might see clearly,
For the first time, the boat inside the painter inside the boat
Inside the eye watching the painter moving beyond himself.
You must remember for us the exact color and design of that.

"THE TREE HAS CAPTURED MY SOUL"

For van Gogh

When they found him mad in the field
On his knees, gripping the hard wooden trunk
Of his own living soul, it could never be said
How it happened, whether the soul of the tree,
Its branches rising and interlocking like bones,
Had disguised itself as skeleton and penetrated
The vision of his body that way undetected;
Or whether his soul willingly turned the vision of itself
Inside its own socket and became the pure white tree
Of its own interlocking; or whether he saw and testified
To the fragmentary parting of his soul caught
Among the wind and branches spreading across his canvas;
Or whether he captured his own body in the turning
Brushstrokes of a thousand yellow leaves and forfeited thereby
The treeless autonomy of his soul here on earth;
Or whether he lost the whole tree of his eye but gained
A vision of the veins of his soul rising and branching
Toward light; or whether the wind turned the soul
Of each yellow leaf inside its own socket
Until his eyes was united everlastingly with that movement;
Or whether he saw the shimmering perception
Of that tree lift his body, light as a soul,

On the tips of its branches forever toward heaven.

But it is known that he came fully awake among them
In the field, his arms around his body
As if it were rooted in the earth, seeing
The illuminating wind of his soul for the first time
In all the possible movements of yellow
Each visionary leaf could offer him.

First Notes from One Born and Living in an Abandoned Barn

Every dusty bar and narrow streak of brilliance
Originating from white slits and roof crevices
Or streaming to the floor all day in one solid column
From the opening directly overhead
Are only light.

The rising tatter of weed ticks under the door
And the quick unseen banging of shingles above
Are named the sudden and the unexpected.

Silence is understood to be the straw-flecked
Morasses of webs consistently filling the corners
With a still grey filigree of dirt, and meditation
Is called orb weaver and funnel spider tugging
At their ropes, working and stitching
With the synchronization of their flexible nails.

The farthest limits to which the eyes can see—
The rotten board walls and the high wind-stopped

Eaves—are the boundaries the mind clearly recognizes
As the farthest edges of itself, and the steel-blue forks
Of the swallows bumping and tapping along the ledges
Of the rafters all afternoon define again
The barriers of the acknowledged. Realization
Is simply the traceable expansion gradually filling
All the spaces known as barn.

And at night the point at which the slow downward swoop
Of the bat first begins its new angle upward is called
Proof of the power of the body's boundaries.
And what it is believed the snake experiences as it slides
The line of its belly along the thigh
Is thigh. The length of the arm is nothing more
Than the length the mouse crawls before its feet
Are felt no more. And what it is imagined the owl sees
As it stares from the eaves directly into the eyes
Of the one it perceives is called identity.

What appears in the opening of the roof at night
Is only what the barn envelopes and holds.
What the mind envelopes and holds in the opening
Of the roof is called the beyond.
And the beyond is either the definition of disappearance
Discovered by the bats, or else it is the rectangular
Body of stars defining the place of the roof, or else
It is the black opening looking down on the starlit
Rectangle creating the eyes, or else it is the entire
Inner surface of the face composed of stars, or else
It is the first lucky guess of the mind at the boundless
Which is exactly what has caused the need to begin tonight
The documented expansion inherent to these notes.

The Tattooed Lady in the Garden   217

THE FORM OF THE MESSAGE

Through the spring afternoon the spangled
Fritillary and the red admiral spread
The only information available concerning floating
Orange and scarlet furls of open sky.
The bullfrog is an obvious messenger bringing
Web-toed proclamations of sloughs
And ditches, announcing details of drift
In the easy hang of its white-legged body in the pond.
And the map turtle is the angel of itself
Declaring red-eyed visions of delicacy in slug
Of snail and clam. And snail and clam embody notices
Of suck and draw, the facts of hard-shelled
Slips of living mud.

The quiet in the budded hook
Of the mossy plumatella delivers the still, perfect
Angel of its own silence, and the prayer of the fanning
Bluegill is the form of its breathing message.
The angel of the primrose willow
Is the swaying leaf of its own graceful prayer.
Whistling and scaling just above the tips of the reeds,
The message of the meadowlark creates the shape
Of its reception in the ear. The pattern of muscle
And breath and ripple in the lark's trilling throat
Is the form of the angel it has always been.
The message that the ear proclaims is the act
Of reception it performs.

Father, this prayer of messengers
I bring to you this afternoon

Is its own message, an angel of good news
In the form of the spring field.
Listen now, for me, to the shape of your ear.

THE TONGUES OF ANGELS

I Corinthians 13:1

The split-second slivers of spiny lizard, sheep frog,
Bufo and chirping marnocki, the stunted ivory knobs
Of tortoise and carp, word from the facile thread
Of the arrow crab, from the yellow tongues of honey
Mesquite, from the red sentence buried in the beak
Of the wheatear, from the mouths of carpenter ants
Perceiving the honeydew language of sucking bugs;

By the coiled power of moth and swallowtail,
The green speech of grass on the tongues of nanny
And sheep, the multilingual form of purple in layered
Larkspur and bloom of chickory, by the quiet syntax
Of the afternoon rising in the air above stubbled
Meadows, the rock tongue of evening mute along the strata
Of the canyon's edge, by the tongues of the sun
Speaking through curtains of blowing lace,

Let me speak, let me learn to speak with love
By the tongues of these loved angels, father, tonight,
To ease, for a moment, the sound of the stuttering cymbal,
My own persistent babble of brass

BEING ACCOMPLISHED

Balancing on her haunches, the mouse can accomplish
Certain things with her hands. She can pull the hull
From a barley seed in paperlike pieces the size of threads.
She can turn and turn a crumb to create smaller motes
The size of her mouth. She can burrow in sand and grasp
One single crystal grain in both of her hands.
A quarter of a dried pea can fill her palm.

She can hold the earless, eyeless head
Of her furless baby and push it to her teat.
The hollow of its mouth must feel like the invisible
Confluence sucking continually deep inside a pink flower.

And the mouse is almost compelled
To see everything. Her hand, held up against the night sky,
Can scarcely hide Venus or Polaris
Or even a corner of the crescent moon.
It can cover only a fraction of the blue moth's wing.
Its shadow could never mar or blot enough of the evening
To matter.

Imagine the mouse with her spider-sized hands
Holding to a branch of dead hawthorn in the middle
Of the winter field tonight. Picture the night pressing in
Around those hands, forced, simply by their presence,
To fit its great black bulk exactly around every hair
And every pinlike nail, forced to outline perfectly
Every needle-thin bone without crushing one, to carry
Its immensity right up to the precise boundary of flesh
But no farther. Think how the heavy weight of infinity,
Expanding outward in all directions forever, is forced,

Nevertheless, to mold itself right here and now
To every peculiarity of those appendages.

And even the mind, capable of engulfing
The night sky, capable of enclosing infinity,
Capable of surrounding itself inside any contemplation,
Has been obliged, for this moment, to accommodate the least
Grasp of that mouse, the dot of her knuckle, the accomplishment
Of her slightest intent.

INSIDE GOD'S EYE

As if his eye had no boundaries, at night
All the heavens are visible there. The stars drift
And hesitate inside that sphere like white seeds
Sinking in a still, dark lake. Spirals of brilliance,
They float silently and slowly deeper and deeper
Into the possible expansion of his acuity.
And within that watching, illumination like the moon
Is uncovered petal by petal as a passing cloud clears
The open white flowers of the shining summer plum.

Inside god's eye, light spreads as afternoon spreads,
Accepting the complications of water burr and chestnut,
The efforts of digger bee and cuckoo bee. Even the barest
Light gathers and concentrates there like a ray
Of morning reaching the thinnest nerve of a fairy shrimp
At the center of a pond. And like evening, light
Bends inside the walls of god's eye to make
Skywide globes of fuchsia and orange, violet-tipped
Branches and violet-tinged wings set against a red dusk.

Lines from the tangle of dodder, bindweed
And honeysuckle, from the interweaving knot
Of seaweed and cones, patterns from the network
Of blowing shadow and flashing poplar, fill
And define the inner surface moment of his retina.

And we, we are the only point of reversal
Inside his eye, the only point of light
That turns back on itself and by that turning
Saves time from infinity and saves motion
From obscurity. We are the vessel and the blood
And the pulse he sees as he sees the eye watching
The vision inside his eye in the perfect mirror
Held constantly before his face.

LEGENDARY PERFORMANCE (1987)

I

AFTER DINNER

Cecil said, "During every night and every day
Of the evolving invention and increased usage
Of the table fork, during every moment and every note
Of the Bach missa performed for the king of Saxony
Before his fire in 1733, through the long rising popularity
Of croquet, played by many fine ladies during summer evenings
In smooth grassy gardens, the light from the exploding
Supernova located in the exterior Galaxy M31 was steadily
Proceeding at 186,000 miles per second straight toward
1929 and Edwin Hubble and his telescope right here on earth."

Sonia said, "If you picture the progress of your thought
As a wooden ball rolling heavily over grass, clearing
Two wire wickets cleanly, then striking a stake with decision,
You might come to understand some totally unexpected truth."

"During every moment of every word of Cecil's speech,"
Albert said, "the weaver ants on the bush beside this bench
Were sewing together two separate leaves by the perfect
Needle and thread of their children's bodies."

"Look at Felicia, having won at croquet, cartwheeling
Across the hill, her feet sweeping in finite arcs
Through every second of the heavens from Capricornus
To Sextanus, from Altair to Corvus."

Gordon, who is writing an article
On stitching of any kind, adds four new elements
To his thesis every evening.

A Fortnight to Remember

Cecil's second cousin has a handicap.
An incurable condition, he can't distinguish
Between his memory and his imagination.

Arriving for a two-week visit, he thinks
He came by circling out of the center
Of the high bush blueberry blooming at the gate.
Later that evening he amused everyone by recounting
The adventures of a confused passenger
On an imaginary train trip.

Believing the winding staircase and the red carpeted
Hallway leading to the guest bedroom to be stanzas
In his newest poem, he has slept on a cot in the pantry
Every night since his arrival. He has been lost
On the path from the garden to the house eleven times
During this visit alone.

And after an outing to the beach
He bored everyone for three days by claiming
To have invented the rock barnacles, the clear,
Sea cucumbers and the calm, country birds
Mewing above the cliffs. Euphoric and vain,
He praised his own genius in creating over a thousand
Species of hunchbacked sand hoppers and their kin.

This morning he is insisting he was born Frederick
Louis Khalibou Yuit of an Eskimo mother and a caribou father.
He believes that he and Cecil used to run the tundra south
To the taiga with the herd. He says when the moon
Smells of rosettes and herbs, he will sing

All the songs his father taught him,
If he can remember them.

Shocked one afternoon to see Sonia,
Whom he regarded as a character in his novel-in-progress,
Serving cheese and poppy seed pastry at tea,
He had to be restrained forcibly and locked for an hour
In the cupola to calm his attempts to verify her reality.

Some days he grips Cecil's arm for hours at a time.

Cecil has learned how to endure
His second-cousin's visits. Sitting at bedtime
Before the fire, when he asks Cecil if he remembers
How they entered the fire one night together
And danced with sizzling hair, throwing their arms
Like light above their heads, and if he recalls
The night the flying fox came to their nursery window
And whispered to them with the voice of a white spruce,
And if he can still find the scars left when the orange slashes
Of a forest evening struck them both hard across the eyes,
Cecil, with a sigh, always says yes.

ASPECTS OF UNITY

1.
This morning at tea Cecil said that violet in flowers
Was the color of accumulated moisture.

Gordon has taken his prism to the east window now
And is making small perfect rainbow-lines
All along the white wall opposite. He says violet

Is nothing more than the shortest ray
Of the visible spectrum.

Albert has used the word *violet* five times
In the hour since tea and the word *violent*
Twice in the last ten minutes.

Felicia, standing before the hall mirror,
Believes her eyes are the color of the shortest rays
Of the bellflowers after a heavy summer rain.

Sonia thinks the words *purple* and *violating*
Pronounced together after dark have definite
Sexual implications.

This makes Felicia wonder if the bean
Of the sieva plant is purple in the dark
Before the sun splits its pod.

Cecil knows nipples made purple by the shortest rays
Of the moon shining on a white body on a white sheet
Can never be found or touched during the light of day.

2.
The only time Albert, Sonia, Felicia and Cecil
Hold hands together is when they run
Down the aster-covered slope from the house
To the lake after lunch.

Gordon, imagining the violet monkshood
Growing on the tundra today, always carries
His satchel in one hand and never participates in the run.

Sonia is curious as to whether a lavender gull flying over
Will look down at them if they all stare at its dark purple
Wingtips at the same time without blinking.

Felicia says violet eyes make gulls disappear in the evening sky.

Gordon believes the properly trained eye can see the lake
At dusk as synonymous with the tundra
Covered by a continuous bed of lavender monkshood.

Cecil knows a game
In which one purple button among many white ones
Must be identified in the dark by touch alone.

Albert, Sonia, Felicia, Cecil and Gordon
Never think the same thing at the same time,
But sometimes, reading outloud together
In the pale violet light of long winter evenings,
They speak the same words at the same time,
And when they do, all, except Albert,
Call it colorful recitation.

NAKED BOYS ON NAKED PONIES

They ride through invisible hollows
And along the indefinite edges of marshy streams,
Fog swirling up to their ears
Over beds of sida and flowering spurge.
The ponies' withers become ivory with pollen
From the blossoming quince, and the bare
Legs of the boys are marked by flickertail
Barley and wild mint. Moisture

On the corn cockle along the ridges
Makes constant suns in their eyes.

Galloping through forests and across fields
Of drying grasses, this is what they create
By themselves—spilled ginseng and screeching
Pipits, dusts rising from the witherod
And the wild raisin, an effusion of broken
Beargrass somersaulting skyward
And mouse-ear chickweed kicked high.

And beside the river they see themselves
On the opposite bank following themselves
Through water chestnuts and willow oak, and they see
Themselves threading among the stand of hornbeam
In the forest ahead. Watching from the precipice
Above the canyon at evening, they know the bronze
Ponies and their riders curving in a line
Along the ledges below.

And at night they see themselves riding upside down
Across the sky, hair and tails and manes
Dragging in the grasses among the long horn beetles
And burrowing owls. And they see themselves galloping
Across the prairie turned upside down, hair
And tails and manes dragging in the dusty glow
Of the starry nebulae. They know they are the definite
Wish of all unexplored spaces to be ponies and boys.

I tell you the speed of the ponies depends absolutely
On the soaring of the rider squeezing tightly
Inside each of their skulls. And the wings of the boys
Depend absolutely on the flight of the ponies
Galloping across the prairies contained in their bones.

And the soaring of the prairies depends absolutely
On the wings of the ponies squeezing tightly
Inside every grass and bone found in the flight of the boys.

And who cares where they are going,
And who cares if they are real or not,
When their ride by itself is that glorious?

THE WITNESS OF DEATH

There was a crisis in the health of Felicia's uncle
During the autumn following his first seizure
Of insanity. Believing himself to be the hoary puccoon
Of the field, how could he endure sitting by the window,
Watching his own slow death advance by dry chill
And musty mold up spine and stem, drawing the throat
Of his blossom tightly closed? What could he suppose,
Seeing the low, cold and quiet sun of the season
Blurring the distinction between stalk and sky,
Obliterating the relationship of petal to earth?

Even wrapped in flannel and fleece and sitting
By the fires, still he shivered stiffly
In the November fogs, whimpering as the damp
Cold evening above the roots eased nearer to his heart.
He complained that his fingertips and ears
Were obviously bitten, shriveled and brown,
The morning after the first heavy frost.

Felicia, wishing to slow his demise,
Closed and locked all the shutters in his room,

But no one could abide the howls
Of his lost soul then left utterly formless,
Bereft of leaf and eye and the steady ritual
Of wasting-away.

Cecil painted a portrait of the hoary puccoon
Of the field in the full orange glory
Of its summer blossom and hung it before his window
As a benevolent ruse. Although the flower
Was glorious and bold in its oils, Cecil failed
To capture on canvas the complete essence of his spirit.
Even Felicia said it wasn't her uncle at all.
The crisis continued.

The day the skin of his face turned as cold
And white as the ice-covered snow over the field
And he lay without trembling for 12 hours straight,
All was considered lost. Then Albert, jumping
From his chair, rushed to the field alone,
Dug through the snow and gathered six whole seeds
From the frozen hoary puccoon. Taking them to Felicia's uncle,
He placed three on his tongue, which he swallowed, and pressed
The others into his tight hoary hand closed beneath the quilt.
(Gordon said his right foot quivered visibly at that moment.)

Now, although Felicia's uncle will not open his eyes,
He sips small amounts of icy water through a thin
Vein-like straw, and he breathes, slowly, unaided
And calm, through every night.

While the doctors and the household prepare for spring,
Sonia comes to kiss the forehead of Felicia's uncle
Everyday, and she touches his temples with perfume

Extracted from the blossom of the hoary puccoon,
Bottled and sent to him, with love, from a well-wisher
Halfway around the world.

THE WELL-WISHER FROM HALFWAY AROUND THE WORLD

Though everyone knows the well-wisher exists (many
Have trinkets sent by him to prove it), no one has
Seen him or heard his name. Like two figures etched
On the opposite sides of a silver coin,
No one can see himself and the well-wisher
At the same moment.

Nevertheless the naked boys on their ponies
Have set out many times to locate the well-wisher.
But they simply find themselves on the path
Between the sugarwoods and the cliffs
Above the sea or crossing the marble bridge
Over the River of Rhom or sleeping at the eastern edge
Of the summer savannah. The well-wisher always lives
On the opposite side of wherever they are.

Therefore Albert, wading in July among the inlet pools,
Looking for thorny sea stars and rock-boring urchins,
Tries to remember that it is winter, at the moment,
For the well-wisher. And when the shadow
Of the purple finch flying over the lawn is seen
Against the bright grass at noon or when the tunnel
Of light made by Albert's torch suddenly appears

Through the black forest at midnight, Sonia is reminded
That the well-wisher exists.

Sometimes Felicia likes to watch the sunset so long
And so carefully that she can still see its glow
Even after the dimmest star of Andromeda can be found.
She wants to see the last moment of the sun's ending
Exactly as the well-wisher is witnessing
The first instant of its beginning.

Cecil, delirious for a week with a late winter fever,
Believed that he and the day were stretched
From horizon to horizon together in two dimensions,
That there was no chamber pot, no dog asleep
Beneath the bed, there being no other side
To the bed. Unable to pronounce the words *deep*
Or *shallow* or *above* or *below,* his eyes looked
Neither up nor down. It was only after the arrival
Of the star-shaped violets sent by the well-wisher
And the simultaneous breaking of his fever,
That he was able to see inside and outside once more.

The blind beggar, who once spent eleven days
In the Deeper Caverns, claims that during his last hour
Beneath the earth when he finally saw nothing of himself
But his blindness, he almost touched the well-wisher.

Gordon, twirling a coin on the table, believes
That death, like the rapid spinning of a flashing
Silver coin, is the only experience during which the unity
Of opposite surfaces might finally be perceived.

THE DOCUMENTATION OF ABSENCE

No one can find Kioka in the winter.

Yet Cecil came back from sledding this evening
Believing it was Kioka's body he had seen buried
In brown, reed–like lines under the ice at the pond.

And Felicia, running yesterday morning to the clearing
Where the snowbirds were squabbling,
Said the birds were dusting in the warm ashes
Left from Kioka's fire.

During a February blizzard, Sonia thought
She could hear Kioka's pony stomping and thrashing,
Screaming as if it were tethered in the sleet
In the open field, and she imagined she could hear
Someone on the roof singing the "Song of Lamentation
For Tethered Ponies" that Kioka learned from his father.

Everyone wonders what it means to be Kioka,
Alive in the blizzard, taking the fury of the icy wind
Into his lungs over and over all night, sleeping
Face to face with the sleet. What will he look like
In the spring, having watched the storm thrashing
Like a tethered pony, having screamed himself
Like wind tied to the end of a rope?

Felicia says icicles are simply the vision of the sun
Caught on the blade of Kioka's knife then frozen and multiplied
Across the northern eaves. That's why
She likes to eat them.

All day Tuesday Cecil, hiking in the snow,
Tried to find the hollow tree where he dreamed he saw
The naked body of Kioka curled and frozen,
Covered with the frost of his own breath.

Gordon says a dream is definite proof
Of the physical absence of its subject.

Felicia has written on her chalkboard,
"Winter comes when Kioka is cold."

Albert, who is tired of telling everyone
That Indian imitators definitely don't hibernate,
Found a single red feather this morning lying
On the unmarked snow on the south side
Of the berry hedge.

————————

A SEASONAL TRADITION

Felicia's music teacher gives a concert for Sonia,
Cecil, Albert, Gordon and Felicia and her insane uncle
In the front parlor every holiday season.
After her traditional repertoire she always plays
One piece on her violin in a register so high
The music can't be heard.

The silence of the parlor during that piece
Is almost complete, broken only by the sputter
Of a candle, a creaking yawn from one of the dogs.

Albert admires the entranced look
On the music teacher's face and the curious trembling

Form of her fingers as she plays. He thinks
He can hear the unheard music in the same way he can hear
Wind among the black strings of the icy willows blowing
In the tundra night. He thinks the silence he hears
Is the same silence found in the eyes of the frogs living
Below the mud at the bottom of the frozen bays.

With tears in her eyes, Felicia says the unheard song
Reminds her of the cries of unborn rice rats
And bog lemmings buried in the winter marsh
And the humming of the white hobblebush blossom still
In its seed and the trill of the unreal bird discovered
In the river trees by the river sun.

Watching the violinist swaying in her velvet gown,
Closing her eyes, pursing her lips, Cecil knows
Sonia is the only possible theme of this composition.

Hoping for a cure for Felicia's uncle, Sonia thinks
The inaudible music might be the unspoken speech
In which he is thought to have lost himself years ago.

At the conclusion of the piece (signaled
By the lowering of the violin) there is always spontaneous
Applause and much barking and leaping by the dogs.

The unheard composition is the one song
Most discussed later over tea and pastries,
And, although it was the subject of the quarrel
During which Cecil knocked Albert's doughnut
From his hand last year, it is still generally considered
The evening's greatest success.

II

BEING REMEMBERED

For Felicia, they were dancers first, turning
In their tight white trousers and purple sashes
Out of the hardwood forest into the hazy sun.

For Gordon's sake, they complicated the coordination
Of their movements, cartwheeling, somersaulting
In circles, shifting their patterns like colored stones
Tumbling in a glass kaleidoscope.

Cecil wouldn't have noticed them
If they hadn't been wearing red patent leather boots,
Boots that moved across the landscape as they danced
Like quick brushstrokes of scarlet
On a canvas of yellow field.

For the blind beggars they wore seven brass bells
Around their ankles to mark each step,
And for the blind beggars they carried
Tambourines to define the place of their hands
In the afternoon. For the naked boys they pranced
Like ponies to the glacial pool. They drank
Like ponies, shaking their heads with a flourish
At the dark blue edge of the summer ice.

Not one yellow aster in the entire meadow
Would have tightened to its stem if the dancers
Hadn't stopped to spin in the grass, their bright hair
Spreading like the petals of a golden flower.

The star-watchers would never have studied them
If it hadn't been for the black satin shirts
They wore, the five suns flashing
Off the mirrored buttons down the front.

A MODICUM OF DECORUM

Eduard, Felicia's tutor, having read
A current best-seller entitled
The Potential Sophistication of Life and Limb,
Is attempting to improve Felicia's behavior.

He has given her a list.

> Somersaulting and leaping confuse clear-thinking.
> Running and bounding lead to chaos in the brain.
> No one can deny that shrieks destroy
> The most delicately balanced tedium.

> Strolling in moderation is tolerated.
> Twisting ribbons and twiddling by small
> Quiet fires is cultivated.
> Sighing is admired.

Eduard, quoting from Chapter IX, has told Felicia
She must envision herself as a heavy, metal bell
Hanging with no pull-cord in a dark, vine-covered
Belfry, her only meaningful reality being the potential
Of her ring. To actually ring then, being the destruction
Of potential and therefore the destruction of meaningful
Reality, is a sin.

Yesterday Felicia, confined to her bedroom
For singing her part in the morning blessing
With too much intensity, wove ropes of pink
And purple crepe paper and hung them from her window.
There they blew in the breeze beside the veranda
Where Eduard was tentatively meditating on the potential
Reality of ringing in bells not yet forged.
Now he is reading aloud to Felicia Chapter XXIV,
"The Abuses of Flags, Banners, Streamers, Confetti,
And Other Paper Paraphernalia."

Felicia, attempting to walk at the pace her tutor
Has approved, thinks if she could camp-out all summer
Heading east, then she might be able to make it
To the field and back once before autumn.

Eduard says a backpack is unseemly.

Last night Felicia, tiptoeing
(which Eduard hasn't yet discussed) across the lawn
To the gazebo, lay inside its latticed walls
With moonlight diamonds covering her body
And giggled with the dogs until dawn.

———————

THE MIRROR OF PIERROT

For Felicia and the unrealized soul of her favorite lost doll

He should never have been set down all alone
In the field like that, a real clown in his floppy
Satin pajamas, dizzy among the trembling pipewort,
Quavering like the brainless wool grass.

Bone-bald in his black skull cap, perpetual
Astonishment on his white painted face, he sits
And stares, his dark lashes as large as teardrops
Circling each wide eye.

How can he ignore the big clicking buttons
Swinging on his baggy blouse as he bends to pick
A prickly daisy for his lapel, or his long cuffs
Falling into the creek as he studies the bravado
Of a crawdad backing under a leaf? Tripped
On the hill by his own pantaloons, he's already lost
One of his tassel-topped silk slippers in a hedgehog hole.

And the starched ruffle around his neck scratches
His ear as he turns to count the jays screaming
Their nonsense among the awkward oaks. He's been teased
For half an hour by a light-headed butterfly flitting
Just out of reach above the raspberry blooms.

Recognizing himself, doesn't he see the wild pantaloons
On the catapulting locust, the bone-tight caps
Of the blackbirds, the white painted faces of the trillium?
He knows the figure he makes sprawled
Among the addle-headed grasses, beside the dumbstruck
Rocks, bewildered under the blank and foolish sky.
He's certain the field is a clumsy buffoon.

Oh, if he could only remember or if he could only
Forget or if he could only imagine someone
Out of sight beyond the hill,
Someone who thinks about him always,
Without laughing.

THE STUDY OF THE SPLINTER EXPERT

An expert on splinters was the guest lecturer
Featured at the academy last week. His career began
As a youthful hobby—a curiosity concerning
The minute lines in slivers of oak and ash, an expanding
Collection of glass splinters, purple, scarlet;
Metal shavings.

Spending two years as a student sorting
Through the refuse left from the explosion
Of a single pine, deciphering patterns in that tangled
Fall of feathered wood, he discovered and classified
Fifty varieties of splinters broken from splinters.

His meticulous investigation of the calls
Of the meadowlark splintering the spring afternoon
Led to his first book, *The Splinters of Time.*
Since then he has completed research on the splinters
Of moonlight made by the needles of icy firs, wind
Splintering the silver surface of the lake, the splintering
Of the wind by the blades of the bur reed.

In any entity he can only see the underlying
Truth of its splintered reality—the red
And yellow splinters composing rattle box
And hibiscus blooms, splinters forming
In the fertile egg of the swamp snake, the potential
Splinters of chill in future snow. He predicts
The eventual development of an instrument able to locate
And describe each splinter of space.

Concerned with the splintering action of analysis itself,
He has carefully studied photographs of himself

Taken as he scrutinized shavings from the femurs
Of unborn calves, shatters of hickory found
Before the rising of the sap. He has attempted
To locate in his own eye that splinter of light
Creating the original concept of "splinter."

Thursday evening he lectured on his recent
Proposal that the sharpest, most painful
Splinter experienced is not of micromagnesium
Or glass silk but the splinter of pure hypothesis.

A well-known seer has predicted that the death
Of this expert will come by steel splinter piercing
His eye and brain, whereby he will enter that coveted state—
The perfect union of object and idea.

Felicia, infatuated with the erudite demeanor
Of the splinter expert, hasn't left her bed during the five days
Since his departure. She is using a calculator to count
The splinters of loss filling the distance multiplying
Between them, and she's afraid that, should she rise,
The splinters of her despair, blending like moonlight
On the floor, would scatter like dust and be lost forever.

THE SHAPE OF SORROW

Felicia wants to contract melancholia today.
She wants to be able to feel her sorrow swelling
The way a shoreline cavern feels the slow rise
Of the sea filling its caves. She wants to say
She is sick with sadness.

Cecil told Felicia that sorrow, when not diffuse,
Is actually the most distinctive physical property
Of hedgerows, marshy shores and thorn fields.
Now she wants to become that single most definite
Point of beauty—the needle of seed shrimp, the sharp
Motion on each blade of swordgrass—which she believes
Is simply the pure concentration of sorrow.

Gordon has a colleague who is making a study
Of the evolutionary development and social significance
Of tears. Felicia is to be the subject of his next paper.
She is saving her tears in sterile
Vials for chemical analysis.

Today Felicia wants to train her vision
So that she is able to detect the pathos
In the jelly eggs of the swamp chorus frog, in the nuptial
Swarms of dixa midges over the meadow pond. Staring
Plaintively from her bedroom window, she has already learned
To see her sadness as the individual wings
Of each mayfly circling above the pond, to see
Her sorrow as the earth's constant line
Maintaining itself against the sky.

She is beginning to love the words
Dementia praecox.

Sonia thinks it might actually be possible
For someone to compose a lasting blessing
For the virtue and periodicity of sorrow.

Felicia says all of this would be easier
If Albert and the dogs would play
On the other side of the house for a while.

The Clockmaker and the Toymaker Are Friends

Because sometimes people want clocks that are toys—
Twelve thimble-sized birds with turquoise feathers
That descend one by one on gold wires to glass
Trees denoting each hour; red, heart-shaped
Clocks sewn inside pillow-bears
Or the muslin breasts of princess dolls.

And sometimes people want toys that are clocks—
A three-inch grieving doll in a purple beaded dress
Who wrings her white wax hands second by second;
A motorized drummer who drums at nightfall
And again at dawn; a mechanical gypsy with an ear
For a clock, who turns her head twice each minute to listen.

The clockmaker is fashioning two tiny crystal
Timekeepers for the toymaker to use as eyes
In his next doleful rag clown, thus giving
Vision to time. And the toymaker is making
A spinning ballerina on a pedestal of pearls
So the clockmaker may mark each turn,
Thus giving moment to frivolity.

When the toymaker dreams of clocks, he sees
The silver wheels of gyroscopes, rolling hoops,
Flashing brass trinkets composing the only pure
Mechanism of time. When the clockmaker dreams of toys
He sees counted rows of metal soldiers, lines
Of falling dominoes, a turning jump rope composing
The only true character of play.

Occasionally the clockmaker and the toymaker
Live on opposite sides of the river and do not speak

To one another for months at a time, so that,
Isolated, they may work simultaneously to distinguish
The perfect unity of their separate crafts.

———————

LOCATING THE SOURCE OF INTENTION

Within the crystal bird that Felicia is admiring
In the window of the curio shop this morning
Is a perfect skeleton of glass bones. The moment
Of the bird's intention to fly appears as a bend
Of purple light curved deep within its wing.
And beneath its glass clavicle is a dram
Of saltwater wavering and shimmering like a heart.

As Felicia looks closer she can see, inside the bubble
Of the bird's body, a transparent egg holding a perfect curl
Of unborn bird, its bones folded as glistening wing
And femur of glass threads. Beneath the vestige of clavicle
There is a sure but wavering salt-point of light.

Looking further she can see, within the loins
Of that unborn bird, a semblance of egg containing
A skeleton of spider-bird bones, a shimmer
Of purple veins connected like night and a hair-bone
Of light forming as heaven's intention to rise like a wing.

And inside the glistening drop of potential egg floating
Inside that embryo-to-be nestled inside the unborn
Bird folded inside the glass bird inside the shop window,
Felicia can sense a definite breath of bones, a waver
Of night wing and a microscopic explosion of light rising

In her eye as proof of the intention
Of a non-existent heart to see.

Felicia is counting backwards now to discover
How many deaths and how many births will be needed
To fully release that flight.

No one knows where the shop owner finds
Such curios to display behind his window
Or how he locates the glassblower
Who executes them.

THE MYSTERY OF UNION

Although naked boys and naked ponies
Are definitely two different things, no one has ever
Seen a naked boy off the back of his pony.

Once, in a dense, pre-dawn fog, Gordon thought
He saw a naked boy slipping down over the slick rump
Of his chestnut mare, but as his feet touched
The gold grassy field he disappeared with his horse
As if they had suddenly become glass in the sparkling mist.

And once Sonia was certain she saw a shining pony
Without a boy on its back galloping toward her
Out of the setting sun, but looking closer,
She saw a boy rising from the flames shimmering
Along the pony's spine, rising until he stood upright
On its back, his hair flying like fire as he balanced
With both arms spread wide.

While he was lost in a mountain blizzard,
The oldest blind beggar by the river believes
He saw naked boys, white with frost and blinded
By the ice-filled wind, leading their blindfolded ponies
With ropes along a rocky ledge. But no one
Can ever understand exactly what a blind beggar sees.

Whenever Cecil tries to paint a naked boy
Riding on a naked pony, the first stroke of his brush
Always proceeds from the boy's slender shoulder
Straight down without a break to the pony's hoof.
He cannot execute on canvas a definite line
Dividing the pressure of knees from the trembling
Of withers. He doesn't know a technique
For painting the mane without simultaneously painting
The fingers that grip the coarse, entangling black hair.

It is Gordon's theory that a naked boy dismounted
Does not cease to exist but instead becomes
The invisible message of an earth devoid
Of mounted motion. And the riderless pony
Does not disappear but becomes instead an alternate form
Of its speed which is the static hoofbeat of time
Unnoticed in the heart.

Felicia wants to ride with a naked boy
On his naked pony. She wants to know
If then she will become blind to herself.
Or maybe, while she is riding on the back
Of a naked pony, she will be able to look
Across the prairie and see god watching.

But as for now, it is true that the ponies
Can be seen grazing on the spring horizon far away.

And the boys are there, leaning down toward the grass,
Stretching full-length along their ponies' glossy necks.
And they watch the locusts spread their wings,
And they take blossoms of red clover and rue
To lace at night through the intertwining dark
Of their long black hair.

GENTLEMEN OF LEISURE

Yesterday Felicia put an invitation
In the evening newspaper addressed
To all true Gentlemen of Leisure:

> Please come tomorrow for an afternoon
> Of sedate conversation, coffee,
> Mints and finger croissants.

As the gentlemen arrive, ringing
Once at mid-afternoon, all is prepared.
They place their kid gloves, their chapeaux
And their canes, without clatter, on the marble stand
And proceed to the parlor to seat themselves
On the couch of bruised-rose brocade, the white-lacquered
Chairs and the maroon-cushioned settee.

Felicia thinks the Gentlemen of Leisure
Are magnificently regal in their lavender
Lamb's wool suits and pearl buttons. She adores
Their subtle aromas of unsmoked tobacco, crushed marjoram
And black cinnamon stem.

There are prolonged silences in the parlor
As the gentlemen nod to one another and muse
And abstractly balance their demitasse. They touch
Their temples occasionally with the lace
Of their wine-colored cravats.

They discuss for a moment the brief verse
They discussed during their visit last year.
And they note the shadow of the fern
In its bamboo stand on the dark polished floor.
They recall the rare virgin canary
Which eats small white seeds in the forest
And sips single drops of silver water
In the afternoon and again at dawn.

All true Gentlemen of Leisure are genuinely
And exquisitely calm inside the outer trappings
Of their serenity. Unlike Eduard, who hypocritically
Preaches the code common to all Gentlemen of Leisure,
They know nothing personally of biological
Petulance or preordained harangue.

Cecil wants to paint a portrait
Of the gentlemen sitting and gazing together
In the parlor, but he cannot find the proper shade
Of mauve. And he feels, besides, that the vulgar
Movements of his brush might irreparably violate
The sensitivities of his subjects.

This afternoon, Kioka has insisted
On erecting his sweat-bath tipi on the lawn
Beside the parlor windows. Even though Felicia closes
The drapes, Kioka can still be heard chanting
In the sizzling and sputtering steam that rises

From the glowing rocks. What a triumph
That only one teaspoon rattles against its saucer
As Kioka rushes suddenly from his bath
Screaming his surrender and runs toward the lake!

Doesn't each Gentleman of Leisure sleep well at night,
Cool and scented with rosebay on the smoothest white
Linen, under a coverlet of combed angora, a low light
Burning by his bed in a cut crystal bowl all night?

Sonia must pray for all true Gentlemen of Leisure
Who lend such glorious affirmation
To passivity.

When they rise to leave, precisely
At the perfect moment of dusk, they hold
Their carved canes lightly and stroll
On the white-pebbled path, slowly through the fog
Just gathering among the budding laurel and the full-flowered
Plum, glancing once this way and once that,
And Felicia holds her breath for the beauty.

III

THE EFFORT TO ELIMINATE IGNORANCE: BIRDWATCHING

Felicia, who can't name the horned lark
Or the Lapland longspur that she has definitely spotted
Across the grasslands, has never been able to see
The chat or the ricebird or the nest of the rock wren
That Albert demands she search for.

Cecil has discovered where sleep exists—
Deep in the center of his own palm. He has seen it
In that creased cavern spiralling
Through stalks of bone. Cecil believes
That the nature of dreams might be revealed
By studying the way the buteo hawk soars skyward
Disappearing into the cupped hand
Of the desert night.

Sonia is compiling a catalog of birds
In which she defines the willet as the first thought
Of wind against the brow, and the godwit
As the manifestation of billowing wheat
Still held in the seed, and the dickcissel as the memory
Of a china tea cup pressed against the lip.
All of her definitions change daily, having monthly
Phases like the moon.

Kioka, who can hear the wheatear when it begins
Its migration southward from the rocky tundra,
Who can smell bayberry on the breath

Of the tree swallow flying overhead and feel the heat
From the domed nest of the king rail across the marsh,
Who can detect, like little flames in his throat,
The rapid respiration of the common snipe,
Says he is not a birdwatcher, has never been a birdwatcher,
And will never consider becoming a birdwatcher.

Gordon contends that birds are simply intermediary figures
In a gradient of winged behavior proceeding from the purely
Imaginary flight of the electron to the paper-hair
Flutter of the velvet hover-fly to the slope-soaring
Of the falcon to the vacuous white feathers
Of the moon to the dark-edged wing of the pure
Conception of flight itself.

Kioka thinks if the correct definition of bird is
"A warm-blooded vertebrate with feathers and wings,"
Then when he dances against the canyon sky wearing
His cape made from feathers of the black-necked stilt
And the black-legged kittiwake, then he at least
Ought to be mentioned in Sonia's catalog.

SEMINAR

"Dominoes, Zebras, and the Full Moon"
Are the subjects of the month-long seminar
Gordon is attending at his alma mater.

His first letter home contained the following information:

Upon entering the speaking hall, each participant
In the seminar must carry a small banner indicating

His primary field of expertise—
Black with white stripes for general zebra experts;
Black with white dots for domino aficionados;
Pure white for professors of the full moon;
White with black stripes for authorities investigating
The effects of zebras on the full moon and vice versa;
White with white-striped black dots for professors
Studying the effects of dominoes on zebra experts;
Descending circles of alternating black and white
For champion muggins players experiencing
Recurring dreams of zebras;
White-striped black with black white-dotted
Dots for all authorities on seminar banners.

A single banner is allowed each participant.
No two participants with the same banner
May speak in sequence.

On the first day a domino expert rose to speak, saying,
"Some black bones of dominoes possess many full moons,
But the deepest side of any domino never
Has a moon of any kind."

This was immediately challenged by a zebra expert claiming,
"There may be more than one undiscovered moon
On the deepest side of any particular zebra bone."

At this moment, an attendant, wheeling a zebra skeleton
Into the auditorium, broke it into pieces
When he tripped on the ramp and fell.
This unfortunate accident, however, led
To Gordon's conclusion that assembling the pieces
Of a zebra skeleton on a stage is remarkably similar
To laying-out matched domino bones on a table.

Upon presenting this insight with all of its implications
To his colleagues, Gordon received a standing ovation.

And when the last bone of the skeleton
Was finally put into place, someone in the audience
Actually shouted out, "Domino!"

Everyone is eagerly awaiting Gordon's second letter
Which will contain news of the preparations being made
For the all-night rodeo and domino tournament
To be held under the full moon.

Because of her intense interest in this seminar
And her great admiration for Gordon, Felicia
Has despised Albert for most of this month.

THE PURSUIT AS SOLUTION

Whenever Albert is bored, he says he wants to know
What's on the other side of the mind. He says
He sometimes has a vision of himself entering
A bird's throat without injuring it, descending
Deeper and deeper headfirst into that warm black center
Until the pressure building at his feet begins to pull
The whole meadow in behind him, every hop clover
And feather foil and smartweed and swamp candle.
And then the hills follow with their grey-green rocks,
Their shagbarks, bitternuts, sourwoods and birches.
And the iron fence around the lawn and the latticed
Arbor house are sucked in too and the warm perfume
Of guests for dinner, crystal salt shakers,
Embroidered napkins. The whole evening sky

Is taken as if it were a net filled with lapping honey bees,
Bot flies, horntails, shrikes and scaups. And even his dreams
Of flying wingless into space and the invisible and the unlikely
And finally light itself are funneled in. Then the bird,
In that vacuum remaining, begins to enter its own throat,
Followed by Albert himself diving in behind himself
And Albert's mind turned inside out.

Sonia thinks Albert should pick
One small thing such as a ceramic thimble
Or a brass button from his great-great-granduncle's
Naval uniform or a six-spotted fishing spider
And try to find the other side of that first,
For practice.

Albert is happy with this suggestion, and now,
On this Tuesday afternoon, he isn't bored any longer
But is out searching along the seashore for a perfect
Short-spined sea urchin or a spiral-tufted
Bryozoan or a trumpet worm or a sea mouse
With which to begin.

Gordon says this whole idea is ridiculous.
Once Albert *knows* what's on the other side of his mind,
It won't be on the other side any longer.

————————

Entomological Research

Cecil thinks the desert blister beetle
Is simply a single moment frozen in the hard-shelled
Body of a bug, a moment grateful to be given
A blue metallic head and six purple legs.

He thinks by watching an entire nest of disturbed beetles
One might see history rearranging itself.

Sonia thinks each purple blister beetle
Is the six-legged proof of a running entomological discussion
Between the desert floor and the sun.

Albert knows the desert blister beetle he studies
Is nothing but the brain finally seeing itself
As the possibility of insect it has always been.
The underside of any brain then
Must be the blue luminescent belly
Of the blister beetle flipped over on its back.

Occasionally Felicia wonders what Albert's brain is
As it recognizes itself in the act of becoming
The hunchbacked blister beetle it studies.

If the blister beetle could perceive itself
As the subject of this research, then its brain might become
The perfect physical image of the words,
Six purple legs and a blue metallic head.

The brain, surrounded by the sun, the desert floor
And the blister beetle it becomes, definitely knows
How to make itself the subject of any entomological discussion.

Someone, grateful for a change in this discussion,
Could suggest that if each blister beetle represented
A note of duration on the musical scale,
Then a startling symphony of revelation
Might exist unheard on the desert floor.

Gordon, with his ear to the sand,
Has told everyone to be quiet twice.

The Love of Enchantment: Felicia Was Kissed in the Garden Last Night

Someone unseen behind her in the sage
And iris odors of the gravel pathway
Definitely took her by the shoulders,
Pushed her hair aside carefully and kissed her
With decision and concern just once,
There at the darkness below her ear.

And there was breath in that kiss
As if the hesitation and impetuosity
Of spring together had finally found
One motion. And there was love
In that motion as when the parting
And reconciliation inside a hawthorn seed
Finally divine together a branch
Full of blossoms.

And now, by her belief in the imagined spell
Created by that kiss, Felicia clearly perceives
The means by which the earth can be taut
With Indian pipe, heavy with matted roots
Of salt marshes, dark with redwood shadows,
While at the same moment it can soar, clean
And shining, a white grain sailing
In the black heavens around the sun.

A new resiliency has risen in Felicia's bones
Since her encounter in the garden, a warm
And dominant, marrow-related alloy sustained
By her spine remembering those fingertips brushing
Her shoulders with praise. Everyone recognizes

The new buoyancy of esteem in the charmed energy
And sureness of her body swimming across
The lily-bordered lake this evening.

Now even Gordon wants to see and touch
That small exalted, transfigured,
Lip-defined, miraculous moment of her neck.

And no one is sorry that, even if just once,
Felicia was kissed and cherished that way
In an ordinary garden rightly declared, rightly
Proclaimed, justifiably announced by Felicia, running
To clasp both of Albert's hands in her own,
As grandly enchanted last night.

HOW THE WHALE FORGETS THE LOVE OF FELICIA

If he breaches at all, he only rises
To a moderate height, rolls little
And falls without luster or surf, silently
In an unremarkable mid-autumn fog.

He rejects the underlying form
Of the fairy shrimp, will not ingest
Fleeing krill if their silver bodies sparkle,
Ignores the possibilities in the strong,
White wings of the manta ray.

In order to avoid the awareness
Of her absence, he must not close his eyes.
In order to avoid the sound of her name,
He must not remind himself to forget.

He deliberately pulls away and bypasses
Brilliant bars of green sun shimmering
Through the dark sea, and he pulls away and sinks
Deliberately from the light salt-vacancies
Of stars ascending like tiny jewels of air
Through the ocean night.

And he never pictures the beauty of barefoot
Riders on horseback when white gulls perch
And flutter on his crusty hump.
And he never remembers tireless dancers
In transparent silks when white waves leap,
Reaching and bowing before a violet sky.

As he moves forward, he doesn't heed or acknowledge
The only direction manifested naturally and forever
Inside the tough hide of his heart, and he doesn't name
The honor of his own broad brow or the honor
Of the comb jellies he passes or the bravery of the bream
And the halfbeaks or the cruelty of the moon's soft skin
Sliding along his own in the night.

How careful he must be never to profess with fervor
The devotion of denial, the clear affirmation
Of suffering.

Indifferent to his own methods, he merely dives
Repeatedly to a depth of dull twilight
Where he meditates without passion on the great
Indeterminable presence of the steady sea, the rock
And return, the capture and simultaneous release
Of its thousand, thousand meaningless caresses.

THE STRUCTURE OF SUSTENANCE

In the month of March, Albert plans
An expedition up the eastern side
Of the nearest mountain.

Kioka says bands of Peruvians coming down
The mountain have reported seeing flocks of hummingbirds
In a meadow near the summit, hummingbirds
With invisible wings, blue-green heads and thumb-bellies
Of scarlet-orange. Kioka believes the trumpet vines
That cover the meadow have swallowed the wings
Of the hummingbirds.

Albert thinks that the hummingbirds, if they exist,
Have changed themselves into Peruvians with ponchos
Of blue-green and scarlet-orange thrown over their shoulders,
That they have come down from the mountain
To repeat their own legends.

The Peruvians seem to go easily up and down
The mountain as if they had invisible wings.
And they themselves say that their women
Go up to the meadow alone to mate
With the hummingbirds in May. They claim their babies
Nurse on trumpet blossoms in the meadow
Until they are old enough to fly.

According to legend,
The ancient Peruvian word for nipple is
Sweet-nectared blossom of orange.

Last fall a black-eyed woman by a mountain road
Gave Sonia a basket of trumpet blossom vines

And old hummingbird nests. Scarlet-gold yarn
And bits of turquoise wool could be seen woven
With spider silk among the threads of the old nests.

Sonia likes to think that hummingbirds are simply
Scarlet-orange trumpet blossoms clipped from the vine,
Given invisible wings and green tongues, that their bellies
Are always full of their own honey.

The title of Cecil's most recent oil painting is
Green Hummingbird Tongue Licking an Orange Nipple.

Gordon is looking through his magazines
For an article entitled "An Analysis of Nectar,
With a View toward Predicting the Structure
Of the Creatures It Sustains."

Sometimes Felicia waits beside the lake at dawn
Until the sky is the exact color of trumpet blossoms.
Then she imagines she is the wing of a hummingbird
Caught inside the orange stomach of a flower
Or a Peruvian baby wrapped in a wool nest, nursing
At her mother's breast.

"Hummingbirds Speaking with Peruvian Tongues"
Is the title of an old song without words.

Albert is spending every day now assembling
And checking his gear. He has ordered bird traps
And vine clippers. And every night Gordon falls asleep
Working on his newest book, *Scarlet-Feathered
Flowers and Egg-Producing Vines in the Legends
Of the Upper Andean Plains.*

Felicia has had a telescope mounted at her window

And will watch for Albert's campfire every evening
In March. He will set a lone pine ablaze at the summit
If he has seen hummingbirds or Peruvians,
And he will shoot an orange flare into the sky
If either has spoken.

Kioka will accompany him, traveling
Out of sight without fire.

It's only January.
"Legend Full of Its Own Nectar" is the name
Of this winter.

THE FACTS OF THE EARTH

*Taken from an entry found in a partially burned journal buried
among the ruins of an old country house.*

Every black-lined shadow of each brown grama grass,
Every winged flicker of every beetle wasp
And sawfly, every stickery slice and quilled seed
Of the multitudinous field is a stark
And isolated detail existing entirely by itself,
And there is no field.

And the field is one solid indistinguishable blade
And blend of brown, a stationary broad wash of constant
Blurred wind, a wide, dull entity of motion
With not a single detail of its own,
And there is no field.

And all parts of the giant crack willow—the lance-like

Leaves and the hairy yellow catkins—are noisy and glaring
And irritable with sunlight. And all parts of the giant
Crack willow—the lance-like leaves and hairy yellow catkins—
Are mute and invisible and irritable with shadow.

The grassland sparrows have abandoned their rufous
Caps and their scarlet bills and are not birds at all,
And the grassland sparrows have irrevocably joined themselves
With their scarlet bills and their rufous caps
And are not birds at all.

Felicia, stationary with her arms at her sides, says
It must be the earth spinning slower and slower around her
That causes such weight.

Albert has disappeared.

Cecil says he has no name.

And for a moment, Sonia thinks that salt
Moving by itself from her eyes, over her cheeks,
Is the most inexplicable phenomenon in the universe.

Gordon is dead.

IV

THE MYTH: RAISON D'ÊTRE

Some say there are wild white ponies
Being washed clean in a clear pool
Beneath a narrow falls in the middle
Of the deciduous forest existing
At the center of the sun.

Some say the thrashing of those ponies
Straining against their bridles, the water flying
From their stamping hooves in fiery pieces
And streaks rising higher than the sandbar willows
Along the bank, drops whirling like sparks
From the manes of their shaking heads,
And the shouting and splashing of the boys
Yanked off their feet by the ponies
As they attempt to wash the great shoulders
And rumps of those rearing beasts, as they lather
Their necks and breasts, stroking them,
Soothing them—all this is the source
Of the fierce binding and releasing energy
Existing at the core of the sun.

The purple jays, mad with the chaos,
Shrieking in the tops of the planetrees,
The rough-winged swallows swerving back
And forth in distress, the struggle of the boys
To soap the inner haunch, to reach
Beneath the belly, to dodge the sharp
Pawing hooves, the wide-eyed screaming

Of the slipping ponies being maneuvered
For the final rinse under the splattering falls—
All the fury of this frightening drama,
Some believe, is contained and borne steadily
Across the blue sky strictly by the startling
Light and combustion of its own commotion.

But when those ponies stand, finally quiet,
Their pure white manes and tails braided
With lilac and rock rose, the boys asleep
On their backs, when they stand,
Fragrant and shimmering, their forelocks
Damp with sweet oil, serene and silent
In the motionless dark of the deep
Riverside forest, then everyone can
Easily see and understand the magnificent
Silhouette, the restrained power, the adorned,
Unblemished and abiding beauty
That is the night.

THE ACCOUNTING

Under the wheel of the gypsy's winter wagon
Or covered with desert sand beside Kioka's footprints,
Felicia is said to have found again the journal
That was lost twice. Although she never recognizes
The old-fashioned hand or the strange spelling
That has dated each entry, she believes in the names
She guesses are written there. And she likes
The journal's binding, the odor rising from its pages

Like soil just given light, like wind coming
From the freshly opened center of an old, old star.

Albert doubts the existence of the journal,
As no one has ever seen it but Felicia,
And she has difficulty reading it, claiming
That every page is too narrow and too fine
For her eyes.

On a blue velvet bookmark given to Felicia
By the gypsies is this saying sewn in sequins:
"Words are remarkably similar to stars
In their ability to determine the past and contain
The future."

Kioka has been lost twice himself
On the desert, walking all night over wide
Sand under a turning wheel of winter stars.
In his own recognizable hand, he has written
On a rock never found again: "One foot
Is named time and one foot is named motion."

If the journal is found again far in the future
And opened to a date far in the past,
Where will Sonia and Cecil be then? found
In the freshly cut center of an old, old star? or lost
In the opened clasp of an unrecognized hand?
Or taken into light like a leaf of soil?

At the desert's far rim Cecil can recognize time as a word
Turning like a wheel so narrow and fine
That edgewise it can't be seen.

Felicia hasn't seen the journal now since she left it
Last night covered with starlight, closed
And locked as tightly as a fine wheel and its word
Turning at the center of an imaginary rock.

She has told Gordon, looking straight into his old
Star-spun eyes, that until she can read in the journal
An account of herself finding a journal twice lost
In which she then discovers an account of herself
Staring into fine, beloved stars, reading her name
Placed on the page like a binding mark between motion
And time, she won't imagine a word of it.

THE EVOLUTION OF FREEDOM

Hands, having freed themselves from water and webs,
From the need to support the body, being finally capable
Of placing, by their own fingers, a ring on every finger,
Wish now for a release from blood and bones,
From the odious limitations of arms.

Every summer evening Gordon searches among the trees
For a completely pure cicada, just one red-eyed locust
That is nothing at all but "insect."

As Sonia watched the ostrich of the Kalahari Desert dance
In the first returning rains, she believed
She had never seen water before.

The eye of the insect watching summer
As it places the evening in ring upon ring among the trees
Is already supporting much more than itself.

268

Gordon understands pure water to be nothing at all
But the desert released from its own limitations.
The ostrich searches the freedom of rain with its wings
As if it had never seen hands before.

THE REVELATION OF THE WILLED HALLUCINATION

Cecil plans to watch the next garden party
From the roof of the highest turret overlooking
The courtyard. He wants to see how the silk parasols
Of all the ladies will look when viewed from above—
The perfect, coral, silk-fringed circle of one, the scarlet,
Crystal-beaded sphere of another, the lavender-jeweled,
The turquoise-tinged ivory, the barely turning, pale,
Yellow chiffon. He thinks the parasols, spined like leaves,
Spiked in the center with pistils, bobbing
And swaying slowly among each other on their invisible
Stems will look, from above, like ruffled blossoms
With silk-skirted feet.

Eventually Cecil wants to imagine that he is looking down
On a garden of moving flowers, as if he were seeing
A full field in spring blossom. He might decide then
To name each parasol as he watches. The splay of orange
Brocade he might call the red-orange wood lily
With its black spots. He thinks he will be able to find
The golden, thread-leaved sundew and identify the wild coffee,
The blackberry lily, the hedge mustard and the rosebay.
He will locate the flower of the bindweed spreading
Its yellow stripes exactly from the center of its pink

Satin dome. The pale, yellow chiffon he might call
The sister of the wild senna.

Cecil wants to concentrate on the parasols
Until he can't be certain they are parasols at all,
Until he can't be sure that their silk isn't really
The soft skin of spread petals, until he begins to believe
That the flowers possess hidden breasts beneath their parasols,
That the fine ladies contain in the deepest crevices
Below their petals, spores and pollen and possibilities
Of faint perfumes, until he is convinced it would be possible
To gather a bouquet of small parasols and place them in a vase
On the piano where they might converse as corydalis,
White laurel, the deep-lined purple and blue-eyed grass.

Finally, in the middle of the party, Cecil plans to startle
Everyone by sounding his brass gong from the rooftop.
He believes at this moment the flowers, non-committal
And indifferent so far in the garden below him,
Will suddenly allow the silk circles of their petals
To fall simultaneously in a unique event revealing
For the first time their eyes and mouths and cheekbones,
The complete, bright astonishment of their upturned faces.

THE CREATION OF SIN

Gordon wants to commit a sin
Never committed before. He says he is bored
By the lascivious; he has slept through
A thousand adulteries. He calls theft
And murder and greed embarrassingly unimaginative.

He spends an hour each clear afternoon
On the lawn beneath the alders, grooming the dogs,
Trying to imagine a sin so novel
It has not yet been forbidden.

Sometimes, in the moment just before he discerns
The fish treading in light at the bottom
Of the spring or when he studies the eye
Of the short-eared owl in the instant before it sees
The shrew, he is certain he has already committed
That peculiar sin without knowing it. In the early morning,
As he watches himself from the icy black cedars
By the window, dreaming in his sleep, he can almost
Define it.

As the sole author of a sin,
Gordon knows he would be obligated to create
Its expiation by himself. Grace by seaside scrutiny
He might claim, forgiveness by clam classification,
Confession by continual shell collection.
He could invent sacred vows—sworn custodian
Of conifers, promised caretaker of ambush bugs
And toad bugs. He could preach atonement by paper
And mathematics, redemption by ritual
Guessing at the matter of stars.

Today he has recorded a unique grassland prayer
On a tape with the whooping cranes. He has gathered
Sacraments of metamorphic meal moths and hardening
Sassafras fruit. And he knows if he could just commit
A truly original sin, it would mean the beginning
Of his only real salvation.

ONE IN THREE

Although Sonia believes her friend, Lettina,
Is a girl visiting from a coastal city, Kioka
Knows a tree that was once a figurehead
Named Lettina. It stands now in the forest on a rising
Hillside like a wooden girl standing upright on the bow
Of a ship, her skirts blowing around her legs
In soft-leafed branches like the pale green
Billowing remembered by a tree sailing
Like a girl through a forest spring.

Consequently, Kioka believes he is the only one
Who knows how to see the depth of the ocean
In the dark seed-point of Lettina's eyes. And he can hear
The salt swelling in the full leaf forming the circumference
Of her heart. He can find the grain of the tree
In Lettina's palm, the flesh frozen as the lapping
Of the sea stopped in wood.

And in the forest, he can put his hand on the trunk
Of the tree and feel how it shudders
In exactly the same way the sea trembles
Beneath a quivering figurehead, in the same way
Lettina grips the bedpost in the middle of the night
Whenever heavy clouds, like great whales, pass by,
Sounding in the dark.

It is one and the same sinking
That exists in the figurehead plunging
Between cold stormy waves and in the tree
Falling between icy crests of winter light

And in Lettina descending into the cold
Drowning of her dreams.

In the core of the tree Kioka has found
The two wooden crosses the figurehead holds
Toward the sky as she races over the seas
Into the center of the still forest, into the crux
Of Lettina's name. Only Kioka sees how a wooden
Figurehead and a single tree in the forest and Lettina
Can rise together as one, facing straight-on the direction
From which their only motion proceeds.

Before her visit comes to an end, Cecil
Wants to paint a portrait of Lettina, depicting
A detailed chronology of the metamorphosis
Of the tree from seed to flower or vice versa,
Illustrating simultaneously the history
Of female figureheads on clipper ships and the evolving
Essence of Lettina's soul, but no one (Kioka never truly
Understands the meaning of the question) will tell him
Where to begin.

ALBERT, STANDING IN THE FOREST AT NIGHT, ASKS HIMSELF, "WHERE DID I COME FROM?"

And the salt-matches in the dark
Of his blood answer silently like the fireflies
Mating in the yaupon hedge before him.

And the shimmerings of a thousand pale moons,
Like poplar leaves blowing in the copse

Across the clearing, answer, "From the stem-and-leaf
Architecture of his flickering
Heart-notion of moment."

And the invisible Angel of Eternity
In his groin repeats, "Out of everlasting light
Broken into time by seeds of white violet
Scattered on the forest floor."

And the fish flashing like soft slips of mica
In the stream, schooled like a synthesis
Of darting, form suddenly as one, a new sentence
Of explanation, adroit and gold-scaled
And lively in Albert's brain.

The image of an Indian standing among the willows
Silently declares, "Out of Kioka's hands
Forming 'Albert' in the ancient sign language
Of his people."

And the distance from the nearest side of his being
Across the void to the farthest side of his being says,
"Originating from the length the whippoorwill's call
Must travel between the nearest white oak
And the farthest white oak where its echo
Waits in the dark."

And with Albert's own accent, his ear,
Designed by forest winds and night crickets,
Is saying to him, "All is born, all born, immediately
And instantaneously with that question."

The Truth of the Matter

Felicia is not really a girl
But a slender stalk of stationary coral,
Particularized yet singular, statuesque
In her tolerance of crabs nesting in her cavernous
Hair, of fish hovering in the shelter
Of her golden flesh. She is dependably columnar
Among the petals of light falling
Around her through the green sea.

Albert is not a real boy but the net
Of a casting spider flying in a wide silver arc,
Weightless, billowing like dawn
In the morning sky.

Sonia is not a girl but the color of wine
Wherever and whenever she is detected—deep
In the tight fingertips of the pink-frilled
Morning glory or beneath the tremulous beak
Of the becard or, on icy February evenings, edged
In black trees along the tops of the frozen hills.

Not an authentic Indian, Kioka is the perfect
Image of himself in buckskin and braids. He even believes
The seven tales he tells of how he touched the abyss
Seven times with his coup-stick hewn
From a seven-year hickory.

Cecil is a salt-grey ocean bird hanging
Like an isolated wave in the sky. His rookery
Is built in cliffs so high the light of the sea
Takes three days to reach it. He knows it is the sight
Of his own tears that tells him when to mourn.

It is by the sound of his own song that he learns
When to celebrate.

These are the roles and this is the cast
Chosen to perform them in a drama entitled
A Brief Glimpse of Reality, written by Gordon,
Posing as an author, in rehearsal now
For its opening night at 8:30 P.M. on New Hallows Eve.

––––––––––

SIGHT AND SOUND

Kioka rides his brown spotted pinto with naked boys
On naked ponies. They were his darlings
From the beginning, his darlings. Their stomachs
Pressed to the ponies' warm backs, their bare
Heels kicking, every one of them rides fast
With both hands free. Nothing will stop them.
They have the whole wide flat prairie of flowering bluet
Before the house, and they have the whole wide shining
Shore of sand before the sea.

Sonia, Gordon and Albert hurry to the second-story
Veranda to watch the naked boys on their ponies
Whenever they gallop past.

Gordon is pleased to discover that the dark
Blind column of the porch where he places his hand
For a moment contains all the knowledge anyone could pursue
Concerning the galloping hooves of ponies bounding
Over a blue prairie with naked boys on their backs.

Even though Felicia is asleep on a distant hillside
And cannot see or hear the ponies, still it is Kioka
Riding with naked boys who makes the only wide prairie
Of Felicia's heart. It is Kioka who gallops without stopping
Along the only wide shining shore of her heart.

Sonia wants to bring the blind beggars
To the second-story veranda when the ponies pass
So that they may watch the wind coming
Through those flower-filled manes to blow
Against their faces, so that they can see, thereby,
The course of their only cure. And she wants the deaf
Beggars to come and grip the prairie-filled porch railing
During that passing so that they may hear
The only method of their healing.

As the ponies pass, Albert, having removed
All his clothes, stands with his eyes closed
And his ears stopped and grips the column
Of the porch as he rises simultaneously and leaves
The second-story veranda to gallop past himself
On a wild pinto pony following Kioka toward the sea.

Cecil has climbed to the highest garret of the house
So that he can see how Kioka and his ponies reach the bay,
How nothing on the sky or the shore hesitates
As they continue straight out over the water, galloping
Across the waves, through the light-filled spray,
Their hooves striking hard against the flat sun on the surface
Of the sea, how they ride high above the deep, becoming
A rearing surging line of ocean rim racing along the sky.
He leans forward watching them into the evening, watching
Until they pass so far out of sight that he can hear them clearly,
Screaming and thundering and roaring at his back.

SPLITTING AND BINDING (1989)

I

THE NEXT STORY

All morning long
they kept coming back, the jays,
five of them, blue-grey, purple-banded,
strident, disruptive. They screamed
with their whole bodies from the branches
of the pine, tipped forward, heads
toward earth, and swept across the lawn
into the oleanders, dipping low
as they flew over the half-skull
and beak, the blood-end of the one wing
lying intact, over the fluff
of feathers scattered and drifting
occasionally, easily as dandelion—
all that the cat had left.

Back and forth, past one another,
pausing as if listening, then sharply
cutting the morning again into shard
upon shard of frantic and crested descent,
jagged slivers of raucous outrage,
they kept at it, crying singly, together,
alternately, as if on cue, discordant
anthem. The pattern of their inconsolable
fear could be seen against the flat
spring sky as identical to the pattern
made by the unmendable shatter
of disjointed rubbish on the lawn,
all morning long.

Splitting and Binding   281

Mothers, fathers, our kind, tell me again
that death doesn't matter. Tell me
it's just a limitation of vision, a fold
of landscape, a deep flax-and-poppy-filled
gully hidden on the hill, a pleat
in our perception, a somersault of existence,
natural, even beneficent, even a gift,
the only key to the red-lacquered door
at the end of the hall, "water
within water," those old stories.

But this time, whatever is said,
when it's said, will have to be more
reverent and more rude, more absolute,
more convincing then these five jays
who have become the five wheeling spokes
and stays of perfect lament, who, without knowing
anything, have accurately matched the black
beaks and spread shoulders of their bodies
to all the shrill, bird-shaped histories
of grief; will have to be demanding enough,
subtle enough, shocking enough, sovereign
enough, right enough to rouse me, to move me
from this window where I have pressed
my forehead hard against the unyielding pane,
unyielding all morning long.

THE DEAD NEVER FIGHT AGAINST ANYTHING

It's always been that way.
They've allowed themselves to be placed,
knees to chin, in the corners of caves
or in holes in the earth, then covered
with stones; they've let their fingers
be curled around old spears or diadems
or favorite dolls, the stems
of cut flowers.

Whether their skulls were cracked open
and their brains eaten by kin
or whether their brains were pulled
by tongs through their nostrils
and thrown into the dog's dish as waste
are matters that have never concerned them.

They have never offered resistance
to being tied to rocks below the sea,
left for days and nights until their flesh
washed away or likewise to being placed
high in jungle trees or high on scaffolds
alone in the desert until buzzards,
vultures and harpy eagles stripped
their bones bare. They have never minded
jackals nosing at their haunches,
coyotes gnawing at their breasts.

The dead have always been so purely
tolerant. They've let their bones
be rubbed with ointments, ornamented
with ochre, used as kitchen ladles

and spoons. They've been imperturbably
indifferent to the removal of all
their entrails, the resulting cavities
filled with palm wine, aromatic
spices; they have lain complacently
as their abdomens were infused
by syringe with cedar oil.
They've allowed all seven
natural openings of their bodies
to be closed with gold dust.

They've been shrunken and their mouths
sewn shut; they've been wrapped
in gummed linen, corded, bound upright
facing east, hung above coals
and smoked, their ears stuffed
with onions, sent to sea on flaming
pyres. Not one has ever given
a single sign of dissent.

Oblivious to abuse. Even today,
you can hit them and pinch them
and kick them. You can shake them,
scream into their ears. You can cry.
You can kiss them and whisper and moan,
smooth their combed and parted hair, touch
the lips that yesterday spoke, beseech,
entreat with your finest entreaty.
Still, they stare without deviation,
straight into distance and direction.
Old stumps, old shameless logs, rigid
knurls, snow-faced, pitiless,
pitiless betrayal.

WHITE PRAYER

For the white tail-like tongue of the echidna
Taking white sap from the ponerine ants;
For the white shadow of the shearwater
Sweeping like a beacon between the black
Night and the black ocean below;

For the noonside paddle of the prickly pear
Pressed flat against the sun, and the white silence
Of the impending scarlet call waiting
Inside the red-winged blackbird settled
Among the icy reeds; and the winter prairie
In the brain of the snow hare changing
His summer fur to white;

For the purest gift of white appearing
As an isolated parabola of light on the forest floor;
For the white mercy the dayflower gives
To roadside ditches, and the white soul of the eye
That can see its own blindness, and the white steps
Of this remembered ritual;

This is a prayer of white praying
For the white prayer buried in the green catacombs
Of bony coral filled with sea, praying for the white
Statement of pale root caught in the core
Of white spruce branches beneath the earth, praying
For the presence of itself with all the promised
Clarity of white within white. May the power
Of its recitation reflect off the seamless walls
Of its own examined boundaries and save us, for a moment,
From the white stare, the smothering fog, the albino terror,
The blankness of death.

II

The Voice of the Precambrian Sea

During the dearth and lack of those two thousand
Million years of death, one wished primarily
Just to grasp tightly, to compose, to circle,
To link and fasten skillfully, as one
Crusty grey bryozoan builds upon another,
To be *anything* particular, flexing and releasing
In controlled spasms, to make boundaries—replicating
Chains, membranes, epitheliums—to latch on with power
As hooked mussels now adhere to rocky beaches;
To roll up tightly, fistlike, as a water possum,
Spine and skin, curls against the cold;
To become godlike with transformation.

And in that time one eventually wished,
With the dull swell and fall of the surf, to rise up
Out of oneself, to move straight into the violet
Billowing of evening as a willed structure of flight
Trailing feet, or by six pins to balance
Above the shore on a swollen blue lupine, tender,
Almost sore with sap, to shimmer there,
Specific and alone, two yellow wings
Like splinters of morning.

One yearned simultaneously to be invisible,
In the way the oak toad is invisible among
The ashy debris of the scrub-forest floor;
To be grandiose as deserts are grandiose
With punctata and peccaries, Joshua tree,

286

Saguaro and the mule-ears blossom; to be precise
As the long gleaming hairs of the gourami, swaying
And touching, find the moss and roughage
Of the pond bottom with precision; to stitch
And stitch (that dream) slowly and exactly
As a woman at her tapestry with needle and thread
Sews each succeeding canopy of the rain forest
And with silver threads creates at last
The shining eyes of the capuchins huddled
Among the black leaves of the upper branches.

One longed to be able to taste the salt
Of pity, to hold by bones the stone of grief,
To take in by acknowledgment the light
Of spring lilies in a purple vase, five white
Birds flying before a thunderhead, to become
Infinite by reflection, announcing out loud
In one's own language, by one's own voice,
The fabrication of these desires, this day
Of their recitation.

––––––––––

THE ORIGIN OF ORDER

Stellar dust has settled.
It is green underwater now in the leaves
Of the yellow crowfoot. Its potentialities
Are gathered together under pine litter
As emerging flower of the pink arbutus.
It has gained the power to make itself again
In the bone-filled egg of osprey and teal.

One could say this toothpick grasshopper
Is a cloud of decayed nebula congealed and perching
On his female mating. The tortoise beetle,
Leaving the stripped veins of morning-glory vines
Like licked bones, is a straw-colored swirl
Of clever gases.

At this moment there are dead stars seeing
Themselves as marsh and forest in the eyes
Of muskrat and shrew, disintegrated suns
Making songs all night long in the throats
Of crawfish frogs, in the rubbings and gratings
Of the red-legged locust. There are spirits of orbiting
Rock in the shells of pointed winkles
And apple snails, ghosts of extinct comets caught
In the leap of darting hare and bobcat, revolutions
Of rushing stone contained in the sound of these words.

Maybe the paths of the Pleiades and Coma clusters
Have been compelled to mathematics by the mind
Contemplating the nature of itself
In the motions of stars. The pattern
Of the starry summer night might be identical
To the structure of the summer heavens circling
Inside the skull. I can feel time speeding now
In all directions deeper and deeper into the black oblivion
Of the electrons directly behind my eyes.

Child of the sky, ancestor of the sky, the mind
Has been obligated from the beginning
To create an ordered universe
As the only possible proof
Of its own inheritance.

THE FAVORITE DANCE OF THE DEAF
AND BLIND BEGGAR

It contains the same precision of gesture
Accomplished by the morning larkspur leaning
Eastward toward light and the same rapid virtuosity
Of the darting fingerling in deep-creek sun
And the single turn of the many—in flocks
Of ricebirds, in schools of mackerel.

He understands, by his own body, the soaring
Of the sun-split leap of salmon after salmon
Through loop after loop of cascading current.
Without sight, without sound, still he knows
The complicated coordination, the passing-by,
The uniting and separating performed by the company
Of willow leaves, yellow catkins and their ribbonlike
Branches blowing together in an erratic wind.

In the closing of his hand, he recognizes
The slow folding of the dancer onstage, the same act
Sealed and completed in the rolling curl
Of the seahorse's tail. As if he saw and heard
The phenomenon from the inside out, the pattern
Of the waltzer's feet on the floor, like the design
Of a wood fern reflected in a pond, he perceives
In its immediate form.

What grace, the way he yearns for the reverence
Of a rising line of smoke which does not descend,
Which has no fall. What evocation, the motion
Of the blooming hyacinth in the motion
Of his beseeching.

Of course, he can comprehend, without speech,
The intricacies of this dance which tambourines
And drums, masks, scarves, mudras, *taconeo,*
The cabriole, the arabesque merely investigate,
Revealing occasionally the placement and position,
The circling and holding that were first performed,
Choreographed permanently in the spatial arts
Of his bones, in the cellular elegance of his blood,
In the old underlying routines of the brain,
Ten billion years before. His favorite dance
Is *this* dance in which he has always participated,
Rising, joining, even asleep, even sitting, still
And bound as he must, inside the enduring darkness
Of his unlimited silence.

III

THE SENSE GOD GAVE

enough to forage successfully for grains
and grass sprouts in the protected shallows
of coastal marshes, to fatten further
on Yukon berries for a month in the fall

enough to thrust the head forward hissing,
raise the feathers and run full force
at weasels near the breeding grounds, to hold
the wings slightly from the body in an icy
rain to shelter the young

sufficient to be reliable sentries
in the courtyards of Egyptians, Romans
and Greeks, to pull the toy, flower-filled
wooden carts of Christian children
at Easter time, to be favorite
family caretaker of cradle songs,
to be roused on a hillside
and scattered forever
by John Whiteside's daughter

enough to nest on the wide nest
of the Arctic tundra, to be as gregarious
as the waves on northern summer bays,
to be flocks of sterling in the moonlight,
the color of fog in fog, to assume
the aura of ancient river flyways,

to assume the name
of snow

enough to be and perfectly be
(even as any saint or angel must)
the full, proliferating,
and ever-multifarious proof
of exactly that measure given

———————

THE ANSWERING OF PRAYERS

Because they have neither tongue
Nor voice, the iris are thought by some
Never to pray, also because they have no hands
To press together and because, born blind,
They cannot properly direct their eyes
Heavenward and, not insignificantly,
Because their god has no ears.

Rising simply from the cement
Of their bulbs, the iris have no premeditated
Motion. They never place one appendage
Deliberately before another in a series
Crossing space. How can they ever formulate, then,
A progress of thought moving from "want"
To "request," from "delight" to "blessing"?
How can they invent what they cannot envision—
A structure of steps leading from "self"
To "beyond"?

Consequently, and some may call it prayer,
They engage themselves in one steady proclamation
Which eventually becomes arched and violet
With petals, pertinently stemmed, budded
With nuance, a subtlety of lissome blades, a sound
Undoubtedly recognized by that deaf god
Who contains within his breast, like the sky-half
Of a spring afternoon, vacancies shaped
As missing floral clusters, purple-streaked
Intimacies. As rooted in his place as April,
It is *their* god who, standing hollow, precedes them
With the absence of brown-wine and lavender bouquets,
Ivory flags on grey-green stalks.

And in the unfolding act of his being filled,
As he becomes weighted, suffused with blossoms
And fragrance, as he feels his heart cupped
And pressed with the intensity of ascent,
In that act of being filled (perfect
Absolution) doesn't he surround, doesn't
He enable, doesn't he with fitting eloquence
Reply?

THE IMPORTANCE OF THE WHALE
IN THE FIELD OF IRIS

They would be difficult to tell apart, except
That one of them sails as a single body of flowing
Grey-violet and purple-brown flashes of sun, in and out
Across the steady sky. And one of them brushes
Its ruffled flukes and wrinkled sepals constantly

Against the salt-smooth skin of the other as it swims past,
And one of them possesses a radiant indigo moment
Deep beneath its lidded crux into which the curious
Might stare.

In the early morning sun, however, both are equally
Colored and silently sung in orange. And both gather
And promote white prairie gulls which call
And circle and soar about them, diving occasionally
To nip the microscopic snails from their brows.
And both intuitively perceive the patterns
Of webs and courseways, the identical blue-glass
Hairs of connective spiders and blood
Laced across their crystal skin.

If someone may assume that the iris at midnight sways
And bends, attempting to focus the North Star
Exactly at the blue-tinged center of its pale stem,
Then someone may also imagine how the whale rolls
And turns, straining to align inside its narrow eye
At midnight, the bright star-point of Polaris.

And doesn't the iris, by its memory of whale,
Straighten its bladed leaves like rows of baleen
Open in the sun? And doesn't the whale, rising
To the surface, breathe by the cupped space
Of the iris it remembers inside its breast?

If they hadn't been found naturally together,
Who would ever have thought to say: The lunge
Of the breaching whale is the fragile dream
Of the spring iris at dawn; the root of the iris
Is the whale's hard wish for careful hands finding
The earth on their own?

It is only by this juxtaposition we can know
That someone exceptional, in a moment of abandon,
Pressing fresh iris to his face in the dark,
Has taken the whale completely into his heart;
That someone of abandon, in an exceptional moment,
Sitting astride the whale's great sounding spine,
Has been taken down into the quiet heart
Of the iris; that someone imagining a field
Completely abandoned by iris and whale can then see
The absence of an exceptional backbone arching
In purple through dark flowers against the evening sky,
Can see how that union of certainty which only exists
By the heart within the whale within the flower rising
Within the breaching heart within the heart centered
Within the star-point of the field's only buoyant heart
Is so clearly and tragically missing there.

IV

For the Wren Trapped in a Cathedral

She can never remember how she entered—
What door, what invisible gate, what mistaken
Passage. But in this place every day,
The day shines as a muted mosaic of impenetrable
Colors, and during the black moonless nights,
Every flickering star lifts smoke, drips wax.
She flies, back and forth through the nave, small,
Bewildered among the forest of branchless trees,
Their straight stone trunks disappearing majestically
Into the high arches of the seasonless stone sky.
No weather here, except the predictable weather
Of chant and procession; no storm, except the storm
Of the watchdogs let loose inside at night.

Now when she perches on the bishop's throne
Her song naturally imitates the pattern
Of frills and flutes found in the carvings there,
The hanging fruit, profuse foliage, ripened
Curves. Her trills have adapted themselves
To fit perfectly the detailed abundance
Of that wooden Paradise.

And she has come to believe in gods, swerving close
To the brightness of the apse, attempting to match
Her spread wings, her attitude, to that of the shining
Dove caught there in poised flight above the Ark.
Near the window of the upper chapel, she imagines

She is that other bird, emanating golden rays
To the Christ in the river below.

Resting on a colonnade opposite the south wall
Of stained glass, she watches how the lines
Of her wings become scarlet and purple
With Mary's Grief. And when she flies the entire
Length of the side aisles, she passes
Through the brown-orange swath of light
From the Journey into Egypt, the green and azure
Of the Miracle of the Five Thousand Fed.
Occasionally she finds that particular moment
And place where she is magnificently transformed,
The dull brown of her breast becoming violet
And magenta with the Adoration of the Magi.

What is it that happens to her body, to bone
And feather and eye, when, on some dark evenings,
She actually sees herself covered, bathed, suffused
In the red blood of the Crucifixion?

Among the statues at night, she finds it a peace,
A serenity, to pause, to murmur in sleep
Next to the ear of a saint, to waken
Nested on the outstretched hand
Of the Savior's unchanging blessing.

Certainly she dreams often of escape, of reversing
That process by which she came to be here, leaving
As an ordinary emissary carrying her own story,
Sacred news from the reality of artifice,
Out into the brilliant white mystery
Of the truthful world.

The Grooming

Under the branches of the elm
and the tall, blooming bushes of black haw,
in the wavering jigsaw of the sun,
you sit, naked on the bench, waiting.
The paraphernalia is gathered,
laid out—warm wash water in a stainless-
steel bowl, rinse water in the deeper
pail, creams, soaps, a sanctuary
of flannel and towels.

She begins, holding each foot
in turn on her lap, carefully,
as if it were a basket of sweet fruits.
Her fingers stroke, wetting, soaping.
She washes the toes, the tender part
of the sole, over the swivel
of the ankle, the swell of the calf.

A hedge of slender sassafras
beside the road sways, almost female
in its graces, as you stand and turn
and she sponges behind your knees,
around each leg (they *are* pillars),
along the inner thighs, without rushing,
to the groin, the slick soap lathered
beneath her hand, the rag dipped
and wrung in rinse water.

She bathes the buttocks next,
and to the front, your genitals,
slowly, carefully. The sassafras sway,
and off in the distance, out of the center
of the rice field, a ceremony of sparrows
appears, releases, dissolves.

Up the strict hollow of the spine,
your torso, your neck, the clean water,
ladled and poured through the disciplined
light of the afternoon, finds its way
back down from your shoulders, following
every wrinkle and bead of nipple
and joint, like rain through leaves
and blossoms of yellow poplar, into the creases
of your sex and out again.

This is the form of absolution:
your hands in her attentive hands,
your arms inside her ministrations.

Listen . . . elbow, your elbow.

Can't you hear, in the sound
of its name, how it has been innocent
forever? And doesn't the entire body, touched
with honor, become honorable? Doesn't the body,
so esteemed and cherished, become
the place of divinity?

The face, the hair, laved,
toweled, rubbed, perfumed,
clean, radiant—you are new,
new as high-mountain snow

not even yet seen, snow so fine,
so weightless, so pervasive, it is one
with the white explosions of the wind,
one with the tight, steady bursting
of the moon, one with the hardest
and safest seams of the night,
by which you now know and so must declare:
the soul can never be more
than what the body believes
of itself.

There Is a Way to Walk on Water

Over the elusive, blue salt-surface easily,
Barefoot, and without surprise—there is a way
To walk far above the tops of volcanic
Scarps and mantle rocks, towering seamounts
Rising in peaks and rifts from the ocean floor,
Over the deep black flow of that distant
Bottom as if one walked studiously
And gracefully on a wire of time
Above eternal night, never touching
Fossil reef corals or the shells of leatherbacks,
Naked gobies or the crusts of sea urchins.

There is a way to walk on water,
And it has something to do with the feel
Of the silken waves sliding continuously
And carefully against the inner arches
Of the feet; and something to do
With what the empty hands, open above

The weed-blown current and chasm
Of that possible fall, hold to tightly;
Something to do with how clearly
And simply one can imagine a silver scatter
Of migrating petrels flying through the body
During that instant, gliding with their white
Wings spread through the cartilage of throat
And breast, across the vast dome of the skull,
How distinctly one can hear them calling singly
And together inside the lungs, sailing straight
Through the spine as if they themselves believed
That bone and moment were passageways
Of equal accessibility.

Buoyant and inconsequential, as serious,
As exact as stone, that old motion of the body,
That visible stride of the soul, when the measured
Placing of each toe, the perfect justice
Of the feet, seems a sublimity of event,
A spatial exaltation—to be able to walk
Over water like that has something to do
With the way, like a rain-filled wind coming
Again to dry grasses on a prairie, all
Of these possibilities are remembered at once,
And the way, like many small blind mouths
Taking drink in their dark sleep,
All of these powers are discovered,
Complete and accomplished
And present from the beginning.

V

THE LIGHT INSIDE OF DEATH

Surely there is a little—maybe like the light
A dark rain carries into the sea on a cold
And broken night or the light held in frozen
Seeds of sumac catching sun along the road
Where a blind man walks alone or the light kept
Beneath the protective wing of a sleeping
Angel that no one will believe in.

Surely in those great depths there is one
Small isolated fin of brilliance that belongs
To death alone (maybe its efficiency, maybe its age),
Flickering like a dim torch no one can recognize
On the opposite side of a foggy gorge, or fluttering
Like a miniature silver fan at the bottom
Of a cavern pool upon which all the concentration
Of the surrounding stones then must focus.

Or perhaps death procures its light solely
By symbiosis, being the only outer edge
Along which the earth's rim can form
Its shining crescent at dawn and the only empty
Frill against which the phosphorescent fern
Can shape the curling glow of its emerging frond.
Maybe death simply borrows the light of the chink snail's
Brain, the twayblade's will, whose presence the pressure
Of its blackness alone has made possible.

But surely death must possess that one tiny,
Intricate light created by the small certainty
Of its own name. And, darling, I know this too,
That in the moment that death comes to cover you,
Lying down carefully over your body, fitting itself
So well, forming belly to belly, matching
Its spreading fingers exactly to your open hands,
Finding its own thighs and its heart and its motion
By finding yours, in that moment, just like a flame
Catching hold suddenly in the center of a lantern
And rising then to fill the dark void of the forest
With its place, death will have no choice,
Must be transformed, illuminated, filled to its farthest
Boundaries by all the glorious sins and virtues
Of your real and radiant grace.

———————

THE NATURE OF WINTER

Why, when the silver-red fox first took
The snowshoe hare in his jaws, when finally,
After the long chase through the snow-filled
Hollow, under the bluff, across the stiff
Bitterweeds, the hare clearing the creek, the hind legs
Of the fox slipping momentarily off the icy rocks
Into that dark rush, and the hare being clever
More than once, darting sideways, doubling back
(Oh, she was snow against the white snow, it's true,
Her black eyes the only thaw of focus visible
To the heaving fox. And she held as still
As a frozen crust of hillside until the last

Second, leaping away again), why, when overtaken
Finally, caught finally, dragged by her flesh
From beneath the cold oak root, snapped up,
The teeth like ivory nails through the ribs,
The spine, the blood muscles of the thigh, hanging
From his jaws, why did she cry out then? Irretrievably
Doomed, why should she have screamed then,
In that empty forest, in that vacant, less-than-sullen,
That paralysis of dusk?

And to whom was she calling? Who could she possibly
Have hoped might answer? Not the solid grey
And snow-blinded sky; not the high, thin-raftered cave,
The deaf structure of the forest; not the crossed bones,
The folded limbs of the brittle hardwoods standing
And breathing still, as they had breathed before;
Not the silver fox whose filled mouth growled
And hummed with the steady engine of pleasure.

The first wine-red, the startling warm violet
Steaming on the snow—maybe it was god's voice,
That cry. Only a god could have uttered it;
Only a god could have heard the lost fur and haunch
And womb and vessel and skull-scream of himself
Beseeching the icy knot, the cold predetermined
Circumstances of himself to save himself.
One chance, the shuddering of his wail,
Maybe this was his one chance quickly
To perceive and declare the divine pain
Of himself before he should forget again,
Expanding back into the tree-cracked
Horizon, the folded white distance,

Into the open black pit at the center
Of the stone, perfect satiation, into the wide
Starry stasis of himself once more.

LIKE GOD

The ash-colored toad
beside the woodpile is always all
that it is not. It is not the quick
flick of August tongue on harp-stringed
katydid tonight, because it is a lump of frigid
and paralyzed earth beneath snow-covered
leaves on a mid-December morning.
And it is not grim, hunchbacked shuffler
after roaches, for it is small slithery
black wing, unbound and weightless,
quivering, cavorting in the moonlit lull
of a spring pond. It is not the bone-dust
that it is, blown by wind through reedy
ditches and hollows but, equally, the first
microscopic swirl of its first mating
rising from a new gathering of water;
and not the spikes of its spadefeet alone
but also the lavender silks of its inner throat;
not the sweet salty red cushion of hidden
lung and heart but the pebble-covered
canvas of its outer hide; never the gold,
acid-etched study of its eye exclusively
but the gaping socket of leather

on the road as well; not the green metal
of its statue by the path, not the cool heavy
mud of its odor in the hand, not the racing
star-ridden composure of its original being
in the heavens . . . how perfectly it ceases!
how marvelously it endures! so secure
and obvious in the glorious absence of all
it is not that we hardly need the word
enigma.

VI

KNOT

Watching the close forest this afternoon
and the riverland beyond, I delineate
quail down from the dandelion's shiver
from the blowzy silver of the cobweb
in which both are tangled. I am skillful
at tracing the white egret within the white
branches of the dead willow where it roosts
and at separating the heron's graceful neck
from the leaning stems of the blue-green
lilies surrounding. I know how to unravel
sawgrasses knitted to iris leaves knitted
to sweet vernals. I can unwind sunlight
from the switches of the water in the slough
and divide the grey sumac's hazy hedge
from the hazy grey of the sky, the red vein
of the hibiscus from its red blossom.

All afternoon I part, I isolate, I untie,
I undo, while all the while the oak
shadows, easing forward, slowly ensnare me,
and the calls of the wood peewees catch
and latch in my gestures, and the spicebush
swallowtails weave their attachments
into my attitude, and the damp sedge
fragrances hook and secure, and the swaying
Spanish mosses loop my coming sleep,
and I am marsh-shackled, forest-twined,

Splitting and Binding

even as the new stars, showing now
through the night-spaces of the sweet gum
and beech, squeeze into the dark
bone of my breast, take their perfectly
secured stitches up and down, pull
all of their thousand threads tight
and fasten, fasten.

The Family Is All There Is

Think of those old, enduring connections
found in all flesh—the channeling
wires and threads, vacuoles, granules,
plasma and pods, purple veins, ascending
boles and coral sapwood (sugar-
and light-filled), those common ligaments,
filaments, fibers and canals.

Seminal to all kin also is the open
mouth—in heart urchin and octopus belly,
in catfish, moonfish, forest lily,
and rugosa rose, in thirsty magpie,
wailing cat cub, barker, yodeler,
yawning coati.

And there is a pervasive clasping
common to the clan—the hard nails
of lichen and ivy sucker
on the church wall, the bean tendril
and the taproot, the bolted coupling
of crane flies, the hold of the shearwater

on its morning squid, guanine
to cytosine, adenine to thymine,
fingers around fingers, the grip
of the voice on presence, the grasp
of the self on place.

Remember the same hair on pygmy
dormouse and yellow-necked caterpillar,
covering red baboon, thistle seed
and willow herb? Remember the similar
snorts of warthog, walrus, male moose
and sumo wrestler? Remember the familiar
whinny and shimmer found in river birches,
bay mares and bullfrog tadpoles,
in children playing at shoulder tag
on a summer lawn?

The family—weavers, reachers, winders
and connivers, pumpers, runners, air
and bubble riders, rock-sitters, wave-gliders,
wire-wobblers, soothers, flagellators—all
brothers, sisters, all there is.

Name something else.

THE REVOLUTION OF THE SOMERSAULT

The first one may have been performed underwater,
A soft green grain of jelly-seed rotating slowly,
Turning by multiple yellow hairs to place
Its cold side in a line of sun below the sea.

Splitting and Binding   309

Or the first one may have been executed by the sea itself
Descending into its own beginning white motion
Over and over, rising again, rolling in a constant
Revelation of action with the shore.

Or maybe it was the heavens during the history before rain
That first performed the act, iris-colored
Clouds defining themselves through the outward direction
Taken by their deepest grey edges folding inward.

The top of the head pressing against the earth, the whirling
Reverse of place between hillside and sky,
Maybe this is the only way to remember
The possible loops of light contained in the recognition
Of stars, to understand how the inside of the soul
Can carry itself closest to open sun, how the circling
Of the spine can prove the central position of the heart.

The somersault may well be the very trick, the confusing
Art, the easy fall and manipulation of perception
Envied and imitated by death.

The tumbling dream of the locust tree
Fulfilled in its corkscrew pod, a blade of grass bending
With dew to meet the field-speckled damp
Of its own pure base—who can know what we know for sure
Whenever we touch the coral-colored somersaults frozen in shell
As the perfect record of the conch's life?

VII

Rolling Naked in the Morning Dew

Out among the wet grasses and wild barley-covered
Meadows, backside, frontside, through the white clover
And feather peabush, over spongy tussocks
And shaggy-mane mushrooms, the abandoned nests
Of larks and bobolinks, face to face
With vole trails, snail niches, jelly
Slug eggs; or in a stone-walled garden, level
With the stemmed bulbs of orange and scarlet tulips,
Cricket carcasses, the bent blossoms of sweet william,
Shoulder over shoulder, leg over leg, clear
To the ferny edge of the goldfish pond—some people
Believe in the rejuvenating powers of this act—naked
As a toad in the forest, belly and hips, thighs
And ankles drenched in the dew-filled gulches
Of oak leaves, in the soft fall beneath yellow birches,
All of the skin exposed directly to the *killy* cry
Of the king bird, the buzzing of grasshopper sparrows,
Those calls merging with the dawn-red mists
Of crimson steeplebush, entering the bare body then
Not merely through the ears but through the skin
Of every naked person willing every event and potentiality
Of a damp transforming dawn to enter.

Lillie Langtry practiced it, when weather permitted,
Lying down naked every morning in the dew,
With all of her beauty believing the single petal
Of her white skin could absorb and assume

That radiating purity of liquid and light.
And I admit to believing myself, without question,
In the magical powers of dew on the cheeks
And breasts of Lillie Langtry believing devotedly
In the magical powers of early morning dew on the skin
Of her body lolling in purple beds of bird's-foot violets,
Pink prairie mimosa. And I believe, without doubt,
In the mystery of the healing energy coming
From that wholehearted belief in the beneficent results
Of the good delights of the naked body rolling
And rolling through all the silked and sun-filled,
Dusky-winged, sheathed and sparkled, looped
And dizzied effluences of each dawn
Of the rolling earth.

Just consider how the mere idea of it alone
Has already caused me to sing and sing
This whole morning long.

WHEN AT NIGHT

Suppose all of you came in the dark,
each one, up to my bed while I was sleeping;

Suppose one of you took my hand
without waking me and touched my fingers,
moved your lips the length of each one, down
into the crotch with your tongue and up again,
slowly sucking the nipple of each knuckle
with your eyes closed;

Suppose two of you were at my head, the breath
of one in my ear like a bird/moth thuddering
at a silk screen; the other fully engaged, mouth
tasting of sweetmeats and liquors,
kissing my mouth;

Suppose another drew the covers
down to my feet, slipped the loops
from the buttons, spread my gown,
ministering mouth again around the dark
of each breast, pulling and puckering
in the way that water in a stir
pulls and puckers a fallen
bellflower into itself;

Two at my shoulders to ease
the gown away, take it down
past my waist and hips, over my ankles
to the end of the bed; one of you
is made to adore the belly; one of you
is obsessed with dampness; at my bent
knees now, another watching, at my parted
thighs another; and one to oversee
the separation and one to guard the joining
and one to equal my trembling and one
to protect my moaning;

And at dawn, if everything were put
in place again, closing, sealing, my legs
together, straight, the quilt folded
and tucked to my chin; if all of you
stepped back, away, into your places,
into the translucence of glass

Splitting and Binding   313

at the window, into the ground breezes
swelling the limber grasses, into the river
of insect rubbings below the field and the light
expanding the empty spaces of the elm, back
into the rising black of the hawk deepening
the shallow sky, and we all woke then
so much happier than before, well,
there wouldn't be anything
wrong in that, would there?

————————

For Passions Denied: Pineywoods Lily

Who knows what unrelieved yearning
finally produced the pink-and-lavender-wax control
of these petals, what continual longing
resulted in the sharp arcing of the leaves,
what unceasing obsession became itself
in the steady siren of the ruby stigma? That tense
line of magenta disappearing over the boundaries
of the blossom is so unequivocal in the decision
of its direction, one is afraid to look too long.

I can understand, perhaps, having a hopeless
passion for gliding beneath the sea, wanting to swim
leisurely, without breath, through green salt
and sun-tiered water, to sleep all night, lost
and floating among the stroking of the angelfish,
the weaving rags of the rays. And I can understand
an impossible craving to fly unencumbered,
without effort, naked and easily over sandstone
canyons, through the high rain of river-filled

gorges, to feel the passing pressures of an evening
sky against the forehead, against the breast.
And I can understand the desire to touch a body
that may never be touched, the frenzy to move
one's hand along a thigh into a darkness
which will never have proximity, to take into oneself
the entire perfume, the whole yeast and vibration
and seethe of that which will always remain
aloof, a desire so unrelenting it might easily turn
any blood or pistil at its deepest crux
to majestic purple.

I don't know what it is that a pineywoods lily,
with all her being, might wish for. Yet whatever dearest
thing this lily was denied, it's clear
she must very greatly have suffered, to be before us now
so striking in her bearing, so fearsome
in her rage.

VIII

The Eyes of the Gardener in the Villa of the Blind

He does it all for them—the narrow flagstone
Path carefully laid through ivory tulips,
Snow-in-summer, dwarf iris, red-tipped
Fern growing among the moss-covered rocks.
He plans the most pleasing perspectives:
Border plants—phlox and hyacinth—before taller
Varieties—delphinium and foxglove—the flowering
Quince and columns of sculpted evergreens
Positioned beyond. That yellow of the torch lily,
So beautiful at dawn against the hedge
Of purple hydrangea.

In the open brick courtyard, he tends and grooms
The spring-fed pond within which swim
The specially bred oriental veiltail and lionhead.
With thoughts of their lingering there, he prunes
The lacy mermaid weeds and nurses
The thin green saucers and violet blooms
Of the floating water lilies. He knows
They can negotiate the three wide steps
Down into the stillness of the hardwood forest,
Past the fringed orchids and rose pogonia
He has placed in the shadows near the trunks
Of the shumard oaks.

When they finally enter in the evening
Through the hinged gate, they walk slowly,

Swinging and tapping their white canes.
They hold their faces slightly raised,
Expectant, as if they believed
They could feel the designed beauty
Of that garden across their brows
Just as they feel the pattern
Of moving clouds and sun on their skin.
Aren't the white centers of their eyes
Actually affected in some way by the light
Of the scarlet larkspur which certainly
Touches them, by the brilliant rays
Of the blaze roses shining here
In this their own garden?

Can't the dark bones of their feet and hands
Assume by reflection the nurtured grace
Of the lilac bushes they envision
To be gracefully growing beside them?

Will they be able to see
The way they are there in the blossoms
Of sweet alyssum and Canterbury bell
Planted specifically for them
And among which they now walk?

How he cherishes them for the purpose
Of their presence! How they adore him
For the perfect mystery of his eyes!

Tomorrow he will mulch and cultivate
The floribunda, the field of narcissus.
He will arrange the hanging sprays of magenta
And maroon portulaca spilling over the low
Rock walls and clear the pond of fallen leaves

Splitting and Binding   317

And weed the east ridges of columbine and sweep
The walk circling the daffodils and violas
And wait again for evening.

————

What the Sun God Saw One Summer Afternoon

Looking long enough, right before his eyes
he saw the sheaths of leaf and tassel
and stem split and fall, layer
after layer, like transparent skins
from around each stalk, until all the barley
and rushes stood complete and naked,
a thousand narrow blades of fire
bending and shimmering across the field.

And the smooth asters and sweet clovers,
releasing their outer shells of texture
and fragrance and color, became small perpetual
explosions poised on their glowing stems.
Without the bronze and violet paper
of their wings or the green of their appendices
or the black beads of their heads,
he could readily identify the dragonflies
as the ignited thrum and simmer shining
over the mud flats of the lowlands.

And in the sky, he watched the red hawk lose,
without relinquishing anything, the scales
and feathers and beak of its body
until it circled over the meadow, a gliding
bird of light alone.

How could he escape knowing then,
on that afternoon, to what *bovine*
and *pepper frog* and *lichen-covered*
granite boulder had always
most resolutely referred?

This was the first gift:
that he came to see everything,
during the moment he saw it,
as steadfastly possessing the one divine
soul of his eyes. What an indispensable,
what a benevolent god! to watch,
to recognize, to thus create and bestow
such necessary majesty.

When You Watch Us Sleeping

When you see us lying scented
in our nightclothes, the patchwork
quilt wadded at our feet, coverlet
kicked aside, when you see us still
at midnight, our bare arms covered
with the moon-shadows of the hemlock
by the window, our hands latent
and half-open on the pillows by our heads;

When you come upon any of us buried
but breathing, close to the earth,
motionless as oak leaves beneath drifts
of oak leaves or curled inside silk
body-vases hanging from greasewood

and vetch or sprawled, languid
under the broad branches
of the baobab in summer heat,
when you hear us humming hoarsely
sometimes, scarcely wheezing, murmuring
like white hens at their roost;

When you watch the green anole
on the banyan, cool and slender
as a pod, the onyx grain of his eye
closed deep in green sunlight,
when you can see how he obviously
possesses in his body, even in the slack
scaly skin of rose beneath his jaw,
even in the posing net of his ribs,
even in the corpuscle of blood
at the tip of his tail,
how he possesses in his body alone
all the power he needs to rise
and declare, not merely truth,
but rapture;

The living body asleep, so great
a sum of beauty that a billion
zeroes follow it, the eyes
sealing the head so tightly
during those moments
that the infinity of possible
heavens inside can be clearly
perceived by anyone;
when you watch us sleeping,
when you see the purest
architecture of the ear,

the explicit faith of the knee,
the old guiltless unforgiving adoring
sweet momentary tremble of claim
in the breast . . .

Aren't you sorry?
Don't you love us?

IX

THE OBJECTS OF IMMORTALITY

If I could bestow immortality,
I'd do it liberally—on the aim of the hummingbird,
The sea nettle and the dispersing skeletons of cottonweed
In the wind, on the night heron hatchling and the night heron
Still bound in the blue-green darkness of its egg,
On the thrice-banded crab spider and on every low shrub
And tall teasel stem of its most perfect places.

I would ask that the turquoise skimmer, hovering
Over backwater moss, stay forever, without faltering,
Without disappearing, head half-eaten on the mud, one wing
Under pine rubbish, one floating downstream, nudged
And spit away by foraging darters.

And for that determination to survive,
Evident as the vibration of the manta ray beneath sand,
As the tight concentration of each trout-lily petal
On its stem, as the barbed body curled in the brain
Of the burrowing echidna, for that intensity
Which is not simply the part of the bittern's gold eye
Most easily identified and remembered but the entire
Bittern itself, for that bird-shaped realization
Of effective pressure against oblivion, I would make
My own eternal assertion: Let that pressure endure.

And maybe this immortality can come to pass
Because continuous life, even granted to every firefly
And firebeetle and fireworm on earth, to the glowing clouds

Of every deep-sea squirt, to all electric eels, phosphorescent
Fishes and scaly, bright-bulbed extensions of the black
Ocean bottoms, to all luminous fungi and all torch-carrying
Creatures, to the lost light and reflective rock
Of every star in the summer sky, everlasting life,
Even granted to all of these multiplied a million times,
Could scarcely perturb or bother anyone truly understanding
The needs of infinity.

―――――

ON BEING EATEN ALIVE

You know the most terrifying ways—giant fish,
reticulate python, saber-toothed cat,
army ants by the hundreds, piranha
by the scores. One can imagine
being scarlet in the blood
of a lion or rolled as pellets
in a wolf's belly or ossified
in the barreled bones
of a grizzly bear.

There are those who have been snatched
away without leaving a trace
into the flames (efficient bowels)
of a pine forest on fire or a burning
barn in August and those
who have been taken on rough tongues
of salt, smothered and lost
in a cavern full of sea.

Splitting and Binding   323

I have seen others disappear
without a cry, wholly ingested,
limbs and hair and voice,
swallowed up irretrievably
by the expanding sac
of insanity.

But I like to think
of that old way, the most common
and slowest, the body disassembled,
diffused, slowly, consumed—particle
by particle, stigma, gradually, by stigma,
cell by cell—converted carefully, transfigured,
transformed, becoming finally both
a passing grain of blue above an early
evening silhouette of oaks and an inflation
of sun in low October fog, both the sigh
of bladed wind in beach grasses
and the sound of singing in the wings
of desert bats, becoming as close
to itself as the smooth night skin
lining the skull, as the white moaning
conch of its own hearing, the body
becoming gradually and remarkably
so indisputably so.

BEFORE I WAKE

The turning of the marsh marigold coming slowly
Into its emergent bloom underwater; the turning
Of the coral sands over themselves and over their dunes

And over the scratchings of the scarab beetles
Turning over the dung of the desert doe; the pivoting
Of the eye of the bluefish turning inside the drawing light
Of its multiple school shifting its constellation
In the dark sea; this is the prayer of sleep
In which I lay myself down to dream.

The quiet enclosed by the burrowing wolf spider
Dragging its egg sac to the surface to sun;
The stillness covered by the barren strawberry
Making its fleshless seed on the rocky hill;
The study in the desert mushroom knotting itself
In the arid heat; the silence of the fetal sea horses
Bound in the pouch of their father; this is the dream
Of the soul in which I lay myself down to pray.

And I've asked the outward motion of the hollow web
Of the elm making leaf, and I've asked the inward motion
Of every glinting fin making the focus of the carp,
And I've asked the involution of the egg buds carried
In the dark inside the cowbirds circling overhead,
And I've asked the tight coiling and breaking
Of light traveling in the beads of the sawgrass
And the net of the sea oats splitting and binding
And splitting again over and over across the open lands
To keep me in this dream tonight through one prayer more.

GEOCENTRIC (1993)

EARTHRISE

A Common Sight

There is at least one eye
for everything here this afternoon.
The algae and the yeasts, invisible
to some, for instance, are seen
by the protozoa; and the black-tailed
seeds of tadpoles are recognized
on sight by the giant, egg-carrying
water beetle. Brook trout have eyes
for caddisfly larvae, pickerel
for dragonfly nymphs; redfin shiners
bear witness to the presence
of flocks of water fleas.

The grains of the goldenrod
are valued, sought out, found
by the red-legged grasshopper who is,
in turn, noticed immediately
by the short-tailed shrew whose least
flitter alarms and attracts
the rodent-scoped eye
of the white-winged hawk.

There is an eye for everything.
The two-lined salamander watches
for the horsehair worm, as the stilt spider
pays sharp attention to midge fly,
crane fly. The cricket frog
will not pass unnoticed, being spied

specifically by the ringed raccoon,
and, despite the night beneath
the field, the earthworm, the grub
and the leafhopper larva are perceived
by the star-nosed mole.

So odd, that nothing goes unnoticed.
Even time has its testimony,
each copepod in the colony possessing
a red eyespot sensitive to the hour,
the entire congregation rising
as one body at dusk to touch the dark
where it exists above the pond.

And I have an eye myself
for this particular vision, this continuous
validation-by-sight that's given
and taken over and over by clam shrimp,
marsh treader, bobcat, the clover-coveting
honeybee, by diving teal, the thousand-eyed
bot fly, the wild and vigilant,
shadow-seeking mollusk mya.

Watch now, for my sake, how I stalk. Watch
how I secure this vision. Watch how long
and lovingly, watch
how I feed.

FELLFIELD

More than from a jelly pod
in waves of kelp; more than from a blue-green
egg in a nest of rootlets and fur;
more than from a fluted seed drifting
toward bottomland, today I feel certain
I came from rocks.

I think I emerged complete
out of those tumbled boulders grouped
across the open hill as if they spoke together
a profound language of position, of pose
relative to virtue.

I know I was here early, in that first moment
after the rocks stopped falling.
I saw them then as they caught suddenly
and held the hill and the sky tight
in their grid, as they pinioned time
like a hide stretched and pegged.

I can say little outright of rocks—limestone,
sandstone, granite, mica. Yet here they make a place
I find so familiar I want to surrender
to the nostalgia, to settle next to them
out of the wild and sleep,
as if they were old grandfathers,
my own culture, as if their configuration
were a lullaby anyone could rely on.

Looking at this expanse of lichen-covered
boulders scattered down the hillside, surrounded
by low brown grasses and blooms of alpine

tundra foliage, I know it's their very pattern
that I've thought so many times before.

When you look at rocks in a fellfield,
I wonder if you feel this way too.

Approaching the Metropolis

Maybe you know also how it sounds
from a distance, the portentous rumble
and whir, the incessant vibrato in the breastbone,
both felt and heard, like timpani in the ears
when the teeth are clenched.

And as one proceeds toward that ceaseless humming
om, that congestion of blaring hell-raisers
and string-pluckers, walking with trepidation
through the still, pine-insulated forest,
nearer and nearer the quaking racket,
it becomes easy to believe that one might
suddenly come upon and witness the vast wheeling,
spitting pistons and flares, the clacking
spokes and golden-oiled engagements
of the entire workings of the inner engine
of the universe itself! That's true.

But as it happens, one suddenly emerges
into the light and rush, surrounded, stunned,
absorbed by the roar of that wide open
field delirious with the machinations
of obsessive blooming, each blossom inhabited,

milked, abused, embraced, forsaken
a thousand times by every gear-shifting,
low-swooping, reckless steam-head, every targeting,
sharp-nosed merchant, fickle poacher and stuttering
thief, every fanatic white-winged sugar-seeker
and buzzing speeding fur-head imaginable
in one spinning frenzy of profit, propulsion
and pause.

So inevitably caught-up, converted! May god,
with the same energy and devotion, bless now,
this and all carnal, egocentric, hard-driving,
fuel-finding, single-minded, death-damning
cities, of any kind.

IN ADDITION TO FAITH, HOPE, AND CHARITY

I'm sure there's a god
in favor of drums. Consider
their pervasiveness—the thump,
thump and slide of waves
on a stretched hide of beach,
the rising beat and slap
of their crests against shore
baffles, the rapping of otters
cracking mollusks with stones,
woodpeckers beak-banging, the beaver's
whack of his tail-paddle, the ape
playing the bam of his own chest,
the million tickering rolls

of rain off the flat-leaves
and razor-rims of the forest.

And we know the noise
of our own inventions—snare and kettle,
bongo, conga, big bass, toy tin,
timbals, tambourine, tom-tom.

But the heart must be the most
pervasive drum of all. Imagine
hearing all together every tinny
snare of every heartbeat
in every jumping mouse and harvest
mouse, sagebrush vole and least
shrew living across the prairie;
and add to that cacophony the individual
staccato tickings inside all gnatcatchers,
kingbirds, kestrels, rock doves, pine
warblers crossing, crisscrossing
each other in the sky, the sound
of their beatings overlapping
with the singular hammerings
of the hearts of cougar, coyote,
weasel, badger, pronghorn, the ponderous
bass of the black bear; and on deserts too,
all the knackings, the flutterings
inside wart snakes, whiptails, racers
and sidewinders, earless lizards, cactus
owls; plus the clamors undersea, slow
booming in the breasts of beluga
and bowhead, uniform rappings
in a passing school of cod or bib,
the thidderings of bat rays and needlefish.

Imagine the earth carrying this continuous
din, this multifarious festival of pulsing
thuds, stutters and drummings, wheeling
on and on across the universe.

This must be proof of a power existing
somewhere definitely in favor
of such a racket.

———————

A VOICE SPEAKS IN EARNEST, BUT NOBODY LISTENS

Folly, I tell them, to build nests
of mosses, lichens, twigs and shredded
grape bark, even a deep, well-made cup
of grasshairs, cobwebs, plant fibers,
or a gourd-shaped, feather-lined cradle
of mud; folly to dig burrows in sandbanks,
among mesquite and prickly pear, to make
alleyways and warrens, to make dens in hummocks,
tussocks, weed clumps, dwarf willows.

Ridiculous, to home in hollow logs, I say,
to roost in cavern crevices, to attach
to sea fans, in eelgrass beds or rubble
bottoms, to wrap up in a sea whip or a vase
sponge, to seek kelp and algal holdfasts.

These barbels, pinchers, beaks, claws,
thorns, sticky stems, spikes and tusks—
absurd, futile—scent glands, ink bags,

twelve-tined antlers, long golden spines,
even beadlike spines in a ring.

Puffings, hissings, hindfeet thumpings,
barking coughs and bugling calls, warning
whistles, buzzes, yaps, pippings, *krees,*
chicarees and *cutta cutta cuttas*—vanity,
all vanity.

Pure folly, I repeat, to put forth lobes
and branchlets, heart-shaped petals, lavender
flowers in wet grassy meadows, bracts and bell-like
blossoms, pink berries, waxy drupes, winged
keys, seeded capsules by the scores.

So surrounded by dark, distant, flaring
combustions, histories and uncertainties,
it's a folly obviously, I tell them, to bring forth
blue-green eggs speckled with olive, white eggs
blotched with brown, black-spotted, clay-colored
eggs, pale eggs laid on sprigs of evergreen, womb
eggs, floating eggs, buried eggs, strings
of jelly eggs in slow riffles. A folly, I say,
to bring forth ever, to give
birth, to bear—stop, listen . . .

A PASSING

Coyotes passed through the field at the back
of the house last night—coyotes, from midnight
till dawn, hunting, foraging, a mad scavenging,

scaring up pocket gophers, white-breasted mice,
jacktails, voles, the least shrew, catching
a bite at a time.

They were a band, screeching, yodeling,
a multi-toned pack. Such yipping and yapping
and jaw clapping, yelping and painful howling,
they *had* to be skinny, worn, used-up,
a tribe of bedraggled uncles and cousins
on the skids, torn, patched, frenzied
mothers, daughters, furtive pups
and, slinking on the edges, an outcast
coydog or two.

From the way they sounded they must have smelled
like rotted toadstool mash and cow blood
curdled together.

All through the night they ranged and howled,
haranguing, scattering through the bindweed and wild
madder, drawing together again, following
old trails over hillocks, leaving their scat
at the junctions, lifting their legs on split
rocks and witch grass. Through rough-stemmed
and panicled flowers, they nipped
and nosed, their ragged tails dragging
in the camphorweed and nettle dust.

They passed through, all of them, like threads
across a frame, piercing and pulling, twining
and woofing, the warp and the weft. Off-key,
suffering, a racket of abominables
with few prospects, they made it—entering

on one side, departing on the other.
They passed clear through and they vanished
with the morning, alive.

THAT'S WHY

> *Both the eye and the mind are notoriously fallible instruments.*
> —STEPHEN JAY GOULD

Can we trust then this scarlet banana flower
of the eye, shining in the lantern light,
or the dawn bat of the retina, seeming to cling there,
smaller than the blossom, taking, with her clean
mouse-tail tongue, nectar from the nectary?

Can the flighty mind be depended upon
rightly to detect the solid grasp
of her wiry nails, the hook of her long deformed
finger into the pod? Should the mind's eye
likewise be expected to see the invisible
tropical forest in the blackness beyond, the spicy
petai, the coveted fruit of the durian?

The bat's mind, we know, sees very well
by other than light. And we can be led
in the night without lantern to the right
blossom by the small heat of her beating heart
sensed even with both eyes closed.

Is it the eye's heart then or the mind's vision
that decides suddenly to call the blossom *mother?*
Is it the mind willed by the heart or the pure

eye alone that wants to name this silent supping
spirit? How can we know if it is merely
a blind heart's error or the mind's mad desire
to perfect itself or the eye through the eye
of the universe that sees *redemption*
as bat belly pressing hard to flower flesh
in a jungle night?

Senseless forest, special flower, sucking
beast, stay. In our certain fallibility,
be infallibly generous. Wait for us.

―――――――

GEOCENTRIC

Indecent, self-soiled, bilious
reek of turnip and toadstool
decay, dribbling the black oil
of wilted succulents, the brown
fester of rotting orchids,
in plain view, that stain
of stinkhorn down your front,
that leaking roil of bracket
fungi down your back, you
purple-haired, grainy-fuzzed
smolder of refuse, fathering
fumes and boils and powdery
mildews, enduring the constant
interruption of sink-mire
flatulence, contagious
with ear wax, corn smut,
blister rust, backwash

and graveyard debris, rich
with manure bog and dry-rot
harboring not only egg-addled
garbage and wrinkled lip
of orange-peel mold but also
the clotted breath of overripe
radish and burnt leek, bearing
every dank, malodorous rut
and scarp, all sulphur fissures
and fetid hillside seepages, old,
old, dependable, engendering
forever the stench and stretch
and warm seeth of inevitable
putrefaction, nobody
loves you as I do.

SEA SAVIORS

My Children (An Old God Remembers)

Knocked suddenly to the ground
from behind, a debilitating blow
to the spine at the base of my neck,
I was lifted, shook, flung by claws
like ice tongs through the thick
of my shoulder. I could feel fat
tongues curled between teeth
pressing hard at my throat,
oily saliva and bellows of sotted
breath at my ear. Razor-dust
perfume of feline, mouse-nest-
berry-ferment fragrance of bear,
green-mud-rotten-tuber-root odor
of lizard, all were there.
I was licked, torn, shredded,
dropped, nudged once, then cuffed
and turned, speared again, dragged
finally down into the undertow.
                              Shining
jelly tentacles wrapped and tightened
around my ankles and thighs. Sharks
targeted, zooming in, white-mouth
sides up, swiping, tearing my buttocks
and breasts. Crabs, fourteen hoary
orange pincers, ripped, scrambled,
stuffing the wondrous machinations
of their mouths. Octopods,

with their rasping beaks, dug in.
Sea vultures and skuas dove and snipped
my earlobes, lips. A suffocation
of sea stars, hagfish, tulip snails
gorged, sucking marrow. And some
that were muzzled and some without
mouths also gathered and fed.
And I was their obsession and I
was their prey, and even those
who only came to watch, all
were satiated, satisfied, filled.

WHAT THE SEA MEANS TO A ROCK BARNACLE IN A TIDAL POOL

He can never understand its complete
essential being, clinging as he must
permanently to the shore rock
of these shallows. He can't know
how it harbors the fluttering
flags of cuckoo ray and banjo ray,
the banners and streamers of zebra fish
and the common squid or how it tolerates
both the fingerfish and the moray eel
in its coral lair or how comfortably
it holds the breaching sperm whale, as well
as flocks of blue tang and extensive
yellow pastures of plankton.

He can never experience its true
depths, being unable to dive

deep enough to encounter the permanent
twilight, the luminous lanternfish
and gulper eels, the glimmering baubles
of the *Stomias boa*. He will never recognize
the red clay bottom or the pelagic
deposits where his own abandoned
cement crust may one day descend
and descend and descend to lie
at last in the general ooze.

Even though he can tickle the feathers
of his mouth through that swaying
salt-flow with a certain skill,
what could the gyral movement
of northern currents or the great
cold-water basins or the mid-oceanic
rift possibly mean to him?

But in the evenings, when he senses
the vast gold glowing of motion
extending itself before him, announcing
presence so emphatically by its alteration
of light, by his own anticipation,
and when that element rises, as it always does,
rushing, submerging, overwhelming him again
exactly like a great grief or a coming
exaltation, then I know he knows,
in the shudder of his own stalk,
something of the power, something
of the abundance, something of the forming
and failing explanation possessed
by that which he will never remember,
that which he cannot name.

TEACHING A SEA TURTLE SUDDENLY GIVEN THE
POWER OF LANGUAGE, I BEGIN BY SAYING:

This green translucent continuance
through which you turn and function, rolling and twisting,
which fluctuates in darkness, which pulses and pushes
insistently against your forehead and your belly
and your genitals, to the top of which you must rise for light,
for breath, is called "The Great Sea."

And by these fingers, of which you have none, I am tracing
the curve of your horned beak, tracing your flippers
intricately scaled in canvas, moving down over the wooden
knobs of your back, down to the leather prick of your tail,
tracing all the boundaries of that which is called "self,"
"Great Turtle of the Great Sea."

And you must try to remember that heavy, ponderous,
slow-shifting silence which is everything you didn't know
you knew before your voice. Say "silence" and listen.
Say "silence."

And your motion is called "gliding, soaring
propulsion of self" and the passing, one after another,
of seaweed clusters and floating eels and rainbow wrasse
and scattered obelia is called "time." Say "compelled,"
say "driven," say "recognition of compulsion."

Understand how you will eventually make the facts of the earth
by the hard drag-marks of your body over the dunes,
how by interference you will make the aggravated existence of bark
and grit and rut and sandbur. Say "egg," say "begat," say "birth,
in the warm sandy loam." Say "birth by the nearest silver egg
buried in the sky." Say "invisible glass turtles pulling up

the black beaches above, leaving in the night
the scattered glow of their daring eggs."
Say "fancy."

Here at the bottom of the sea, beneath the pock-marked
boulder, beside the extending and withdrawing feathers
of the polyps, in the definite turn and focus
of your reflective eye, here is where you must begin now
to be engaged in the making of your brain, each new word
bringing a salt-pulsing neuron simultaneously
into existence. Listen, I am telling you,
it is from the awareness of this precise moment
that the creation of yourself begins.

Sea Dragon Fish in His Garden/Chu Chung Li, 91st Birthday Anniversary

He celebrates, remembering so well the wavy kelp,
the movement of the fronds and seaweeds surrounding, the hang
and sift of the limber green vines of his body
blowing, swaying in the windy ocean current. He recalls
the magenta shift of the silk of his flanks, the bronze
eyes turning as his drifting edifice rotates
presently around itself in the steady stream.

He relives and relives the clock of his two pulsating
side orifices, the regular suck and blow.
How marvelously natural, he sometimes thinks,
to have twenty swaying hands shaped like leaves.

And he remembers sitting inside his camellia garden
like this, his legs crossed, in the flux and flotsam
of evening; he recognizes his recognition as the only
stationary point of bone around which the dusky azure
hedges, the blurred borders rotate slowly. He drifts,
an occasional violet petal floating past
in the regular suck and blow of the breeze.

He chokes, shudders, a spasm, and the turning
sea-edifice pauses, the circling of the garden,
the orifices, the flowing blossoms halt . . .
until he catches his breath and all begin again.

Under the sea, in the silent pock and flicker which appear
as sunlight floating through waving camellia and lavender
foliage, he rocks, he celebrates, he closes his eyes
in his bald bronze skull, moves his fingers down
the easy satin border of his kimono, light leaves
brushing the lapel, the flowing sash, as if all
were truly once tangible.

———————

LIFE AND DEATH: ALL THE LOST ACCORDIONS AND CONCERTINAS

You may wonder yourself what happened to them.
They're at the bottom of the sea.
Some people saw them floating downward,
discarded, sinking slowly into that foreign plane.

They were humming and chording
all the while, inside a confetti of bubbles,

their bellows expanding, opening
like the folded fins of butterfly fish.
Their leather straps were fluttering
behind them like ribbon fish, writhing
like eels, attached like lampreys.

A cargo of concertinas sailed
the salt surface momentarily, bobbing
like a fleet of air-filled jellyfish.

Down they all went, schools and cities
of them, turning and tumbling,
mother-of-pearl buttons gleaming,
keys and reeds quivering.

They recline there yet where they settled,
half-buried in muddy sand, tilting
on cliffs of coral, bobbled and nosed
by jacks and rays. Their bodies
teeter, bowing, contracting
to the tempo of the surf.
They wheeze and blow nightly
with the currents, singing like sirens,
shimmering in their treble, tenor treble.
Their sound is the same sound
you can imagine hearing if beds of waving
seaweed were a chorus of violins.

They take in and give forth their element.
They breathe and moan, those eternal
lungs. They speak. They are greater
than ghosts.

Their soliloquies circle the wide sea,
rippled and meditative, are heard
by nursing blue whales,
who answer.

IMMEMORIAL

when Kioka lifted the flap and ran
    out the door of his sweat bath tipi   headed
       toward the glacial melt   his steamy naked
      body dripping

      he ran right through the perfect
oval moment of the day   right through the first
    loop of the night-to-come   right through the first
      spreading ring of his own shouting

             and kept on going

    dancing through all the horizon's spinning hoops
        in and out every secondary hue
     of his own nature   emerging from the violet hallway
a shade of iris   emerging from the crimson corridor
    sun-red   emerging from the sapphire sheath
           a bean-pod green

     his face pressed forward   his hair
flying   he pushed beyond the five unlatched
    doorways of his name   sprinted through the bull's eye
of his own pointed finger   raced through
        the needle-eye of his grandmother's mettle

                    through the last strategic spyhole
cut by his grandfather

                    passing through the circle
of his linked arms   passing through the gate
      of his own "amen"   down the spiralling tunnel of his sex
through the open mouth of his own death

                                        he dove finally
      straight into the depths
                                    of that icy pool
                  only to rise
            out of the stillness again shooting
      above the water   waving and cursing and blowing
                  fiercely and it's a fact

            nobody can run like Kioka can.

Diving for Gold: The Bottom of the World

That which is far off and exceeding deep,
who can find it out?
            —Ecclesiastes 7:24

Slipping down beneath thick shelves of ice,
into the green-blue shadows and planes,
the frigid, salt-smothers of the sea, your cords
and tubes and tanks, the mask, into the crude
currents that press against the limbs
and spine, that swing loose ties
and straps like a prairie wind;

it's worth it, even the shock
and cold-plastic rigidity of the fingers,
even the buffeting, even the freezing,
solidifying recitations and rules, the ice-crystal
constrictions of the breath; downward,
inward and down through the easy sluice
of the sea, into the slick swallow of the cold
sea, sinking so far and so deep that finally
the sound of *deep,* the pronunciation
of *deep,* the ringing of *deep,* recedes
and returns, circles and tides, involutes,
turns itself upside down, the head below
the feet now, the motion like rising
yet descending still, the voice of the self
heard resolutely from without now,
the hollow of the heart informing now
from both sides of the eyes;

the body a particle thus suspended
weightless at mid-heaven of the vast,
encompassing ocean; looking clearly, far,
farther into any direction than before,
you might discern what you foresaw
seeing—those million, faint campfires
of stars everywhere, their still threads
of smoke, the old, well-fed hunters
hunched beside them telling your story,
fiery constellations shining like grains
of gold along every crest and ridge
and creviced valley of the billowing,
black mountains extending above
and below, away and beyond.

AMEN

It was just an intriguing system
of I-beams and metal arches and long,
narrow rungs of steel, a dusty, complex
scaffolding of crisscrossed pipes
and iron rafter upon rafter; linked
towers of empty frames, a skeletal maze
supporting, occasionally, a stretched
bend of corroded lattice, a rusty
round rim filled with wire spokes
that never turned. It was a mountainous
concoction of extension ladders, street
grates and chinning bars, a network
of trusses and bolts and welded
T-joints, a great black cockeyed
grid looming a thousand twisted frames
high and miles deep against a still
impenetrable background of grey, until . . .
high up, the 45th story maybe,
(it takes a spyglass to spot it)
in a coordinate far east of the center,
out from the dark behind a mottled
gooseneck pipe, swims a single yellow dot,
fluttering, gliding past a crooked
saw-edged strut. It's a shining, weaving,
bud-sized mobility, fins flittering,
rosy gills pumping, each scale
a prickling, a shimmering. Look at it
holding now before a distant corridor
of dented columns, its saucy
double-fantail flipping, flipping
against the current.

GOOD HEAVENS

GOOD HEAVENS

1.
The common garden snail can't watch
the heavens and enumerate—600 young
stars in Perseus, one more hour
until full moon. It can't make lists—
pinwheel of Andromeda, comet fireball
of Tempel-Tuttle. It has never called
its slither the soft finger of night
nor its wound shell a frozen
galactic spin. Yet its boneless,
thumb-sized head is filled and totally
deaf with exactly the same tone
and timbre as the sky.

2. *Winter Midnight*
It seemed I was looking into the face
of a vendor, skin so dark
I couldn't focus at first,
the stark structure of his skull
tighter, blacker even than his eyes.
It was a vendor with his wares—glass
bulbs and seeds, silver goats, loops
and strings of copper, brass-cathedral
charms, polished couples on sticks
copulating, twisted bracelets
and rings—spread like a market
of stars on the blanket at his knees.

I thought I saw borders, ways
and measures in his onyx face.
A shifty hawker, a familiar swindler,
it was an old, skinny vendor on folded
knees, kneeling purple bones, a skeleton
of vestments, a posture of spirals
and stocks hovering above and below
his spread of sockets and hoops,
reaching, rocking, merchandising
at my elbow: *Kum, laydee, bye,*
kum bye mine.

3.
To imagine stars and flaming
dust wheeling inside the gut
of a blind, transparent fish
swimming out of sight in the black
waters of a cave a thousand years ago
is to suggest that the perfect
mystery of time, motion and light
remains perfect.

4.
Good—because the heavy burnings
and fumings of evolving
star clusters and extragalactic
cacophonies—because the flaming
Cygnus Loop, still whipping
and spewing sixty thousand years
after its explosion—because
the churning, disgorging womb
of the Great Nebula and the rushing
oblivions left from the collapse

of protostars—because suffocating
caverns of pulling, sucking gases
and pursuing, encircling ropes
of nuclear bombardments—
because erupting cauldrons
of double stars and multiple
stars flinging outward great
spires and towers of searing
poisons—because all of these
for this long have stayed
far, *far* away from our place.

ELINOR FROST'S MARBLE-TOPPED KNEADING TABLE

Imagine that motion, the turning and pressing,
the constant folding and overlapping, the dough
swallowing and swallowing and swallowing itself
again, just as the sea, bellying up the hard shore,
draws back under its own next forward-moving
roll, slides out from under itself
along the beach and back again; that first
motion, I mean, like the initial act
of any ovum (falcon, leopard, crab) turning
into itself, taking all of its outside surfaces
inward; the same circular mixing and churning
and straightening out again seen at the core
of thunderheads born above deserts; that involution
ritualized inside amaryllis bulbs
and castor beans in May.

Regard those hands now, if you never
noticed before, flour-caked fists and palms knuckling
the lump, gathering, dividing, tucking
and rolling, smoothing, reversing. I know,
from the stirring and sinking habits
of your own passions, that you recognize
this motion.

And far in the distance, (you may even
have guessed) far past Orion and Magellan's vapors,
past the dark nebulae and the sifted rings
of interstellar dust, way beyond mass and propulsion,
before the first wheels and orbits of sleep
and awareness, there, inside that moment
which comes to be, when we remember,
at the only center where it has always been,
an aproned figure stands kneading, ripe
with yeast, her children at her skirts.
Now and then she pauses, bends quickly,
clangs open the door, tosses another stick
on the fire.

SNOW THINKING

Someone must have thought of snow falling first,
before it happened. That's what I believe,
someone way before me, way before anyone
could write "snow" and then see it happen—
in the cracks between the mud bricks
of the patio, assuming the shapes
of seeded sedum and wineleaf, covering

the tops of overturned flowerpots,
so much whiter than the sky it comes from—
as we do sometimes.

I think it must have come (the being
of the motion of snow, I mean, furling out
of the black, this method of winding
and loosening, this manner of arriving)
first from deep inside someone, as we say,
out of some quiet, exuberant graciousness,
far beyond neutron or electron, way before
eyes or hands, far before any crudeness
like that.

It had to come from someone first,
before snow, *this expression of snow,*
the swift, easy, multi-faceted
passion possessed and witnessed
in descending snow. It must be so.
Otherwise, how could we, as ourselves,
recognize it now—*the event of snow,*
so clearly eloquent, so separate,
so much rarer than *snow?* It's there.
We know it—the succumbing to sky,
the melding, nothing too small
for the embracing, a singular gentleness.

And don't we know now, without seeing it,
without touching it, that outside the window
the snow is coming, accumulating over the walls
and hedges of the garden, covering
the terra cotta, filling all the filigree
and deficiencies of evening?

I believe that snow snowing is the form
of someone singing in the future
to a new and beloved child, a child who,
staring up at the indistinguishable
features of his mother's star-filled face
in the dark, knows, without touching
or seeing, the experience of snow, opening
his mouth to catch and eat every spark
of the story as it breaks and falls
so particularly upon him.

––––––––––

CARRYING ON THE TRADITION
OR
THE MAN IN THE MOON BRINGS HIS DAUGHTER FOR LESSONS IN MARBLE SCULPTING

She learns selection, visits
remote quarries, studies veins
and faults, the translucent, buried
strengths, the art of release and recovery.

She practices at home with pick
and point and chisel claw, completes
a flawless egg in a nest of bristles, a rapture
of eels in a crystal bowl. She doubles
the radiance in the wings of her first
yucca moth. How does she accomplish it—each thin
glass-white leaf in a forest of oak, the frosted
grid of the spider, even the flickering
rustle of ice-chips flying in a winter wind?

She's ideal, a gift, and she's ready now.
Standing before her father's mirror,
she takes file and chisel in her lily hands,
begins, carefully sculpting the silk bloom
of her transparent pajamas, the distinct
apple-white arch of her lifted arms.
She watches her work bring forth
the sanded glow of her belly
and thighs, the light from each link
of her bracelets and bands.

Until she perfected her art,
no one had ever seen the albino monkey
grinning on her shoulder, the blind man
standing in the shadow at her back.

Now she is buffing, waxing the sharp
polish of her cheeks, highlighting the orblike
curve of her brow, the surf of her hair.
Almost finished, she peers hard
at her mirrored face, narrows in, determined
to discover and depict with brilliance
the old lunacy shining in her eyes.

SELENE'S GENEROSITY

The plains-dwelling warthog (normally diurnal,
rooting for bulbs, tubers, fungi in the noonday
sun) has occasionally been seen feeding
in the light of the full moon.

Coarse black bristles covering her barrel
body from head to shoulders, she is naked
beyond, down to her rump, prissy stick legs,
cloven hoofs. Her weak eyes are tiny
beads buried in the huge, grey gourd
of her head. It would take both arms
of a strong man straining to cradle,
to carry, such a massive head severed.

Even awash in the night perfumes
of worms, molds, grub-rich humus and soil,
she can scent the scat, the spray, menses,
sperm, the spittle of leopard, wolf, feral
dog, approaching boar.

Clair de lune, of course. Lumpy
from her last mud wallow, she grunts
in her odoriferous gut, shovels
through the dirt with her upturned
teeth-tusks, with the cartilaginous
disk of her mucous-dripping snout.
Anyone there to see could see
the pustule-like warts on her misshapen
head shine silver.

By the moonlight, towards dawn, she stretches
on her stomach, dozes in a dew-drizzle.
Moisture gathers in the deep
depression between her petal ears.
One sparrow, two, come to take sips,
a quick splash, at that glittering
pool held tight as pearl in the bristly
cup of her buzzing black skull.

WHY LOST DIVINITY REMAINS LOST

I look for it, but there are always
distractions—eleven magpies cawing, rocking,
crowded in one small-boned locust tree.

I search, but my concentration
is broken by the pattern of leaf shadows
moving on the wall, the fragrances of pine sugar,
sage, dry red grasses in the air.

I say prayers, but the evening thunder,
the gully wind . . . I have to stop
and check the sky.

Once I shouted the word, called out
across the field, "Divinity?"
But if there was an answer, five prairie dogs
rising on their haunches beside their mounds
at that moment to stare straight at me
took my attention completely.

Some holy men and some holy women
can sit on spires and nails and try
to remember for days at a time
without being distracted. Even that mountain goat
we saw yesterday appearing suddenly
out of the rocks on the edge of the cliff,
even her kid appearing just as suddenly
at her udder, couldn't cause those holy
ones to blink. But I don't know how
to know what they know.

I try to meditate. I try to set my mind
firmly on the task. Again, just devils
I suppose—the night that is nothing
soothing around my face, my hair,
and the stars, seeded by an uneven hand,
so profuse, so demanding, so clearly
insistent in their silence.

———————

DISTANCE AND DEPTH

Whether looking down through
a pond's surface, past a brown mossy
tavern of twigs into a floating nest
and through the membrane of a single
translucent egg globule, down
into the drama and complex carnival
of that jelly mote, its lipids,
ashes and crystal inclusions,
through its loops and plots
and domestications, past bound
messages, gates, stringy messengers,
past storms, sparks, signs and orbits,
on down toward the tense purple
nebula of chaos at its core;

or whether watching far out over
the flat grasses and gullies, skimming
the plains past low opuntia, hidden
beeflies, jumping mice, the burrows
of dogs and deer and all that multitude,
right up to the first rising red rock

range and past that to the next sheer
evergreen plateau and on beyond
to the ultimate highest blue snow
of the peaks with names, past them
to the ragged ridge of the sinking moon
and behind that into the easy black
where the eyes seem suddenly turned
hard and fast on themselves;

whether distance or depth, either way
it's evident there are fields and fields
and fields aplenty, more and more
space than is needed, ample space
for any kind of sin to be laid down,
disassembled, swallowed away, lost,
absorbed, forgotten, transformed,
if one should only ask
for such a favor.

———————

BY DEATH

In that moment she became two, one sitting
among the red flags of the blackbirds
in the reeds, the other standing fixed
like a poplar in a fence of poplars.

In the next second, there were four
of her, one watching evening from the sill
beside the bed, another laced through the night-
spaces between the fireflies.

In a further splitting, she was eight,
and in the next sixteen, one blue
by paper lantern, one amethyst by evening
smoke, one ringed like ice by a winter
moon, one ringed like a lily-pond by rain,
one marked by murder, one veined
by acquittal.

And there were thirty-two of her then
and again sixty-four, and she was simultaneously
over a plain of summer cress and under
a reef of evening coral, within a knob
of shyster thistle, within a bud of thresher
shark, sailing by roots of bony fish,
soaring by fins of tamarack and phlox.

With the next turning she became
a hundred and twenty-eight of herself, groomed
the horse of Orion, dwelled in the light-remnant
of Vela. She was wind through the scaffold
of pity, a nesting owl among the eaves of praise.
Then two hundred fifty-six—she was stone as well,
and zephyr, then legion, then too various
to be reckoned, too pervasive to be noticed,
too specific to be named.

THE MANY FACES

To Complete a Thought

"In order to define the issue . . ." he begins,
as an orange one leaps from the piano, lands
in the middle of the room on the floral
carpet, bounds again, climbs halfway
up the silk drapes and stops, legs spread,
hanging as if suspended there.

"Time in a timeless . . ." she pauses,
as the calico jumps from her lap, scrambles
up the drapes, chasing the swishing
orange tail of the other.

A short-haired yellow one skids
around the corner, at this point, sliding,
skittering, batting at a rolling bell, jangling
and spinning it down the marble hallway.

"Heredity definitely plays
a role," he replies.

"It's a simple matter of give
and take," she responds, as a grey one falls
from the chandelier, lands on the head
of a tabby, slides off, raking
one ear with a hind claw (just a slight
suggestion of blood).

Two toms race through the open
door at this moment, thud along the couch, fly

from the top of the chintz armchair
to the mantlepiece, spilling a brass jar
of round rum candies.

"Even god as a concept . . ." he continues,
while an old matted white one sips perfumed
water from a vase of camellias
sitting on a buffet before the mirror.

"If we could just catch hold . . ."
she whispers. Three thin black ones,
sitting on the icy windowsill outside, peer
into the parlor with indignant longing.

She sighs, stretches, slowly licks
her finger, wets and winds a neck curl
into place, while he watches,
swaying, hind quarters wriggling
until he pounces, catches and pulls loose
in a sudden release of one motion
the trailing sash of her cashmere robe.

THREE'S CHARM

Whenever we make love, we bring in
the panther to sit on his scrolled
pedestal in the corner of the room.
We like him there, the power of his engine.
We like his reek, the odors of licorice
and scorched grasses he carries with him.

Sometimes he ignores us, licks his fur methodically,
chewing and sucking between each claw,
droning on with his eyes closed
through the whole event.

But usually he perches erect on his pedestal
and watches, tail twitching. We glory
in his interest. We dramatize our thrashings,
growl for his pleasure, squeal repeatedly
for his delight. We flip and writhe
like stranded fish on a rocky shore
just to put him in a frenzy, just
to make him jealous.

Some nights we lose ourselves completely
in his presence, grow weightless
with the distance. We see only his eyes
and the fires of his gleaming teeth
as he hisses. He's a constellation,
our sign, the tips of our bodies
burning in his own black sky.

And we wait for those evenings
when he crouches low, draws his head
down into the bat-blades of his shoulders,
actually leaps right for us on the bed.
We get our fingers deep into his furry
hide, as we wrestle him quickly
to the floor. I grab his rump,
my partner his head, and we drag him
back to his corner, force him to mount
his lacquered pedestal again. We collar
him then, bind him there with chains

where he belongs. We laugh at him,
poke him and smack his muzzle,
though we know how much we need him
as we lie down together again panting,
furious with his fury, ears
flat, fangs exposed.

UNDER THE BIG TOP

Though I walk through the valley of the shadow . . .
            —PSALM 23

They're always here. One of them tumbles
in her maroon and silver-sequined tights before me,
as if she led, down the road. She somersaults, flips
mid-air over a hedge row, her bodice sparkling, over
a patch of butterfly pea. She does handstands
off curbs, cartwheels down alleys, leapfrogs
past parking meters. Crossing any bridge
with her is ceremony, a ritual of back bends
on thin wooden railings, toe-dances
on suspension cables.

How can I fear, one going ahead armed with chair
and fake pistol, two going ahead in epaulettes and brass
buttons, with marching drum, bold tasseled baton?

Another keeps a constant circle of blossoms
and pods spinning around my head. Tossing
and catching, he weaves almonds, apples, limes,
pomegranates, once the spotted eggs of the wood pewee,
once the buds of the Cherokee rose. So deft,

nothing he handles falls or shatters or bruises.
Even in the night far ahead I can see his torches,
their flames spiralling high into the black
dome, down again into his waiting hands.

And this one, such comfort, shuffles at my pace,
following one step behind. Holding his purple
pint-sized parasol above my head, he recovers
from each of his stumbles, tripping over stray dogs,
paper cups, raindrops, stepping on the dragging
cuffs of his own striped trousers. He keeps up,
guffawing when he hears me laugh, stopping abruptly
if I cease. And when he sees tears in my eyes,
he takes out his cowboy hankie, honks his schnoz,
shakes his doleful head, with chin trembling,
presses two sad fingertips sincerely
to his garish grin.

THE YEAR ALL THE CLOWNS WERE EXECUTED

Many saw them taken away, crowded
in the wagons, chained together,
their oblong white faces peering
through the slats, eyebrows arched high
with bewilderment. All those joeys,
some were wearing cup-sized black
bowlers on their bald heads,
others topless top hats
resting on their ears, orange neckties
down to their knees. A few
blew on bubble pipes and pondered

the sky as the wagons bumped along.
One in baggy blue coat, a tin foil
star pinned to his chest, beat
the others repeatedly
with his billy club balloon.

Their painted tears
looked real.

Later, after the last wagon
had disappeared into the mountains,
that was a bad time for all merchants
selling floppy chartreuse satin pajamas
with big ball buttons, tent-sized
trousers of tartan plaid and purple
stripes. The Squirting Plastic
Flower Company and the Six-Inch Bicycle
Factory had to close shop completely.
Fox terriers, trained to wear
bonnets and ride in baby buggies,
lost their jobs. Soon the youngest
children couldn't remember a shivaree,
the parade of stunts, midget cars
or prancing piglets, the "walk-around"
on the Hippodrome track.

Then toward the end of that year,
visionaries began to appear, the first one
claiming to have seen the stiltman at dusk
striding in his gold metallic suit
through a copse of slender prairie
poplars in the shadowy evening sun,
another swearing to have witnessed

Petrolino himself wearing his pointed
hat topped with bells, ducking down
and popping up among the swaying
cattails, frightening all the blackbirds
in the most comical way. A third, watching
a distant field of autumn milkweed,
testified to seeing confetti
fly into the air from the old
empty-water-bucket gag.
Even a grandmother living alone
heard Grimaldi singing "An Oyster
Crossed in Love" beneath the scraping
branches outside her window
just before dawn.

But on a windy evening at midnight,
when a whole party of laughing people
together saw one of their favorites
stumbling on the sidewalk in the bluster,
tripping up the curb, reeling
against a trash can, somersaulting
again headfirst, sprawling
and pitching, taking his pratfalls
down the street like a blowing tangle
of open newspaper, then no one dared
deny any longer the truths
of spirits and souls, that bold new
rumor of resurrection.

GET ON BOARD

While all the seas harass themselves
with whipping waterspouts and typhoons,
while all the seas draw back
out of themselves into still poplar
prairies and sheaths of ice, while Lily,
her spine pressed against the oak, murders
her baby in the forest, and Hubert
at tea time hands Rose a lemon wedge
and cream—all along it continues
to move along, that wagon, its bed
planed and pegged like a floor,
its sides like a farm wagon
slatted and high.

Where the mottled mongrel, chained
to the shed, meets the returning howl
of his own barking at midnight,
where the spotted salamander
at the pond's edge relinquishes
its color and motion to the blooming
milfoil, where the eye of the snow hare,
alone on a white plain, becomes
the only true vortex and blizzard of winter,
there it passes also, creaking
and swaying, the hub of each wheel turning
like a coin spun on a table, each spoke
circling like a lighthouse beacon.

It passes the fallen and fern-cradling
tree from which it is constructed,
passes the ocean valley from which its lumber

will grow, passes the sleeping infant
who has forged its axle, passes the grave
of the smith who will ring its wheels,
passes blind Edith who points and shouts,
"See the flaming wagon crossing the sky,"
passes Uncle Morris reciting, "There lies
the wagon, broken, upside down in the ditch,"
passes itself, sides hung with orchis
and lavender, wheels laced with sage,
inside the visionary's mind.

It sways and rumbles, traveling always
both subsequent and prior to every moment
of its path. Don't you know it? Can't you see?
You, riding along with all of its passengers,
standing up, laughing now, waving
your hat, hallooing and hallooing?

THE MAD LINGUIST

It takes several scholars working together
to translate her orations. Even then
no one understands completely. Just listen
to the multiple tentacles and bivalve forms
in the language of this one, the constructions
winding like the whorls of a whelk's shell
around their axis. The trained ear can hear
the many small coordinated spider claws
of nuance there, a rapidity of staccato
syllables sounding like the sharp toes
of purple shore crabs scurrying over the sand.

And listen to the strangeness of this speech,
logic that progresses in a network
of ever-smaller branches spreading outward
as a poplar spreads clear to the thin
veins at the edges of its yellow leaves.
Here every verb contains a subtle allusion
to ascension; predicates rise vertically
out of pines into the sky.
What an ideal language for describing
the emotional state of anyone who feels
the recitations of seven thousand
riverside birches trembling in his bones.

She is equally at ease in the tongues
of temperature and sun, voicing the same slow,
careful vowels that barely sound in a warming
April field, the scrape and rasping whisper
of shifting stones being pushed aside
by the roots of patridge peas. She pronounces
each syllable with the quiverings found
in the buds of verbena, the throbbings
in the pods of the swallowtail.
Will the deaf and blind of spring,
who hear only by their armless, legless
bodies lying beneath the soft soil,
now be able to understand
her every assertion?

"All spoken words presuppose the existence
of an audience that perceives them," she quotes
from an ancient language that pauses
and plunges forward in leaps and lurches
like a prehistoric grizzly pouncing once

in the rushing snow-melt, pouncing again,
catching finally and lifting to the shore
the sweet flesh of the struggling silver fish
we know so well.

———————

THE PROCESS

First she gave all that she carried
in her arms, setting those trinkets down easily.
Then she removed her scarlet sash and gave it
for bandage, her scarf for blindfold, her shawl,
her handkerchief for shroud.

She let her violet kimono slip from her shoulders,
giving it too, because it was warm and could surround,
enwrap like dusk, and because it held her dark-river,
night-swimmer fragrances tight in the deep
stitches of its seams.

And she cut off her hair, offering its strands
for weaving, for pillow, lining, talisman,
for solace.

She gave her bracelets, the rings
from her fingers—those circles of gold jingling
like crickets, those loops of silver
chiming like spring—and gave her hands as well,
her fingers, the way they could particularize.

Her feet and their balance, her legs
and their stride, she relinquished;
and her belly, her thighs, her lap—wide, empty,

open as a prairie—her breasts full of sunlight,
like peaches and honey, like succor. She gave away
her bones—ribcage for scaffold, spine,
smaller knuckles for kindling, for sparks,
for flame.

And what remained—her face, her visage
reflective, transparent as sky—she gave
and even her word, her name, its echo,
until all, everything was given and everything
received, and she was no one,
gone, nothing,
god.

———————

THE GREATEST GRANDEUR

Some say it's in the reptilian dance
of the purple-tongued sand goanna,
for there the magnificent translation
of tenacity into bone and grace occurs.

And some declare it to be an expansive
desert—solid rust-orange rock
like dusk captured on earth in stone—
simply for the perfect contrast it provides
to the blue-grey ridge of rain
in the distant hills.

Some claim the harmonics of shifting
electron rings to be most rare and some
the complex motion of seven sandpipers

bisecting the arcs and pitches
of come and retreat over the mounting
hayfield.

Others, for grandeur, choose the terror
of lightning peals on prairies or the tall
collapsing cathedrals of stormy seas,
because there they feel dwarfed
and appropriately helpless; others select
the serenity of that ceiling/cellar
of stars they see at night on placid lakes,
because there they feel assured
and universally magnanimous.

But it is the dark emptiness contained
in every next moment that seems to me
the most singularly glorious gift,
that void which one is free to fill
with processions of men bearing burning
cedar knots or with parades of blue horses,
belled and ribboned and stepping sideways,
with tumbling white-faced mimes or companies
of black-robed choristers; to fill simply
with hammered silver teapots or kiln-dried
crockery, tangerine and almond custards,
polonaises, polkas, whittling sticks, wailing
walls; that space large enough to hold all
invented blasphemies and pieties, 10,000
definitions of god and more, never fully
filled, never.

OLD SPIRAL OF CONCEPTION (1994)

Till My Teeth Rattle

Why is it always arresting—
the sight of that same metal-sharp
disc of moon slicing slick and clean
as if it spun on a motor through
purple autumn clouds?

Likewise, I'm startled, taken aback
this morning, by three long-tailed
weasels humping cattywampus across
the gravel road, disappearing
into the weed-tunnels of oxeye daisy
and dock in the roadside ditches.

There's a whole prairie of popped
yucca pods, an overdone, unrestrained
confetti-spilling deluge of seeds
that's stopped me before, and I admit
I've stared—a tribe of darkling beetles
on the path, all standing on their heads,
black rear-ends to the wind. Like this,
like this, like this.

Whoever said *the ordinary, the mundane,*
the commonplace? Show them to me.

Wait a minute—a hummingbird moth
so deep now inside a rose petunia
that its petals flutter too, like wings.

There's no remedy, I suppose—this body
just made from the beginning to be shocked,
constantly surprised, perpetually stunned,

poked and prodded, shaken awake,
shaken again and again roughly, rudely,
then left, even more bewildered,
even more amazed.

––––––––––

IN MY TIME

It's easy to praise things present—the belligerent
stance of the woodhouse toad, the total
self-absorption of the frostweed blossom.
It's simple to compliment a familiar mess
of curly dock, the serene organization
of common onion reeds, the radish bulb
and its slender purple tail. And I like the way
the jay flings dirt furiously this morning
from the window box, the ridiculous shakings
of his black beak.

But it's not easy to praise things yet-to-come—
the nonexistent nubs of mountains not risen
from beneath the floor of the sea
or a new sound from some new creature,
descended maybe from our golden peepers
and white-chinned chuggers, that sound
becoming synonymous, for someone else,
with spring.

How can I appreciate light from an aging
sun shining through new configurations neither pine
nor ash? How can I extol the nurturing

fragrances from the spires, the spicules
of a landscape not yet formed or seeded?

I can praise these flowers today—the white yucca
with its immersing powder-covered moth, the desert
tahoka daisy and the buffalo gourd—but never
the future strangeness that may eventually
take their places.

From here now, I simply praise in advance
the one who will be there then,
so moved, as I, to do the praising.

THE NEED TO ADORE

There is a need, a craving I have
to adore something as charitable
as the rambling scarlet sea fig, fruit
and blossom surfeiting the shore,
and something as certain as the undeviating
moon moving, like a gold marble
down a groove, exactly along its golden,
autumn corridor.

I have a passion to love something
as ministering as the morning penetrating
clear to the bottom of the pond, touching
the earth-side and sky-side of each leaf
of white water crowfoot, hornwort,
enclosing the blooming parsnip, petal-side,
stem-side, surrounding tadpole shrimp,

carp and cooter and mollusk, mud-side,
rock-side, to love something possessing
such lenient measures of inner
and outer circumference.

I know my hunger to worship something
as duplicitous as the peaceful aardwolf
and as fearsome as hounds on a fallen doe,
something as pliant and amenable as honeysuckle
vining a fence, as consummate as stone,
as fickle as jellyfish threads in a sea current,
to worship with abandon that which is as weak
as the neckbone of a button quail, fast
as fires on the Serengeti, silent
as the growth by grains of rock spires
in a damp cave, something that sails
in waves like needlegrasses across
the summer afternoon and something that falls
like fragrances of pine mold and mushroom
in forests filled with rain.

There is a need, my obsession, to submit
wholly, without reservation, to give entirely
to something lucent enough and strict enough,
fabled enough and fervent enough to encompass
all of these at once, something rudimentary
enough to let me enter, something
complete enough to let me go.

Emissaries

How will we convince them,
when we return, of the beating crimson
of the honeycreeper's body, the quaking
violet rump of the velvet cuckoo wasp,
or simply of an easy night rain
over hills, that dizzy falling, grains
of moisture the size and multitude
of stars, a rain not lull and loop
alone but a perfect elucidation
of sleep? How can we describe it to them?

How will they understand the scaffold
of logic or the shape of mercy,
with neither the informing patterns
of the swallow's nest nor the radiating
structure of needles on a slash pine
in their memories to help them, without
even the razzling of poplar leaves
in an evening wind or the intensity
of spotted trout braced against clear
currents in their speech to help them?

How will they know how to perceive
without ever having witnessed
the grasping talents of the moon snail,
the salt-marsh snail?

Maybe they won't be able to attend
to us at all, not realizing how the sooty
owl attends, how the black-tailed jack
and the hoary cress and coyote thistle

of the grasslands rise alert and still
to listen, as if listening were a place
with boundaries each created.

And when we tell our stories,
can they follow the plots, never having seen
the spreading revelation, word by word,
of the wood lily, or the unfolding
revelation of a fruit bat's skin wings?
Can they recognize resolution,
never having watched the constellations
completing their circles around Polaris,
never having studied the rising
and sinking vortexes of a sharp-shinned
hawk circling above a gorge?

Be sure to remember the surprise
among the ashy leaves, that ashy flick
of five-lined skink, living slizard,
and the surprise of burnished mushrooms
sprouting in a ring through black forest
trash. Take notes on the spotted cleaning
shrimp at work with its silver wands
on the mouth of a great reef fish. Assimilate
each polished prick and sun-sharpened claw
of the jumping cholla and learn now
to imitate the bask of the seal,
the sleight of willows in a storm,
to recite the rigid blue illumination
of ice shelves under pressure.

We'll need all these, everything, when we return

to that place after death to tell them, back
to the silent, uniform darknesses we were
before being born on earth.

If Dying Means Becoming Pure Spirit

Then I think it must be like falling,
that giving-up of the body.
Who wouldn't try to catch hold
of something fast, jerk forward, reaching
with the fingers spread, before the hands
were gone, before the arms
disappeared?

I could never willingly withdraw
from my ribs, pull out of the good bars
and cage, leave the marrow, the temple
of salt, of welling and subsiding, abandon
complacently the swallow, the tongue, the voice.

How could I regard a crab apple
flustered with long-stalked blossoms
or a sycamore hung with nutlets and tufts,
with no face to catch the shadow-splatter
of their limbs and leaves? How could I apprehend
mixed fields of cordgrasses and barleys,
with no breath to detect the scent
of their sedges and clefts?

Even though it's said the spirit
is weightless, still, I think it must be

like falling a terrible fall,
to leave the body, to speed away
backwards, cut off from the humming
a cappella of pines, the skeltered
burring of grasshoppers, from the fragrances
of low wood fires beside a river, clean
ice on stalks of cattail and rye, lost
to the purple spice of scattered
thunders, no belly left to feel
the wide, easy range of the earth.

I admit to being angry
and frightened tonight at the thought
of such a plummeting.

———————

THE LAYING ON OF HANDS

There's a gentleness we haven't learned yet,
but we've seen it—the way an early morning haze
can settle in the wayside hedges of lilac and yew,
permeate the emptiness between every scaly
bud and leafstalk until it becomes bound,
fully contained, shaped by the spires,
the stiff pins and purple-white blossoms
of that tangled wall.

There's a subtlety we haven't mastered yet,
but we recognize it—the way moonlight passes
simultaneously upon, through, beyond
the open wing of the crane fly
without altering a single detail

of its smallest paper vein. We know
there is a perfect consideration
of touching possible. The merest snow
accomplishes that, assuming the exact
configuration of the bristled beggarweed
while the beggarweed remains
exclusively itself.

If I could discover that same tension
of muscle myself, if I could move, imagining
smoke finding the forest-lines of the sun
at dusk, if I could place my hand
with that motion, achieve the proper
stance of union and isolation
in fingers and palm, place my hand
with less pressure than a water strider
places by the seeds of its toes
on the surface of the pond, balance
that way, skin to bark, my hand
fully open on the trunk of this elm tree
right now, I know it would be possible
to feel immediately every tissue imposition
and ringed liturgy, every bloodvein
and vacuum of that tree's presence, perceive
immediately both the hard, jerking start
of the seedling in winter and the spore-filled
moss and liquid decay of the fallen trunk
to come, both the angle of tilt in the green sun
off every leaf above and the slow lightning
of hair roots in their buried dark below,
know even the reverse silhouette of my own hand
experienced from inner bark out,
even the moment of this very revelation

Old Spiral of Conception

of *woman and tree* itself where it was locked
millennia before in those tight molecules
of suckers and sapwood.

Without harm or alteration or surrender
of any kind, I know my hand laid properly,
could discover this much.

Eating Death

Suppose I had never distinguished myself
to myself from the landscape
so that reaching out to touch a leaf
of chickasaw plum or a spiny pondweed
underwater were no different to me
from putting my hand on my knee or pulling
my fingers through my hair.

And that which was not tangible
I understood as my expression to myself
of my inclinations—my violet serenity
synonymous with distant levels of blue
rain against a ruddy hill, my opening circling
into sex identical with the gold and russet
revolution of the sun into dusk.

In the new forming of lilac
or pear blossoms I realized the color
and fragrance of my balance redefined
every spring. I knew the horizon
as that seam made by the meeting
of my sight and my word, and recognized

the night and the day as my own slow
breathing in and slow breathing out
of light.

Then surely the small ebony hobble
I'd notice one evening appearing
out of an ancient canyon syntax, I'd understand
simply as a further aspect of myself.
And as it became larger, slowly obliterating
the purpose and combustible prairie-presence
of myself, I wouldn't be frightened, knowing
that it came to me from my own depths,
its empty eyes my creation, its steady
grin the white stone of my history.
And when it lifted and spread
its cloak finally, as if it were my will
filling the sky, and I called it my name,
it would be easy to be taken and covered
by my own possession, to put my mouth
against it, my star-pocked arms tight
around its neck, to draw in, sucking,
swallowing, consuming completely
every quiet fold and release
of the last event of my life.

BERRY RENAISSANCE

1.
Its range is worldwide—swamps, pine
and rocky barrens, thickets, dry uplands,
sphagnum-dominated bogs, backyard

gardens—and its names inclusive—cranberry,
nannyberry, strawberry (wood, Indian,
meadow and beach), chokeberry, poison
baneberry, dewberry, dahoon.

2.
And these are true in certain circles:
at night, a sky-full field of ripe, white
berries; berries of rain that break
on the face; berries, mistletoe and blue,
transformed to pearls and sapphires worn
on eartips and wrists; rose-colored
berries, one at the tip of each breast,
that men like to nibble.

3.
Of clustered spears and heart-shaped
leaves, of terra-cotta-tinted, lavender
blossoms, of aromatic ovaries, bristled
anthers and stamens, of probings and fiddlings
deep within, of open-eyed sun staring,
of vigil, of transfiguration, of such
is the palate of raspberry liqueur,
blackberry cordial.

4.
Jumpers in bandana midriffs and short,
handkerchief skirts that fly up to their waists,
jumping fast on their toes, one foot,
both feet, running in, running out, sing
this double, jump-rope chant:

   Bearberry, wolfberry,
    huckleberry, grape,

patridgeberry, coralberry,
sea and mountainscape—
how many berry-boys did she pick?
one two three four . . .

5. *Gospel and the Circle of Redemption*
There are times when I want to be stained,
marked all over by berry wine, baptized,
mouth, fingers, chin and neck, between my toes,
up my legs like the wine-makers of Jerez
who walk round and round in tubs
of berries all day, who return then
to their homes at night wreathed
in berry halos, heady with ripe flower
bouquets dizzy with bees, their bodies
painted, perfumed by purple sun syrup,
their breath elderberry delicious. In the dark
all night, even their sleep is guarded,
lullabied by berry ghosts.

I want to be so immersed, so earth-wined myself
that I'm mistaken for a berry entire.
I want to be plucked, split and gulped whole
by a bacchanal god, swallowed alive by a drunken
savior. I want to rise then from his soul
as his own wild laughter spreading
over the landscape like a berry-colored
evening engulfing blackbirds and cowbirds
and hillside forests and even
every blessing of his own vineyards
and even the way he reclines there,
lordly, generous.

Apple Disciples

It has always very adequately maintained
its dependents: spider mites, woolly aphids,
brown-tailed moths and flat-headed
borers, canker worms, webworms, green fruit
worms and the red-banded leaf rollers,
all.

It supports, as well, powdery mildew, black rot,
rust, apple scab, apple canker and the hearty
crown gall.

In the field, in the orchard, domesticated,
wild, even at this moment, it endures mincing
mother mice and rutting mice, the needle nips
of jumping mice and dusky-footed wood rats
of temperate zones, also jack rabbits sawing,
mule deer and fallow deer scraping, crunching.

Its tendernesses have been encircled
by the black, biting nails of the apple-eating
porcupine, those sweet dimpled swellings
gnawed clear through to their cores and beyond.
(The stickery pigs waddle off to their burrows
afterward satisfied and full.)

This rosaceas, in its fragrance and sugary
tang, even has the power to draw fearsome
black bears, cinnamon bears all the way down
from their mountain dens to munch and bask
in its frosty shade.

For its pristine example, we also pamper it,
prune it, peel its various parts alive, chop it,
grind it, beat and burn it, crush its droppings
under iron-rimmed wagon wheels, smash
its rotten balls against Old Man Troutman's
barn, get drunk on its golden urine, screech,
bellow, sing of fornicating, fornicate
under its blossomed branches.

Even god, remember, learned early
how best to use such perfect fruit.

———————

Still Life Abroad

1.
Over the split cantaloupe, its staid,
orderly seeds and corky hide, over
the pall of four plums and the paralysis
of their shriveled leaves, past the still,
steely fish, white stone cheese, biscuits
and bread . . . the little brown hairy hand
moves quickly, brushes the pitcher
of cream, rattles the basket of clams,
suddenly snatches two cherries
from the heap on the plate, jerks back,
disappears. Off-frame, rushing feet,
hysterical chittering can be heard
receding down the invisible hallway.

2.

Within the red serenity of each apple
in the bowl, a seething fortune of molecules
is expanding, uniting, transfiguring.
And at the epicenter of the onion's circle
of steady waves, even in that dark funnel,
there is a hard rush, a gathering
and differentiation of cells rudely forcing
upward toward light a sharp flume of green.
Beneath the quiet surface skin of the bulging
plum, many million microscopic teeth tear,
rip—pulp, fermentation. Tangled in the noiseless
core of one fragrant peach, twist and rear
many fearsome beasts, many fires.

3.

Mary is offering the Baby Jesus an apple.
At least it looks like an apple
from where we stand. But it could easily be
her breast, the blush of the full nipple
cupped in her hand like a pip, held
toward his parted mouth. Or it could be a ripe
bonbon of manna, a heavenly food, or the earth,
juicy, buzzing, spice-popping globe.
It might be the very ovary, the original
blood-and-butter egg of knowledge.
Maybe it's Buddha's ball. Maybe it's Satan's
burning red eye. A jewel, it almost flames,
it almost illuminates.

What should the Mother of God offer
her luscious naked boy-child leaning now
within her arms, against her belly?

And who has the power to forbid any fruit
to the Mother of God and her son?
They make righteousness themselves, moment
by moment. I think it's the apple. Notice
the excitement in his reach, the calm,
rather timid confidence of her inward
gaze. And although no one can be certain
about the future, it seems apparent to us
from the zeal on his baby lips
that he means to accept.

FOREPLAY

When it first begins, as you might expect,
the lips and thin folds are closed, the pouting
layers pressed, lapped lightly,
almost languidly, against one another
in a sealed bud.

However, with certain prolonged
and random strokings of care
along each binding line, with soft
intrusions traced beneath each pursed
gathering and edge, with inquiring
intensities of gesture—as the sun
swinging slowly from winter back
to spring, touches briefly,
between moments of moon and masking
clouds, certain stunning points
and inner nubs of earth—so
with such ministrations, a slight

Old Spiral of Conception

swelling, a quiver of reaching,
a tendency toward space,
might be noticed to commence.

Then with dampness from the dark,
with moisture from the falling
night of morning, from hidden places
within the hills, each seal begins
to loosen, each recalcitrant clasp
sinks away into itself, and every tucked
grasp, every silk tack willingly relents,
releases, gives way, proclaims a turning,
declares a revolution, assumes,
in plain sight, a surging position
that offers, an audacious offering
that beseeches, every petal parted wide.

Remember the spiraling, blue
valerian, remember the violet, sucking
larkspur, the laurel and rosebay
and pea cockle flung backwards, remember
the fragrant, funneling lily, the lifted
honeysuckle, the sweet, open pucker
of the ground ivy blossom?

Now even the darkest crease possessed,
the most guarded, pulsing, least drop
of pearl bead, moon grain trembling
deep within is fully revealed, fully exposed
to any penetrating wind or shaking fur
or mad hunger or searing, plunging surprise
the wild descending sky in delirium
has to offer.

THE POWER OF SUN

1.
I think those who have its name
are luckiest—most fortunate sun bear,
sun grebe and sun bittern, sunflower,
sun spider, sunfish, sunbeam snake.

And the name is apt, for the sun bear
rises, reveals his orange-crested chest,
flares with huffings and hot, bellowing
pronouncements over the quiet of damp
liverworts, mosses and mangroves,
just like the morning.

The amethyst, green-headed sun
bird sucks and shimmers his wings,
perching on yellow petals and beams
of buds, like summer sun. And the sunstone
glows as reddish as a spangled dusk,
and the sun spider is golden and swift,
like a tight circle of sun focused
through a glass, spiking its way
across the grasses. Sunfish—rock bass,
bluegill and pumpkinseed—are buoyed
all over with flashing spines and shafts.
They float and yawn light through
and through underwater.

Maybe the name comes first, the word
a binding predestination fulfilled
only subsequently with a proper being,
as a sea wind wild and whipping

against a fractured cliff comes first
and then the cypress emerges, gnarls
and knobs itself to fit the shape
of that buffeting.

Think how the sun starfish can press
its limy rays outward, striving
to fill the possibilities of sweeping
combustion in its infinite name
all of its life.

And back, back inside that first final
locus of black beginning void, I believe
the sound of *sun* must suddenly
have been sung, and then, of course,
it had to happen.

2.
Someone said my real name to me
last night. Someone whispered
to me, before I knew, the name he knew
me to become last night.

Sun breath he murmured into my mouth;
sun hands sun-caressing he said,
kissing the ends of my fingers;
he called me *sun voice low and catching
through parting forest rain; ruddy
sun beaded nipples* drawn and bitten
by his lips; *sun thighs* he whispered,
tasting with his tongue, *rocking slow
with salt on the sea; light as solar wind,
self-luminous body* he called me again
and again. And I rose easily to my name

as if over the rim of the earth at dawn,
exhumed and spacious, shining
in his arms, as boundless and blinding
and released in that given radiance
as death by its name could never hope
to be in all of its dark freedom.

ARE SOME SINS HOSANNAS?

Those sins, for example, of amplitude,
of over-abundance, like the unrestrained
seeding of the blue yucca, the mink frog
and dusky crawfish frog, the spore-gorged
tumbling puffball? You've seen this transgression
in the cottonwood too, covering the river,
burdening the summer with more drifting,
white fluff and flurry than anyone
ever requested, replicating over and over
and over, as if being were worth it.

Are certain sins, of arrogance for instance,
a form of praise, the way the mullein
and the vinegar weed shoot straight up
from the earth unabashed, taking
overmuch pride in their stances, pointing
their flower-covered batons toward the sky
as if they were a righteousness?
This is the same haughty act the stalks
of sotol and steeplebush, the audacious
lodgepole pine and towering lousewort perform.

Is the noise of too much joy a madness
condemned by more moderate gods
who surely know better? Hush, hush
chortling heathen toads, unredeemed, triple-
chirping field crickets, ceaseless
sinning *tsee* of waxwings, spring-forest
sweet-sweet-sweet of wood warblers.

If some sins are truly jubilations,
then with you here beside me again
tonight, I'm certain I offend
many gods myself. I confess it and repent,
repent with the most contrite
voice I can manage, pulling my pillow
over my face, lying on my hands to try
to stop this rude sacrilege, my uncontrollable
crooning of happiness, incessant caressing,
touching your body everywhere, a sliding
vine of butterfly pea openly curling,
binding, such decadent opulence, my long,
excessive murmurs of immeasurable
adoration.

———————

THIS KIND OF GRACE

Let's bless the body before love.
By rights we should, every detail.
We could use water, spring water
or rose, minted or bay rum. A touch
to the shoulders—*bless these.* A drop
behind each knee—*sanctify here.* A sprinkle

to the belly, yours, mine—*in heartfelt
appreciation.*

I could dip my fingers into oil cupped
in my palm, sweet citronella, lavender,
clove, trace your forehead, temple
to temple, the boldness of that warm
stone—*so glorified*—perfume the entire
declaration of your spine, neck
to tail—*so hallowed.*

We'd neglect nothing, ankle, knuckle,
thigh, cheek. And for the rapture
of hair, scented with sweat or the spices
of cedary sages and summer pines,
in which I hide my face—*praise
to the conjoining hosts of all
radiant forests and plains.*

And imagine how I'd lay my hand,
move my hand carefully on and around
and under each axil and hummock and whorl
between your legs, the magnificent maze
of those gifts—*thanks to the exploding
heavens, thanks to all pulsing suns.*

For these cosmic accomplishments:
this delve of your body, a narrow
crevasse leading into earth-darkness;
this assertion of your hands, light
winds lifting, parting, pressing
upon supine grasses; this rise, the tip
of a swollen moon over black hills;
this sweep of union, hawk-shadow

falling fast across the open prairie
into the horizon; *for this whole blessed*
body, for what we are about to receive
together tonight . . . truly, ardently,
ecstatically, boundlessly
grateful.

FETAL BAT: THE CREATION OF THE VOID

Tender in its absolute predestination—four
long, deformed finger bones, plum-round
body, umbrella wings—it's an inevitability
begun by bat penis, sperm dart, bat
ovum, bat pocket of womb where it flutters,
flickers sporadically, warm and drowned
in swaying pearl-clear waters.

The fetus folds in its place, tightens,
settles again, shoulder-hunched knuckles
drawn to its ears, a vestigial claw
to its chin. Its eyes are thinly lidded.
Its tongue, slender, pliable as a single
leaflet of summer fern, moves back
slightly in its throat as if to suckle.

A pea-sized heart swings inside
the tiny night of its chest inside the night
behind its mother's teats and blue
coming-milk inside the still stone cavern
of night where she hangs by one foot upside
down inside the universe of night

with its shifting, combusting summary
of stars wheeling inside, outside.

When this fetus emerges,
feet first, born alive, clinging
to its mother's breast, legs curled
beneath her armpit, drying the fine fuzz
of its face and features, the translucent
dun and veined-scarlet silk skin
of its wings stretched wide, it screams,
screeches wildly, setting every petal
of yucca and sweet chicory that blooms
inside its rare garden to shivering,
to ringing.

What a very first phenomenon
it makes as it occupies so perfectly
such a definite empty space, the only void
of itself which we recognize now
never anywhere, until this moment
of its birth, existed at all.

INFANTICIDE

Sometimes they were put in baskets, little nests
of rushes and leaves. (Someone had to weave
these water-cradles for them—the threading
fingers of grandmother, auntie, midwife.)
They were placed in their casket-boats
and launched, and if they couldn't swim,
whose fault was that?

Some were curled, heads touching knees,
in their womb positions inside clay jars,
then set along temple porticoes
in case some passing worshipper might want
a baby for a slave. Their fretting
voices in the corridors were as common
and hoarse as dry cicadas, till they died.

Some were burned for expiation to the gods,
in ceremonies, shrill trumpets and cymbals
covering their cries. Some were placed naked,
still bloody, on icy pinnacles in dark snow.
Some were strangled, some tortured
to death, some eaten, a few hours old.
After all, nobody knew them yet.

Some were flung off canyon cliffs,
even on a spring afternoon, the prairie
colored with clover and milkvetch,
or even on a damp autumn morning,
the plums red and sweet and fragrant.

Mary Hamilton bore her baby alone
in the King's forest, leaning back, pressing
against an oak, her skirts pulled up,
and all the while watching the patterns
above her, layered leaves, sky pieces,
branches and boughs constricting, widening
with the wind. Then she killed him with a knife.

Gone, murdered by deliberate
acts—I don't think anyone
ever counted them all—those cursed, born
during lightning storms or under a bad

moon or feetfirst or blind, born
during war or a hard journey, into starvation,
those with the wrong fathers, the girls,
the unwanted. It was the custom,
and there were reasons, burdens.
Even mothers said so.

From every stone-cut or gnawed
umbilical, from every bud-sized
fist, every thumb and finger petal
folded inward, from every perfectly
stitched violet thread, every temple pulse,
every rib shudder of this elegy,
relieve us.

GODDAMN THEOLOGY

It was easier when you were a jonquil
and I was a fingertip pressed at the juncture
of your radiating petals and stiff stem.
And it was not so difficult
when I was a Persian guitar
and you were the knee on which I lay,
my neck held easily in your hand.

But there were problems
when you were two hundred years of years,
twisted like taffy, twisted and looped
like a dry bristlecone in dusty snow,
and I was just a beginning sliver
of clear, tadpole breath in a whorl

of waterweed. I didn't know
what to say.

And when I thought I knew your name,
and I called it out loud many times,
that's when you were a deaf sheaf
of catacombed coral with more
than one title and no tongue.

I was whole, a burning ball of peach
hanging from a branch. You were multiple,
sparks struck from a hammer against rock.
I split into a showering orbit of mayflies
in the evening sun. You congealed
into a seeded cow patty in the field.

When the painted pony and I were galloping
fast through rabid waves on the beach,
there you were, a tiny spire of ship
sailing off the edge of the sea.

The night I woke in white, my body moon-grey,
you were curled, a black hump of quilt
at the foot of my bed, dead asleep.

And later when you were falling rapidly,
heavily, raindrops and pockdrops and bullet
marks, a mob in the mountain lake, I was precise
wing and talon over the prairie, jackknifing
and stabbing, lifting the mouse by her spine.

When I was crying, crying and truly
sorry, you were a spray of chartreuse
and scarlet tinfoil confetti on my head.

406

That's when I knew for certain
it was going to be much more difficult
than we'd ever imagined before.

————————

The Natural Nature of Late Night Prayers

Most are generally horribly tangled,
like the broken-twig broom of a witch hazel
or the sticky, irregular web of a branchtip
spider, like the leaf-jumble of a squirrel's
nest empty since last season or the stumble,
the bandy-legged hops of a drunk man
down a curb, the zip-zag dance of fire
up a dry pine. Like thistles and fur, late
night prayers are usually snarled, embrangled.

The ones I know are always more knotted
than smooth, like long hair wet with salt
and whipping in an ocean wind, like long hair
stroked and gripped and left against a pillow
after love, always crumpled like hoarded
riffraff (limp seaweed, crab bones, jelly
strings, seadollar teeth, plastic kelp)
wave-wadded on a shore. Prayers accumulate
rubble in the dark like rat hovels.

To be unresolvable must be the ordained
nature of after-midnight prayers; for never
neat, never orderly, never sorted, never
clear-headed, never singularly purposeful,
always shaken with knocks, overburdened

with rattles, bound with ear-numbing
babbles, my own, crooked mottles, stutters,
sheet-wringings and whines, now again
beside the bedpost my rambling accusations,
now again my mad apologies.

TRIAL AND ERROR

The right prayer might be a falling
prayer spiralling down in the throats
and raised wings and white warmth
of tumbling pigeons, the joy
of a beseeching abandon, or a crossing
prayer in the fingers of oak branches
over themselves, their display
of a hopeful wind, or a drifting
prayer in the cerise petals
loosed and dropping from a stalk
of wild betony, a proclamation
in dissolution.

It may take two every night, maybe three
every dawn—prayers offered of one fact
against another—milkweed against winter,
reflected face against water, rapid
barking against fear.

I can compose any kind, prayers wrapped
in seaweed, rolled in grape leaves,
prayers sent spinning tied to butterfly
kites crackling in the sky over the sea,

prayers in wax bound to stones sunk
past coral cliffs or ice canyons
to the ocean floor, prayers delivered
with moans or howls, rattling gourds
or timbals, prayers in the cadence of rain,
prayers in the absence of breath.

I'll send them out in signs, lanterns
on rooftops, candles on cairns, backward
prayers like the dark side of the moon, prayers
hung upside down by the knees, prayers
beginning with praise, beginning with *Our Father,*
with *Darling Mother,* with *Darkling Son,* fading
off fast to *In the beginning* . . .

I'll become by myself, I swear,
whatever prayer it takes, teeth, eyelids,
ears, beatitude of knuckles, invocation
of spine, a solid skeleton of the perfectly
linked linguistics of prayer, hands
pressed together before me,
my whole body speaking,
waiting.

————————

GOD ALONE

It was important on this April night
to open the windows, all of them, east
and on the west, pushing the panes
as high as they would go, to allow
the wind free passage through the rooms,

to allow the night occupancy
as if it were a word come into the body
to render the bones definitive.

And the house became the spring
night—the hallway a vernal hallway
rushed with flowing field grasses, all
the tugs and crescents of sex-in-flight.
The wooden casements, railings and rungs,
were carved, their curves traced,
by the calls of peepers, crickets,
killdeer, those cries possessing
every mirror too, in and out, like streaks
and bells of light. Quilts and counterpanes
became shadowed with yellow-budded willow
and lilac priorities, like patterns
laid out, wound and stitched fast.
In the dark, a garden of grape,
honeysuckle and rosmarin took root,
spreading, blooming, vining a leafy
network through the bedroom mid-air.

And the April night, rich with black
stellar vacancies and portents, became
the house, took the grace of pliant
curtains lifting and parting, took
the form of doorways, cornices,
ceilings, pressed to the frame of every
room angle, curled inside the painted
rings and links of porcelain curios
on the shelves, settled in the open
drawers of the bureau, the hollowness
beneath the bed, became fluted

with the fanned linen of the lampshade,
rigid with the wooden chair, spindled
with beveled legs and back. Shaping
itself to faces and fingers, the night
became human. It gave and received
the same breath with all who slept there.

Divine is the spring night filling
the house with fragrant tumbling,
with the cylindrical sounds and high-climbing
purposes of a sun-tilted earth; and equally divine
are the rooms providing the boundless black
with measurement, with place, with the reflections
and honor of artifact; and equally divine
is the hand that raised all the sashes.

———————

ANOTHER LITTLE GOD

You don't know how important
it might be—the blue-white light
from a star like Vega caught in the eyedots
of nocturnal grass frogs and yellow-bellied
toads, caught in the senses of fishing
bats, mouse-tailed bats.

And I can't say either how much
it might matter—that same ping
of light multiplied by each reflective
grain of crystal sand along a beach
beside the Gulf, held by each slide

and scissor of beak rushes
in a southern marsh.

Maybe particles and spears of light
from Vega penetrate the earth, descend
through silt and loam, touching,
even enlivening, even partially defining
the microscopic roots of bellfowers,
purple vetches and peas, the creases
and shackles of worm snakes and grubs.

The translucent eggs of the plumed moth,
the fins of the redbelly dace might need
a star's blue-white light, like water,
like air. Breath might require it,
breathing starlight into the heart.
You don't know. After all, we've never
lived without it.

If starlight spears through each oily
sperm link of reedbuck and potto,
if it enters every least bulb
of snow flea, wheel bug, hay
louse, if it corridors through all bone
crystals, around each spurl and bole
of the brain, inside timbre and voice,
piercing the whole stone and space
of *believe,* then, if only for one
complete name under the sky tonight,
lie still and remember.

LIFE IN AN EXPANDING UNIVERSE

It's not only all those cosmic
pinwheels with their charging solar
luminosities, the way they spin around
like the paper kind tacked to a tree trunk,
the way they expel matter and light
like fields of dandelions throwing off
waves of summer sparks in the wind,
the way they speed outward,
receding, creating new distances
simply by soaring into them.

But it's also how the noisy
crow enlarges the territory
above the landscape at dawn, making
new multiple canyon spires in the sky
by the sharp towers and ledges
of its calling; and how the bighorn
expand the alpine meadows by repeating
inside their watching eyes every foil
of columbine and bell rue, all
the stretches of sedges, the candescences
of jagged slopes and crevices existing there.

And though there isn't a method
to measure it yet, by finding
a golden-banded skipper on a buttonbush,
by seeing a blue whiptail streak
through desert scrub, by looking up
one night and imagining the fleeing
motions of the stars themselves, I know
my presence must swell one flutter-width

wider, accelerate one lizard-slip farther,
descend many stellar-fathoms deeper
than it ever was before.

Creating Transfiguration

It only took staying still, standing
in the right place at the right time, arms
held out sideways straight from the body,
standing still like that on the shore, the winter
wind blowing ice-fog and freezing spray
in from the sea in swelling shrouds
and moanings all night;

to stand there, ice slowly shelling
the body in smooth white glass,
forming, hour by hour, thick glistening
pillars around bone, frost tassels
of tangled hair, clear, solid ribbons
of sea frozen in fringe hanging down
from the fingers and chin, furrowing
like tears stopped on the cheeks;

only to stand still letting the stinging
sea-drizzle fasten to face and breast
in the dark, form choirs of ice on spine,
ribs, knuckles, name; to stay at dawn,
staring unmoved toward the horizon, crystal
body gold in the sun, steam rising
like a holy spirit of light in the sun;

then to let them all, waking, come,
some running, some on knees, some bringing
candles in paper cups, peaches dried
with clove, some carrying violet lilies
and spindled whelks, others placing markers,
smooth stones, like loaves of bread, piled
in cairns on the sand for signs, all
circling round and round, all imbued
and radiant, all promising,
all transfigured.

THE FANCY OF FREE WILL

All of us here were taught
that we were born believing
in the beauty of the deliberately twisted,
the supervised tangle, the cultivated
knot. So we adore any loveliness
that turns in on itself, compounding
the strength of its simple charms—the bud-stitched
apple inverted four times, the five-knuckled
thumb, the bisected line melded
to its opposite ligament.

We know that no two crafted knurls,
knitted creatures or finely gnarled
blossoms can ever be exactly the same,
this uniqueness thus proving
their worth and superiority.

And how could anything growing
without the guidance of shaping straps
and stakes and restricting wires
ever hope to become the beauty
beyond itself?

The artist of my body wore
black satin lounging pajamas
every time she came. She carried
into my room her satchels filled
with splints, adjustable buckles, tight
nylon sheaths, choking thongs and staves,
metal strips, measuring rods in many sizes,
all enchanting, magical materials
which she fitted in ingenious ways
to the raw material of my limbs
and torso. If there was pain,
I thought of the wondrous perfume
she wore—the third generation of mulled
and humped gardenia gourd.

Unless told to turn, to widen,
to squeeze, I lay still
as she worked, tying, splitting,
sometimes separating, sometimes
inserting, binding and directing my bones
and flesh, always consulting her design.
She was a saint in her concentration
and mastery.

Now tonight, if you doubt
we're right, just watch the adoration,
the rapture on this boy's face

as he unwinds the binding cords
from my refined feet, as he removes
the tight swaddling cloths around one thigh,
the metal braids banding the other. He kisses
each warm convolution he discovers,
each devised angle, caresses with his fingers
the surprising crevice, the damp
revelation. His lips and tongue
are around each epiphany
as he uncovers it, learning a new
language, slowly, eagerly, flushed.
See his hands tremble with pleasure.
He's exalted, a witness to god momentarily,
as he anticipates the hidden art beyond,
unhooking, unbelting, easing away
the final brace, lifting carefully
the last silk shift.

FOR ANY KNOWN FACT: NUDE WALKING ALONE ON A BEACH IN MOONLIGHT

One might easily become confused
about proper designations. The beach
is as white, as tense and dedicated
as the moon, it could be stated.
Or should one say the moon presses
through the black sky as steady, reflective
and waxen as a nude body sequined
with spray walks through the night?

The sound of such convoluted thinking
has the same sound as the surf, perhaps;
for the speaking surf has many tongues
that divulge and stutter, prod forward
fondling, withdrawing.

The black sea surface glitters
with bobbing, stuttering moons as flat
as light. Likewise the black body
of any single fish is covered
with thousands of glassy moons, and each drop
of spray on a nude body—jewelling the neck,
beading the lashes, tresses and ear tips,
sparkling down the ivory legs—becomes moon
and mirror simultaneously.

Along the beach of the one distant,
completely naked moon, a strolling figure
might be detected. The moon is a mirror,
surely, but is a mirror a forbidden window
becoming itself by its own reflective act,
or is it just a dull word of unenlightened
imitation?

To turn and walk deliberately out
into the convoluted surf, to feel
the dedicated sounds of that surf
rising gradually to cover the thighs,
the breasts, the eyes, to say the sinking
lungs are filled with waves of fondling
moons, the heart stopped with silent
salt-light—it could be called *suicide,*
but that's just a single word, a thrashing

sound covered with reflective scales,
a stuttering word that might mean to see
suddenly, in this black and alabaster
world, an orange-violet reflection
in a transfigured window, a startling
scarlet-blue sphere of body
and image as one, or it might mean
merely to watch, without interfering,
as that barely recognizable figure
of white light unclothed in the mirror
steps precisely and manifestly off
the edge of the moon.

The Image in a World of Flux

As black as tropic heat on a windowless
night, black as the center of poison, black
as the scorched edges of an old prayer, the cat
sits upright, tail curled around her paws.

She's the only consistent being here
for as far as anyone can see, surrounded
as she is by shooting and sinking pellets
of plains, by fields that startle in rattles
and coughs, rivers that mend in curtsies,
relinquish in spells, reclaim
in gales and graveyards.

Yet she sits, a composition of bone
and bevy, throat strumming, satiated,
oriental, dozing. Her reflection on the sky

in the swarmy sea is split open and sealed
constantly, copped and bound, snatched
in hooks of salt, rocked by pistons
and wheels of water, fang and whisker
drawn under, yawning and licking lifted up.

Her reflection rests serene in puzzled
fragments on the glass dome smashed
and glued together again and again.

As still as a marble saint in a vault,
as stopped as *12:00 midnight* spoken aloud,
she's the measuring rod, the magnetic pole,
the spine, the axis around which the rackets
of the surf strike, ameliorate, reverse
themselves, define their exploding equations,
deny their names in fog and ice. She's the base
tagged and abandoned repeatedly.

Watch out. Watch out. There's a sudden
conflagration. A flame catches hold
at the corner of this picture beginning
to crisp and curl under, smoke and ashes moving
rapidly in a diagonal across the world
toward my fingers.

But see, she's leaping, leaping,
white now, invisible, up and out, escaping
to clutch a bare branch as real and definite
as this network of black cracks we see spread
in its steady place across the blank,
blank ceiling over our heads.

The All-Encompassing

Philosopher in Meditation,
     by Rembrandt

The philosopher is the old, bearded
man in the red beanie, dozing,
it seems, in the sun by the window.
Before him on the table lies his ponderous
volume open to the indirect
light of the day.

But the philosopher could be
the bent firekeeper by the wall
behind the stairs. He stirs, rouses
the coals, studies the combustion.
He's hunched and crotchety there,
concentrating obviously as he constructs
his viable conflagration.

The solid spiral, helix staircase,
curving down the middle of the room,
could be the philosophy, each step leading
naturally and logically to the next.
It's the physical form of ordered thought
reaching a grand staircase conclusion.
The carpenter, then, is the missing seer.

Yet the small round door (dwarf-size)
behind the old man, rightly accepts,
by portal philosophy, that it must meditate
on its closed and locked condition
until a key appears, at which time
it must assimilate the revelation of *open*.

Old Spiral of Conception   421

Does the blind black in the corners
beyond the reach of the window radiance,
as well as the cavern maw at the top
curve of the stairs, match the oblivion
in the sleep of the thinker? If so,
then the sun works a philosophy itself
by realizing the window ledge, the pottery
on the sill and idle book, the folded hands,
the dropped chin. And the old scholar
sleeps in the light of the known.

O philosopher's meditation, don't you understand,
even the baskets and barrels and pots
and smoke of this hovel that split
and bang and cling, and the firekeeper
cracking his throat and the bucket
of ashes and clinkers on the hearth,
and each separate meditation in its place
and time, all these must take their positions
in the rhetoric of the system?

If I hear the ancient housewife rattling
and creaking now down the curve of the stairs
(old gene, spiral of conception, old twist),
dogs scrambling at her heels, broom
and dustpan knocking, if she enters here
with her raucous retinue, cursing and barking,
jolts the sleeper, sweeping under the old man's
stool, cuffs the firekeeper, sets the pans
and spoons swinging, then all previous
suppositions fail, and we must begin again.

EATING BREAD AND HONEY (1997)

BOOK ONE

THE SINGING PLACE

For the orange, saucer-eyed
lemurs indri of the family sifaka,
it is the perfect forest of the hot,
humid zones. There, at sunset and dawn,
they all pause arboreally and chorus,
howling, hooting, shaking the shadows
overhead, the fruits and burrowing
beetles inside the many-storied
jungle. They are the ushers,
the chaperones, the screaming
broadcast of darkness and light.

The house cricket, the field cricket,
the dead-leaf cricket make song places
of the warmest, darkest niches
they can find, at the bases of stones,
in grass stem funnels, the mossy
underbark of southside tree trunks.

For the sage grouse, male, the real
singing place is where he actually sings,
there inside the thimble-sized, flesh-
and-blood place of his voice, that air
sac burbling and popping, puffing
through the morning as he struts
and bows before his hens on the open
spring lek. Breath, I believe,
is place.

Eating Bread and Honey   425

And maybe even the bulb and tuber
and root suck of the big black slug
of wet pastures could be called a long,
slow mud music and meter of sustenance,
by those lucky enough to be born
with a pasture sense for sound.

The whine and wind of heat
through ragged gorges make sandstone
and basalt a moving song. And place,
I think, is moments in motion.

As on the white-statue plains
of the moon's most weird winter
where no dusk scream or lingering suck
or floosing air sac of song has ever
existed, utter stillness is a singing
place too, moments where I first
must find a shape of silence,
where I then must begin
to hum its structure.

———————

OPUS FROM SPACE

Almost everything I know is glad
to be born—not only the desert orangetip,
on the twist flower or tansy, shaking
birth moisture from its wings, but also the naked
warbler nestling, head wavering toward sky,
and the honey possum, the pygmy possum,

blind, hairless thimbles of forward,
press and part.

Almost everything I've seen pushes
toward the place of that state as if there were
no knowing any other—the violent crack
and seed-propelling shot of the witch hazel pod,
the philosophy implicit in the inside out
seed-thrust of the wood sorrel. All hairy
salt cedar seeds are single-minded
in their grasping of wind and spinning
for luck toward birth by water.

And I'm fairly shocked to consider
all the bludgeonings and batterings going on
continually, the head-rammings, wing-furors,
and beak-crackings fighting for release
inside gelatinous shells, leather shells,
calcium shells or rough, horny shells. Legs
and shoulders, knees and elbows flail likewise
against their womb walls everywhere, in pine
forest niches, seepage banks and boggy
prairies, among savannah grasses, on woven
mats and perfumed linen sheets.

Mad zealots, every one, even before
beginning they are dark dust-congealings
of pure frenzy to come into light.

Almost everything I know rages to be born,
the obsession founding itself explicitly
in the coming bone harps and ladders,

the heart-thrusts, vessels and voices
of all those speeding with clear and total
fury toward this singular honor.

THE FALLACY OF THINKING FLESH IS FLESH

Some part of every living creature
is always trembling, a curious
constancy in the wavering rims
of the cup coral, the tasseling
of fringe fish, in the polyrippling
of the polyclad flatworm even under the black
bottom water at midnight when nothing
in particular notices.

The single topknot, head feather,
of the horned screamer or the tufted
quail can never, in all its tethered
barbs and furs, be totally still.
And notice the plural flickers
of the puss moth's powdery antennae.
Not even the puss moth knows how
to stop them.

Maybe it's the pattern of the shattering
sea-moon so inherent to each body
that makes each more than merely body.
Maybe it's the way the blood possesses
the pitch and fall of blooming grasses
in a wind that makes the prairie
of the heart greater than its boundaries.

Maybe it's god's breath swelling
in the breast and limbs, like a sky
at dawn, that gives bright bone
the holiness of a rising sun.
There's more to flesh than flesh.

The steady flex and draw of the digger
wasp's blue-bulbed abdomen—I know
there's a fact beyond presence
in all that fidgeting.

Even as it sleeps, watch the body
perplex its definition—the slight shift
of the spine, the inevitable lash shiver,
signal pulse knocking. See, there,
that simple shimmer of the smallest
toe again, just to prove it.

———————

WHERE DO YOUR PEOPLE COME FROM?

Great-grandfather originated
inside the seamless shell of a hickory nut,
being enabled, thereby, to see
in blindness the future brightness
of combusting seeds and the sun's dark
meat captured in walls like night.

Three aunts came up through the roots
of raspberries, rhododendrons and oaks
and so perceive prophecy in the water-seeking
lines of the moon, in the urging branches

of the incantatory voice. They perceive
the sweet fruits and blossoms thriving
unwitnessed in the plane above the stars.

My sisters were spun outward
from the pinion and swirling-lariat swim
of seals under ice. They walk on earth,
therefore, with bodies as smooth
and radiant as daylight through snow.
Each opens to her lover with the same
giving grace hidden in the fur-warmth
of a seal inclining toward surges,
turning passion round, round in currents
slowly, then heading fast for heaven.

From the line between rock and sky
come my brothers who hold measure
and lock in one hand, hold flocking
violet-green swallows and thin, shining
robes of rain in the emptiness
of the other hand, brothers who swell
with the blue space of mercy
in their stone-steady bones.

My cousins rose right out of the *cheery,*
cheery, cheery chu cry of the painted redstart.
Thus they think in terms of three two-turning
leaves and one hanging plum, seven-syllable
gods, three open windows and a single latched
door, six stitches of scarlet silk—three
in, three out—and a final knot.

And I, rising up through sedimentary
earth—fossil femur, jaw and shell,

burrow and track—speak as I must,
in just this way, of all beginning
points of origin.

———————

ORANGE THICKET: TO SPEAK IN TONGUES

A god lives inside the orange,
a divinity partitioned who discusses
the eight sections of his own being
one at a time with his seven other voices,
an important lesson for the versification
of all future scriptures.

And the orange tells time. It ticks,
sliding in sequential explosions
from its green pea-skull emergence
out of white petals into the measured
dissolves of its wrinkling mold
and powder collapse into a nothing
and new beginning zero.

Some ancient oranges are at the bottom
of the sea, having fallen that far
off the railings of ships sailing
the Indian Ocean or having been dragged
down inside the cargo bays of sinking
ships Italy-bound. There, in the fright
of that deaf and smother of black
salt and tonnage, they testify still
to the existence of sky noise and sun.

The Maltese, red-pulped, doesn't speak
in sound but postulates to summer, evidences
to the round scarlets and brass vowels
of dawn, the burnished sermons of dusk.

Orange-girls with their carts filled, orange-
wenches rolling their loaded wheelbarrows,
vendors of orange-wood walking sticks—all
shout orange praises through the streets
every day in their wondrous rags.

In Parfait Amour, the orange as bitters
speaks with limes, rose spirits
and spices, to all lovers who will taste.

With a tangible voice, a sweet speech
of rind oils and juices, with a cry
of passion that possesses weight
in the hands and baskets of Moors
and Chinese queens, the orange
wants, above all in its spiritual
sizzle, never to die.

Murder in the Good Land

    Murder among the creek narrows
and shafts of rice grass, among lacy
coverlets and field sacks, among basement
apple barrels and cellar staples
of onion and beet;
               beneath piled stones,

razed, broken and scattered stones,
beneath cow bridges, draw bridges, T girders
crossed, and cables, beneath brome, spadefoot,
beneath roots of three-awn

        and heaven; murder
in the sky between stalks of spikesedge,
between harrier and wolf willow, between
the bedroom walls of formidable sluts
and saints, in the sad blindnesses
of moon and mole, in light as curt
and clearcut as blades of frost
magnified;

     through blanks of winter wind
through summer soapweed, through welcoming
gates and bolted gates, throughout the blood-rushing
grief of the swarmy sea;

       murder beside gods
down heathen colonnades, down corridors of scholars
and beggars, down the cathedral colonnades
of orchards in harvest;

       murder with the clench
of white clover, with the slip of the wandering
tattler, with the slow splash of window
curtains flowing inward

       with morning air; murder
in the winsome, murder in the wayward,
murder in canyon wrens, in the low beating bell
in the womb, in bone rafters,

       in mushroom
rings and rosy rings; murder, murder,
murder immortal, pervasive, supreme
everywhere in the good land.

NEARING AUTOBIOGRAPHY

Those are my bones rifted
and curled, knees to chin,
among the rocks on the beach,
my hands splayed beneath my skull
in the mud. Those are my rib
bones resting like white sticks
wracked on the bank, laid down,
delivered, rubbed clean
by river and snow.

Ethereal as seedless weeds
in dim sun and frost, I see
my own bones translucent as locust
husks, light as spider bones,
as filled with light as lantern
bones when the candle flames.
And I see my bones, facile,
willing, rolling and clacking,
reveling like broken shells
among themselves in a tumbling surf.

I recognize them, no other's,
raggedly patterned and wrought,
peeled as a skeleton of sycamore
against grey skies, stiff as a fallen
spruce. I watch them floating
at night, identical lake slivers
flush against the same star bones
drifting in scattered pieces above.

Everything I assemble, all
the constructions I have rendered
are the metal and dust of my locked
and storied bones. My bald cranium
shines blind as the moon.

_____

OF POSSIBILITY: ANOTHER AUTUMN LEAVING

Here they come like miniature herds
of headless ponies without hooves,
stampeding, rearing, trampling one another.
They corral to circle upward themselves
like airborne droves of crippled brown
crows, rising in fragments of dust spouts,
raining down singly in swiveling pieces.

As if they were blind, they batter
against barricades, pile along brick
walls, boulders, wooden fences, filling
gullies and clefts, multitudes deep
as if they had no need to breathe.
Even with bodies without lungs,
there's a ghost cusp and sigh, a hollow
desert buzz to their rousing.

They sweep all night in the dry-moon
rasp of their rattling trance.
They scutter and reel up the windowpanes
on their hundred pins, over the roof
in their thorny flocks. Though totally
lacking bones or the tatters of bones,

Eating Bread and Honey

still they shrivel and quake.
Though totally devoid of hearts
or the rubbish of hearts, still
they are brittle and heedless.

Even without souls, they shiver and rend.
Even without devils, they make ritual
processions of their deprivations. With no
word at all, they lie. They stutter.
They testify to themselves. Even lost
and without a god, they make visions
of the invisible, become the buffet,
the possessed, the very place of wind.
They are the time and tangible nexus
of all heavenly spirits. Even without tongues,
they clatter their tongues.

———————

CREATION BY THE PRESENCE OF ABSENCE: CITY COYOTE IN RAIN

She's sleek blue neon through
the blue of the evening. She's black
sheen off the blue of wet streets,
blue daunt of suspension in each
pendant of rain filling the poplars
on the esplanade.

Her blue flank flashes once in the panes
of empty windows as she passes.
She's faster than lighthouse blue
sweeping the seas in circles.

436

Like the leaping blue of flames
burning in an alley barrel, her presence
isn't perceived until she's gone.

She cries with fat blue yelps, calls
with the scaling calls of the ragmen,
screeches a siren of howls along the docks
below the bridges, wails with the punctuated
griefs of drunks and orphans.

She scuttles under gates, through doors
hanging by broken hinges, behind ash
bins, into a culvert, shakes off the storm
in an explosion of radiance, licks
the cold muzzles and genitals of her frenzied
pups, gives them her blue teats, closes
her yellow eyes.

No one ever sees her face to face,
or those who do never know they do,
denying her first, pre-empting her lest
the place of pattern and time she creates,
like the blue of a star long since
disintegrated, enter their hearts
with all of its implications.

THE DEATH OF LIVING ROCKS AND THE CONSEQUENCES THEREOF

The god of rocks said *stop,*
and all the rocks stopped still
where they were—wolf rocks, pouncing
or suckling, packed in the forest,
snake rocks singling over the desert,
rock toads, their round pebbly
humps huddled along streambeds.

They all stopped—whale boulders
impassive on the floor of the sea, seal
rocks piled shiny and herded in spray
on the shore, a rock puma, granite
teeth bared, her rock kittens scattered
and halted halfway down the hill,
closed mica butterfly wings.

Whole swaths of gypsum stems
and flowerets became paralyzed
where we see them now, unmoved
in the wind. Pipes of organ rocks
and the red bugle rocks beside them
posed statuesque over ravines
and gulches without music.

On the day the god of rocks
said *stop,* all the rocks of the earth
stood still, without further expression,
without further response. And the god
of rocks, simply a possible reflection
of his own rock creation, became bound himself,
eyes staring marble white, voice a solid

layer of shale, the words *live again*
soundless and locked irretrievably
on his silent, stone tongue.

———————

THE CONSEQUENCES OF DEATH

You might previously have thought
each death just a single loss.
But when a plain grey titmouse dies,
what plunges simultaneously and disappears too
are all the oak-juniper woodlands,
the streamside cottonwoods, every elderberry
bush and high spring growth of sprouted
oak once held inside its eye.

And when a sugar pine splits, breaks
to the ground, falling with its fiestas
and commemorations of blue-green needles,
long-winged seeds, the sweet resin
of its heartwood, there's another
collapse coincident—a fast inward
sinking and sucking back to nothing
of all those stars once kept in its core,
those clusters of suns and shining
dusts once resident in the sky of its rigid
bark and cone-scales. We could hear
the sound of that galactic collapse as well,
if we had the proper ears for it.

And when a mountain sheep stumbles,
plummets, catapulting skull, spine,

from cliff side to crumbling rock below,
a like shape of flame and intensity
on a similar sharp ledge on the other side
of the same moment, out of our sense,
loses balance, goes blind.

Because of these torn paper-shreds
of gold-lashed wings, this spangled
fritillary's death, somewhere behind the night
a convinced declaration of air and matter
and intention, silenced, speaks no longer
of the god of its structure.

————————

AGAINST THE ETHEREAL

I'm certain these are the only angels
there are: those with raised, sneering
lips revealing razor-pure incisors that rip
with a purpose, dominions in the moment
when they spread like flying squirrels,
sail like jaguarundi across the celestials
with sickle claws thrust forward.

This is the only rite of holiness
I know: fierce barb of bacteria, that hot,
hot coal, that smoldering challenge
glaring, for twelve millennia at least,
in all directions from its dark, subzero
cellar of frozen, glacial rock.

This is the noise of heavenly

hosts: trumpet-blaring chaparrals
and shinneries, cymbal-banging greasewood
and jojoba deserts, burble of hellbinders, slips
of heliotropes, tweakings of brush mice
and big-eared bats, wheezings of rusty wheels,
grasshopper sparrows, autumn leaves ticking
across gravel on their paper pricks.

I aspire devotedly and with all reverence
to the raspy links of lampreys, the tight
latchings of pawpaw apples and soursops,
the perfect piercings and fastenings
of sperms and ovipositors, clinging
grasps of titis and chacmas.

Aren't you peculiarly frightened, as I am,
by the vague, the lax, the gossamer
and faint, the insubstantial and all
submissive, bowing transparencies,
any willfully pale worshipping?

This is the only stinging, magenta-cruel,
fire-green huffing, bellowing mayhemic
spirituality I will ever recognize:
the one shuddering with veined lightning,
chackling with seeded consolations, howling
with winter pities, posturing with speared
and fisted indignations, surly as rock, rude
as weeds, riotous as billbugs, tumultuous
as grapevine beetles, as large black, burying
beetles, bare, uncovered to every perception
of god, and never, never once forgiving
death.

SERVICE WITH BENEDICTION

Chunk honey, creamed honey, buckwheat
honey on buckwheat bread—like glass lanterns,
there's enough concentrated summer sun caught
in these jars of comb honey to give us
ample light to travel by on a winter night.

Sesame breads, sausage breads, almond
breads, sweet panettones, cassava cakes
and millet cakes, all are laid out
on the table before me beside these bowls
of molasses honey and heather honey, wild-
wood honey gathered by wild bees, hallows
of honey, orisons of bulging loaves.

So I eat sun and earth by the slice
and spoonful, suck yeast breads soaked
in alfalfa honey, dip crusts dripping
from the dish to my mouth, lick gold
sugar from my fingers. I swallow
pure flower syrup brought from the sky,
chew the kneaded spike and germ of fields
and gardens. Surely I become then
all the arabesques of bee dances
and the cultures of beebread balls rolled
from nectar pollen. I comply easily
with the lean of heady buds and grasses
waxing and waning at their cores
sunk in the earth.

Two gifts, I heard the temple bakers say,
when, for immortality, the priests immersed

his dead body naked before burial
in a cistern of amber honey.

Allow me now in the fullness of this morning
to consume enough clover honey and white
wheat fire to see my way clearly
through the cold night coming.

BOOK TWO

ANIMALS AND PEOPLE: "THE HUMAN HEART IN CONFLICT WITH ITSELF"

Some of us like to photograph them. Some
of us like to paint pictures of them. Some of us
like to sculpt them and make statues and carvings
of them. Some of us like to compose music
about them and sing about them. And some of us
like to write about them.

                  Some of us like to go out
and catch them and kill them and eat them. Some
of us like to hunt them and shoot them and eat them.
Some of us like to raise them, care for them and eat
them. Some of us just like to eat them.

                  And some of us
name them and name their seasons and name their hours,
and some of us, in our curiosity, open them up
and study them with our tools and name their parts.
We capture them, mark them and release them,
and then we track them and spy on them and enter
their lives and affect their lives and abandon
their lives. We breed them and manipulate them
and alter them. Some of us experiment
upon them.

        We put them on tethers and leashes,
in shackles and harnesses, in cages and boxes,
inside fences and walls. We put them in yokes

and muzzles. We want them to carry us and pull us
and haul for us.

And we want some of them
to be our companions, some of them to ride on our fingers
and some to ride sitting on our wrists or on our shoulders
and some to ride in our arms, ride clutching our necks.
We want them to walk at our heels.

We want them to trust
us and come to us, take our offerings, eat from our hands.
We want to participate in their beauty. We want to assume
their beauty and so possess them. We want to be kind
to them and so possess them with our kindness and so
partake of their beauty in that way.

And we want them
to learn our language. We try to teach them our language.
We speak to them. We put *our* words in *their* mouths.
We want *them* to speak. We want to know what they see
when they look at us.

We use their heads and their bladders
for balls, their guts and their hides and their bones
to make music. We skin them and wear them for coats,
their scalps for hats. We rob them, their milk
and their honey, their feathers and their eggs.
We make money from them.

We construct icons of them.
We make images of them and put their images on our clothes
and on our necklaces and rings and on our walls
and in our religious places. We preserve their dead

Eating Bread and Honey   445

bodies and parts of their dead bodies and display
them in our homes and buildings.

We name mountains
and rivers and cities and streets and organizations
and gangs and causes after them. We name years and time
and constellations of stars after them. We make mascots
of them, naming our athletic teams after them. Sometimes
we name ourselves after them.

We make toys of them
and rhymes of them for our children. We mold them
and shape them and distort them to fit our myths
and our stories and our dramas. We like to dress up
like them and masquerade as them. We like to imitate them
and try to move as they move and make the sounds they make,
hoping, by these means, to enter and become the black
mysteries of their being.

Sometimes we dress them
in our clothes and teach them tricks and laugh at them
and marvel at them. And we make parades of them
and festivals of them. We want them to entertain us
and amaze us and frighten us and reassure us
and calm us and rescue us from boredom.

We pit them
against one another and watch them fight one another,
and we gamble on them. We want to compete with them
ourselves, challenging them, testing our wits and talents
against their wits and talents, in forests and on plains,
in the ring. We want to be able to run like them and leap
like them and swim like them and fly like them and fight
like them and endure like them.

We want their total
absorption in the moment. We want their unwavering devotion
to life. We want their oblivion.

Some of us give thanks
and bless those we kill and eat, and ask for pardon,
and this is beautiful as long as they are the ones dying
and we are the ones eating.

And as long as we are not
seriously threatened, as long as we and our children
aren't hungry and aren't cold, we say, with a certain
degree of superiority, that we are no better
than any of them, that any of them deserve to live
just as much as we do.

And after we have proclaimed
this thought, and by so doing subtly pointed out
that we are allowing them to live, we direct them
and manage them and herd them and train them and follow
them and map them and collect them and make specimens
of them and butcher them and move them here and move
them there and we place them on lists and we take
them off of lists and we stare at them and stare
at them and stare at them.

We track them in our sleep.
They become the form of our sleep. We dream of them.
We seek them with accusation. We seek them
with supplication.

And in the ultimate imposition,
as Thoreau said, we make them bear the burden
of our thoughts. We make them carry the burden

of our metaphors and the burden of our desires and our guilt
and carry the equal burden of our curiosity and concern.
We make them bear our sins and our prayers and our hopes
into the desert, into the sky, into the stars.
We say we kill them for God.

We adore them and we curse
them. We caress them and we ravish them. We want them
to acknowledge us and be with us. We want them to disappear
and be autonomous. We abhor their viciousness and lack
of pity, as we abhor our own viciousness and lack of pity.
We love them and we reproach them, just as we love
and reproach ourselves.

We will never, we cannot,
leave them alone, even the tiniest one, ever, because we know
we are one with them. Their blood is our blood. Their breath
is our breath, their beginning our beginning, their fate
our fate.

Thus we deny them. Thus we yearn
for them. They are among us and within us and of us,
inextricably woven with the form and manner of our being,
with our understanding and our imaginations.
They are the grit and the salt and the lullaby
of our language.

We have a need to believe they are there,
and always will be, whether we witness them or not.
We need to know they are there, a vigorous life maintaining
itself without our presence, without our assistance,
without our attention. We need to know, we *must* know,
that we come from such stock so continuously and tenaciously
and religiously devoted to life.

We know we are one with them,
and we are frantic to understand how to actualize that union.
We attempt to actualize that union in our many stumbling,
ignorant and destructive ways, in our many confused
and noble and praiseworthy ways.

For how can we possess dignity
if we allow them no dignity? Who will recognize our beauty
if we do not revel in their beauty? How can we hope
to receive honor if we give no honor? How can we believe
in grace if we cannot bestow grace?

We want what we cannot
have. We want to give life at the same moment
we are taking it, nurture life at the same moment we light
the fire and raise the knife. We want to live, to provide,
and not be instruments of destruction, instruments
of death. We want to reconcile our "egoistic concerns"
with our "universal compassion." We want the lion
and the lamb to be one, the lion and the lamb
within finally to dwell together, to lie down together
in peace and praise at last.

BOOK THREE

THE ART OF RAISING GIBBONS AND FLOWERS

We think they go well together—the translucent
vanilla orchid, the slipper orchid, the ginger
fragrances of the fiddle leaf, the swollen,
juice-filled buds of magnolia grandiflora,
Turkish tulip, Susa crocus, and the Siamang
gibbons who pound and scream, quarreling
and sweating, stinking inside their tight
cages where we have put them in the garden
under the iron oak trees.

They shake the bars, their snouts
dripping, piles of fecal matter covered
with green flies in the corners of their cages.
How they reek, puffing their red throat sacs
to holler and hoot in chorus at dawn and dusk.
The petals of the fringed iris and the tea-scented
China rose certainly shimmer then with that roar,
and even pollen spores and feeding butterflies
are shaken loose by the fetid blast.

But it all makes a nice contrast, we think.
So we allow the ranging wisteria to venture over
the east brick wall without pruning, the grape
hyacinths to spill supremely beyond the borders
of the walk. The spirea and trumpet vines
billow up through summer at will
like surf in a storm.

And the wide, white cups of gloriosa
blossoms hang down soft, confident
and abundant from the branches of the iron oak
where their vines have climbed. In an evening
breeze, we see them brush the roofs of those rank
cages, dawdle there in an evening breeze.
They sway and hush out of sight. Their perfume
and nectar-rain are dizzying. Their petals
shine with moonlight, just barely beyond
the reach of the horny black fingers stretching
through the bars to scratch, to encase.

Later we come close to the cages to watch
the gibbons sleeping, the straggly hairy
nakedness of their curled bodies. We imagine
they dream that the crusty callouses and bunions
of their hands and feet have turned to camellias,
to petals of pale nolana, that they sip the liquor
of honeysuckle and drink the ices of violets
and orange blossoms. We imagine they dream
that their arms and torsos are supple
vines and sturdy trunks rising unrestrained
into the night, carrying moonlight
on the blossoms and graces of their bodies
up through the sky and back to the source
of that shining.

There's a certain pity and hope
made evident by this, which is the art
we carry with us like a penance out of the garden,
along the path, and down the darkened
hallways to our beds.

PARTNERS

1.
I like sleeping with the old table leg
close beside me under the covers in bed.
It's so placid, still and sturdy
in its slumber. It tolerates my knee
hooked over its finely lathed middle
and the way our ankles and feet
couple beneath the blanket.

Without attention or liberty (unlike
window or mirror), it withdraws wholly
and satisfactorily into the tight
oak of its own parameters.

Hardly restless, it never resists
itself or cants recitations to maker
or scholars. Its respiration is a lasting
lullaby, more predictable than my breath.
Its heart is less phantom, more upholding
than my heart.

During winter snows, I seek it,
I cradle it to my bed, I tuck it.
We somnia close, union and loss,
all through the night of the night.

2.
I like sleeping with great-uncle's
sea-crusted rope. I wind it in the familiar
route up my legs, round my waist, between
my breasts, a repeated necklace.

My sleep composes to its spirals,
follows its blind underwater passages,
the lines of its many past knots
loosened and lost.

The light of its fragrant coils
is the silver of its lovely residue:
dried spittle, fish flakes, moon oil.

With its head-end like a thumb
stuck in my mouth in the dark, subsumed,
I suck the salt-jack of its prehistoric
waves and currents.

3.
I take the carefully tuned guitar along
to sleep with me at night. Wrought
below the frets with ivory crescent moons
and their ebony crescent shadows,
it reclines best on its back, keeping
to its own pillow, keys resting
against the fringed satin.

With a mere accidental brush of my hand
across the center of its nakedness
in the dark, I feel the two of us
and the entire bed, springs and boards alike,
become a humming, six-stringed doxology.

The guitar surrounds a hollowness
as desperate as my sleep inside
its framework, as immeasurable as the night
inside its boundaries, as possible
as any truth inside its fabrication,
and sings the same.

KISSING A KIT FOX

The kit fox has fine lips. Often black
or grey, they are as demure as two slight
fronds of Mayweed in fog, yet a little fuller.
They are capable of pulling back,
disappearing up and into the nether
to reveal his impressive fangs.

The lips of the kit fox taste
sometimes of the sweet spring water
he drank in its dark rock the moment before.
They taste also sometimes of the rank
bone marrow of the dead peccary
he licked in the ditch for a meal.
His lips and breath today tasted
of the peanut of desiccated
grasshoppers burned dry.

The needle teeth of the kit fox
when kissing sometimes pierce the lover's
tongue with sevenfold hot spears
like the sun. Often too they puncture
the lips of the lover and bring blood
to the mouth like the moon. A few cherish
this pain when kissing the kit fox,
because they believe they then may speak
with the authority of scars
on the nature of day and night.

And when kissing a kit fox,
some are lucky, for he will occasionally
wrap the thick ragrances of his plush
tail around the lover's neck up to the ears,

or better, across the eyes and over the nose.
One may then fall completely into the lush
swoon and smother of his race and art—cactus
juice, thorns and the musk of fear, snake
seed, fecal rat.

Some say kissing the kit fox
is a story, because it has both character
and event, both union and scorn.
But some say it is a song in syncopation
that they may tap to themselves
in loneliness for comfort. Others say kissing
the kit fox is a place one may enter,
a location with boundaries fixed in space,
a measurable site in a portion of time.
I say kissing a kit fox is like memory,
because it is a mere invention of pleasure
and pain, a creation of wild risk
with wound and fetish, certain evidence
of either the unlikely or the lost.

——————

KALEIDOSCOPE: FREE WILL AND
THE NATURE OF THE HOLY SPIRIT

At the beginning, the Lady of Wild
Things is placed cheek-to-cheek
with her long-fingered, woolly black
lemur aye-aye, while Baby Bob, decked
and dingled in silver fleece, sleeps
where he was laid—in his cradle
under a creamy summer moon. The nootka

Eating Bread and Honey   455

rose can only spread and spin itself
like a philosophy all night
over the crooked garden walk.

Suddenly, a playful twist of the instrument,
and there's the Lady upside down
at the top now, her purple silk tights
tight up her legs certainly kicking
in the sky. The full wondrous tail
of the aye-aye is curled seductively
around the fat cheeks of the tilting
summer moon during this moment, and Baby
Bob, spilled from his cradle, finds
himself wound close, locked in the prose
of nootka roses.

The inevitable rotation again,
and Baby Bob is sucking sweet cream
from the fallen moon nestled-in now
beside him. The lemur aye-aye, landing
sprawled in a seduction of nootka roses,
tickles with one long finger the purple
dingles at the center of each cheeky
blossom. Spinning crookedly, the Lady
can't help chasing the wondrous tail
of the wild black night circling fast
and free in her eyes.

All are tumbled once more, and a new
crescent moon is set to swaying as a result,
rocking like an empty cradle of light
suspended mid-garden. The Lady of Wild
Things Tamed kisses, as she must, the sweet
creamy cheeks of Baby Bob pressed against

her perfect nootka rose mouth. Decked
in silver fleece pajamas and flipped
topsy-turvy, the aye-aye walks
on its hands across the summer night
like a shiny moon with black feet
thrust upward among the dingling stars.

The whole world is shaken again,
and this time the shiny round rock
of the moon is stuck firmly in the aye-aye's
mouth, whereby its eyes are lit brightly
to shine like summer. The night has become
a cradle of philosophy rocking a sleeping
nootka rose to stone (perfect definition
of a pink moon blooming) which the Lady
is compelled to pluck and wear
in her ear for cheer to Baby Bob.

O Lady, take the full moon like a monocular
glass, hold it to your eye, if you can,
and study. O aye-aye, with your crooked
finger beckon the rosy summer night,
gently tickle Baby Bob's cream-dabbled
chin, play dingle long and loudly
on the truth of these turnings.

INSIDE THE UNIVERSE INSIDE THE ACT

The plum, just picked, is smooth
and cold as a river stone in the hand,
egg-smooth along the lips, soft

as lips against the lips. Its quick
puncture at the teeth is discrete,
the tongue of its brown-syrup-
fragrance. Inside this event
of bone and tree, this consummation
of plum weather and sugar pulp
swallowed, is a singular universe
created alone of ripe purple,
pit, savor and summer signature.

The staggered moonlight off cracked
and shackled grasses of ice, the white
piece of moonlight the baby wants
to lift from his blanket, the smoke
of moonlight in the panting breath
of the cougar caught in a trap—
these are not the same moonlight.
Even in the same instant of winter
evening, each is a multiple, rare
universe itself determining the universe.

What unique writing is plucked
by the rain's passage across the lake
this evening? What line of the world
is only recorded by water falling
at dusk on water? How should
the histories of electrons read now
inside these dissolving signals
of storm? And what reality at last
is created, set spinning like a globe
in orbit, by the act of asking questions
of the rain within the rain?

Night and the swift prescriptions
of stars rise, collapse, join,
and dissemble, change relevancy again
and again inside this hour—my hands
in love, in light along your face,
your hands beneath my thighs, my legs
parted for you, hidden, vulnerable
underbelly exposed for you.

Every leaf of every plum in moonlight,
all rain prophecies, all dissolutions
of all swallowed suns are shaken
forever inside the rile of our bound
bodies, inside our cries
of compassion for far-flying
distances and their poor solitudes.

Now inside this first remembering—what new
place becomes? what time begins?

THE CENTER OF THE KNOWN UNIVERSE

It's exactly here—mark the moment—the tip
of my breast kissed and held
in his mouth, now the one clear grain
around which all goldfish gather to nip
and feed and fleck their fire, now
the circling ring where all river
waters descend, swelling and surging,
this tight bud in his mouth
whose petals, thin as light, I feel

as they loose themselves singly,
peel away like breath, falling
by falling, dissolve only to rise again.
By this falling I understand
how resurrection is central
to knowing.

And this moment is congruent,
the very same moment where Mother
often held Father cradled to her breast,
the same exact moment where Mary nursed
the Christ child feeding, that bud,
that mouth pulling. Astral bodies,
we remember, were drawn into orbit
around that place. By this I understand
how event gives order to matter.

Found nipple nestled in the warmth
of his nudging mouth, inside the curled
and sucking funnel of his tongue—
this is the central bead of the only
universe I know, the very pin
around which the open window, the white
sheet pushed to my knees, the house,
its dishes and doors and eaves,
the curlew calling in the fields outside,
all go whirling. It is the hub where I
in my own knowing go swinging round,
eyes closed, head above, head below.
My toes, my fingertips define
themselves properly only by measuring
their circumferences circling this axis.

God bless the small, central power
and point of this loving instant
upon which all angels, forever countless,
bore and spin and pivot, naked angels
embracing naked angels, mouths at breasts
everywhere inside the center of this moment
holding time and its great wheeling
lariat fixed and found and knowable.

PLACE AND PROXIMITY

I'm surrounded by stars. They cover me
completely like an invisible silk veil
full of sequins. They touch me, one by one,
everywhere—hands, shoulders, lips,
ankle hollows, thigh reclusions.

Particular in their presence, like rain,
they come also in streams, in storms.
Careening, they define more precisely
than wind. They enter, cheekbone,
breastbone, spine, skull, moving out
and in and out, through like threads,
like weightless grains of beads
in their orbits and rotations,
their ritual passages.

They are the luminescence of blood
and circuit the body. They are showers
of fire filling the dark, myriad spaces

of porous bone. What can be nearer
to flesh than light?

And I swallow stars. I eat stars.
I breathe stars. I survive on stars.
They sound precisely, humming in my nose,
in my throat, on my tongue. *Stars, stars.*

They are above me suspended, drifting,
caught in the loom of the elm, similarly enmeshed
in my hair. They are below me straight down
in the deep. I am immersed in stars. I swim
through stars, their swells and currents.
I walk on stars. They are less,
they are more, even than water,
even than earth.

They come with immediacy. They are as bound
to me as history. No knife, no death
can part us.

THE KINGDOM OF HEAVEN

    inside of which careen
the wrecked suns of obliterating
stellar furies and smelting quasars
ejecting the seething matter of stars
in piercing shocks wrenching and spewing
blasted flares and ash of incinerated
planets whose roaring eruptions
and scorching thunders, in the slightest

proximity, would boil and melt the ear
to spent char long before those sounds
could ever reach the ear as sound
    inside of which exist
the serenities of this fading summer
evening, the motion of wind in slow,
shifting passions down from redcedar
and netleaf, across the easy flight
of creeks and bluegrasses, within
the peace of possibilities created
by a single cricket in his place,
the assurance of blindnesses behind
my eyes closed on this hillside,
earth pressing against my body
    inside of which wheel
fine solar particles and microscopic
constellations issuing and collapsing,
waging transformations, gatherings
and dissolutions through bones and veins,
circling and spinning in pursuits and purposes
with bloody powers and strategies
    inside of which is one
deity proven by the faith of sleep
and the imagination to exist throughout
these realms of such measured light
and destruction

FRACTAL: REPETITION OF FORM
OVER A VARIETY OF SCALES

This moment is a single blue jay,
a scramble of flint, sapphire iron,
spiking blue among the empty brambles
and vines wound like skeins back
upon themselves through the dun forest
of thistle spurs and thorns.

And this moment is as well the brambled
skeleton of the jay, anthracite spine,
thorny blades and femurs, tangle
of knuckled twigs flittering
through an equal flitter of jointed
sticks, vines and husks of wind.

And as well again, this split second
is the singular blue-black pod of jay heart
thiddering among a bramble of rib bones
inside the tufts, the bristled
capsules of forest and winter barbed
and strung with dusk.

And the jay's call is this same
instant, a cry of release slivered
and shaped by the tangle of bones
and scrub woods, by the bolus wound
of winter air, thatched and spurred,
through which it travels.

And this moment is a single point
of sun wrapped and templing in the black
pathways of the blue jay's eye, like a heart

shuddering in a tangle of bones,
like a bird in a shifting knot of forest,
a call in a skeletal patch of winter,
winter in a weaving clutch of dusk, a moment
tangling within the string and bristle
of its own vocabulary.

God is a process, a raveled nexus
forever tangling into and around the changing
form of his own moment—pulse and skein,
shifting mien, repeating cry
of loss and delivery.

WITHIN ONE MOMENT, ALL POSSIBLE MOMENTS

Across the plains, over the threadleaf
and the gripping thistle, Mignon comes running
up to the edge of the crevasse, stops short, peers
down into those shifting halls, the seeping
guano, the latched and bundled
fluttering pods of the netherness.

Running across the plains, her eyes
on the metal marker ahead, a pole
of the circumnavigating medicine line,
Mignon, not aware of the crevasse, falls
sideways into it, is transformed in that deep
harrow to a planted seed of Reseda ordorata,
mignonette rooted, little greenish-white flower.

Mignon, lithe and fleet, becomes
her running so thoroughly that she crosses

the crevasse in one stride, never seeing
nor knowing afterward in her hartebeest
bed, beneath her antelope covers,
within the gazelle of her sleep, anything
of the immobile gulf of its terror.

From a mile away, she sprints right for it,
dives deliberately headfirst straight down
into that crevasse, her long, full skirts
falling completely over her head,
revealing beneath, in place of legs, a jester
in a spotted jacket who seizes a juniper
with his bejangled hands, holds tight,
blinking at the sudden light.

Mignon steps into that element slowly,
carefully, one foot off the dusty grass,
then the other, sinks, the blackness pulling
like a drawstring over her head. She floats
through scattered incendiary dust; occasionally
here and there, she hears a hist of tight flames
beading tighter. She drifts directly
for the spot where the moon used to be.

After leading her mother right
to god's mouth, shoving her over and down
into that chasm, Mignon closes the crevasse,
as if it were a book, turns off the light
beside the bed, pulls the blanket to her chin,
shuts her eyes, steps out in her running shoes
onto the quiet snow-covered plains.

Before I was a ghost, I was born.
This event was continuous—as the separating
and peeling away of beetles and barnacles,
birchleaves and curlleaves from the sun
is continuous, as the unraveling of sage,
salt cedar and thrasher from the day
is continuous.

I was born a ghost; for there were no
boundaries between me and the fragrances
of wild grape and licorice. The light
of fireflea, fox eye, dropseed, and candelabra
tree, all entered me freely. I gazed myself
without shape or form right into the hard
glass monocle of the moon, descended bodiless
through water into the fibrillating black
dollop of tadpole. I penetrated the boll
of the buckbrush, merged with the thump
of the bushtit. In one sudden opening
of layered clouds, I became all the moments
in a moment of summer night.

I was a ghost forever before I was born,
bearing in the present moment everything
to come and all that has been—the past
distance and data of *now* held in the ovary
of an ancient grandmother's son
of an unborn son.

When I was born into death,
I was a living ghost, being the only spirit

of fingers, the sole shock and spell of river
litany spoken. I was the animus of ponder
and strain, the revenant of hope, the feeding
soul of slaughter and consume.

I was born becoming the beginning
of a ghost dying. This finality
was continuous—as the distinction
of barnacles and beetles, curlleaves
and birchleaves from the sun
is the finality of birth, as the unraveling
of sage, salt cedar and thrasher
from the day is the continuous present.

THE IMMORTAL SOUL

It longs for the spine-shudder
coming with an October persimmon
sucked clear to the seed. It craves
pipe and whistle music played to neon
reflections on night rivers, seeks
the structured sounds of cello and strings
with the same desire as it seeks the sway
and draw of rain and wind witnessed
on the way. It falls in with the confusion
of waxwings and red ash disappearing
together in a union of their own making.
Word of its privileged place is as certain
as the royal totality of a crow is certain,
heard once calling across a fertile meadow.

Its first five ways are the first
five fragrances of bog and booth
willow, beaked sedge, warming
mud, expanding mosses, encountered
in the first thaw of spring. The ten
directions of its faith are its two hands
spread before a blue-yellow flame
burning in the snow. The ways
of its passion are all the directions
revealed by wet, white needles
in a pine forest filled with riverfog.

Its deepest alienation from god
comes when the eyes are closed and sleeping.
Its most jolting connection to god comes
in its plunge headfirst off rocks down
into the pummeling pressure and sudden
buffeting of a cold surf. Its most complete
connection to god is its definition
found by the most loved of lovers.
And when the soothing voice of the one
lover is at its ear whispering devotion
and possession, telling truthfully
of such fictions, the soul then believes
with all of its body in its own immortality.

Abundance and Satisfaction

1.
One butterfly is not enough. We need
many thousands of them, if only
for the effusion of the wayward-
swaying words they occasion—blue
and copper hairstreaks, sulphur
and cabbage whites, brimstones,
peacock fritillaries, tortoiseshell
emperors, skippers, meadow browns.
We need a multitude of butterflies
right on the tongue simply to be able
to speak with a varied six-pinned
poise and particularity.

But thousands of butterflies
are surfeit. We need just one
flitter to apprehend correctly
the will of aspen leaves, the lassitude
of lupine petals, the sleep
of a sleeping eyelid. To examine
adequately one set of finely leaded,
stained wings of violet translucence,
one single sucking proboscis (sap-
and-sugar-licking thread), to study
thoroughly just one powder scale, one
gold speck from one dusted butterfly
forewing would require at least
a millennium of attention to all melody,
phrase, gravity and horizon.

2.

And just the same, one moon is more
than sufficient, ample complexity
and bewilderment—single waning crescent,
waxing cresent, lone gibbous, one perfect,
solitary sickle and pearl, one map
of mountains and lava plains, Mare
Nectaris, Crater Tycho. And how could
anyone really hold more than one full
moon in one heart?

Yet one moon is not enough. We need
millions of moons, glossy porcelain
globes glowing as if from the inside out,
weaving among each other in the sky
like lanterns bobbing on a black river
sea-bound. Then we could study
moons and the traversings of moons
and the multiple meanings of the phases
of moons, and the eclipsing of moons
by one another. We need a new language
of moons containing all the syllables
of interacting rocks of light
so that we might fully understand,
at last, the phrase "one heart
in many moons."

3.

And of gods, we need just one, one
for the grief of twenty snow geese
frozen by their feet in ice and dead
above winter water. Yet we need twenty-
times-twenty gods for all the recurring

memories of twenty snow geese frozen
by their feet in sharp lake-water ice.

But a single god suffices
for the union of joys in one school
of invisible green-brown minnows
flocking over green-brown stones
in a clear spring, but three gods
are required to wind and unwind
the braided urging of spring—root,
blossom and spore. And we need
the one brother of gods for a fragged
plain, blizzard-split, battered
by tumbleweeds and wire fences,
and the one sister to mind
the million sparks and explosions
of gods on fire in a pine forest.

I want one god to be both scatter
and pillar, one to explain simultaneously
mercy and derision, yet a legion of gods
for the spools of confusion and design,
but one god alone to hold me by the waist,
to rumble and quake in my ear, to dance me
round and round, one couple with forty
gods in the heavenly background
with forty violins with one
immortal baton keeping time.

BOOK FOUR

"GOD IS IN THE DETAILS," SAYS MATHEMATICIAN FREEMAN J. DYSON

This is why grandmother takes such tiny
stitches, one stitch for each dust mote
of moon on the Serengeti at night, and one half
one stitch for each salt-fetch of fog
following the geometries of eelgrasses
in fields along the beach.

And this is why she changes the brief threads
in her glass needle so often—metallic bronze
for the halo around the thrasher's eye,
ruby diaphanous for the antenna tips
of the May beetle, transparent silk
for dry-rain fragrances blowing
through burr sages before rain.

She inserts her needle
through the center of each elementary
particle, as if it were a circling sequin
of blue, loops it to its orbit, sewing thus,
again and again, the reckless sapphire sea,
a whipping flag of tall summer sky.

Sometimes she takes in her hands
two slight breaths of needles at once,
needles so thin they almost burn
her fingers like splinters of light.
She crochets with them around each microscopic

Eating Bread and Honey   473

void, invents, thereby, an ice tapestry
of winter on the window, creates a lace
of peeper shrillings through flooded
sweet gale, secures a blank jot of sight
in the knitting of each red flea
of zooplankton skittering mid-lake.

God's most minute exuberance is founded
in the way she sews with needles
as assertive as the sun-sharp loblolly
that she sees with her eyes closed;
in the way she knots stitches
as interlocked as the cries of veery,
peewee, black-capped chickadee and jay
that she hears with her ears stopped;
in the way she whispers to her work,
recites to her work, spooling every least
designation of spicule shade, hay
spider and air trifid, every hue
and rising act of her own hands. *Try
to escape now,* it reads, *just try.*

Mousefeet: From a Lecture
on Muridae Cosmology

Mousefeet are often as small, exact
and precocious as eighth notes penned
across a composer's score. Most are no
larger than two quarter-inch W's printed
side by side. All mouse toenails
are just about the size of poppy seeds.

Yet one encounters mousefeet
everywhere.

The leaves of the wild radish,
for instance, are simply green mousefeet
held bottomside up with thin toes spread
to the sun. And the leaves of aspens
and certain poplars make many mousefeet-
twitters-and-jumps themselves in any brief
skimpering mousebreath wind.

Each hister beetle, we know,
is just one fat, black mousefoot
transformed to bug.

Raindrops hitting dusty cement
sidewalks make trails of splayed mousefeet
running in every direction. And there are pale,
blue footprints of mice all over the moon.
Just get a telescope and check
for yourself some night.

Whitefooted mice in May create,
everywhere they step through the field,
those tiny white yarrow blossoms
so commonly seen. I've been exalted
as well by the musky whiffs of mousefeet
fragrances (moldy loam and leaf rot) rising
with wild cherry and green brier perfumes
through the damp night grasses,
haven't you?

Falling snowflakes caught on a dark wool
scarf are easily identified as the frozen,

crystal bones of pygmy mousefeet lost
in ice a century ago. You can feel
the prickle of cold scurry in your mouth
if you eat them.

And even after predators have speared
live mice and swallowed them whole, still,
those mousefeet are there, ticking
in the flick of the rattlesnake's tail,
scraping in the weasel's growl, running
and leaping with light in the cougar's
steady eye.

Be careful where you tread.
There are mousefeet, tiny folded fans
of knuckles and pins, thousands of them, curled
in the roll of the surf, inside the tight
furl of marsh fog, planted deep in pea pods,
and cockle rocks, in the earth in burrows
below us as we speak.

And be careful where you fly. They are startled,
a fleeing, overlapping four footprint dash
like dying dots of fire tracking
the black in multitudes across the night.

And be careful to listen
to exactly what your prayers are meaning
as you sing; for those mousefeet pervade
and determine, ping and sloop, dicker
and dodge through all invented cadences,
imposing on every voice and ear the tittering

character and mad, precise, alpha-and-omega
pickering machinery heard so prominently
every time in God's perfect reply.

RAPTURE OF THE DEEP: THE PATTERN OF POSEIDON'S LOVE SONG

The blue ornata's spiderweb
body sidles and pulses among the turning
cilia wheels of the microscopic
rotifera tilting over the feathery
fans of the splendidum slowly extending
and withdrawing
                        their fondling tongues
inside the body of the summer solstice
where the sun with its ragged
radiances organizes transparent
butterflies and paper kites of light
into flocks of meadow-drifting
throughout the green sea surrounding
the design
            of string worms palolo
floating in the gripping and releasing
event of their own tight coils
toward a reef of chitons pulled
from their rock bases by the violent
bite and suck of a spinning
squall

curling themselves then
into their round coat-of-mail shells
as if they were each one made
by the sound of long O moaning
inside a sailor's ancient prayer
to Mater Cara
                    tumbled and tumbled
by the waves beneath which the frilled
shark a singular presence in a dimension
of lesser constellations suspended
mid-sea whips with a graceful pattern
of pitiful evil
                    toward a nebula
of cephalopods undulating
below an arrangement of rain
shattering the evening suddenly
out of the linear into the million
falling moments
                        of one moment
pebbling the open plain of the sea
through which plankton ascend
like a legion of flittering spirits
or the single body of a multiple
deity swallowing stinging salt pieces
of stars
                to the surface to bask
beneath the violet order
of the traveling moon touching
all points in the declaration of birth
to death
                to stone embodied by shoals
of glass-threaded cod fluctuating

in their progress like schools of storm
petrels creating descent and angle
from a totally flat sky playing
a layering of flight
                    shadows off the eyes
of soaring dolphins breaching
with the contrapuntal rhythm of a passage
from Bach as over and within
this universe
                    the hand of an ecstatic
wind its fingers spread wide
with blessing moves in a seizure
of joy through every trembling spray
and pulse and skeleton forming
the reality of this whole
prolonged consummation

GOING FOR WATER AND LIGHT

Is it possible to draw up
in a bucket (that emptiness submerged
into the river and raised) both light
and its water? to pour water and light
together into the glass bowl
on the dinner table and not lose either?
by that crystal glass to cut light
into its needles of green-violet
and fire while keeping water
all the while whole?

Though moving water may remain

the one color of itself when seen properly,
yet light on rivers can be the copper-black
evening light of autumn or the blue-cinnamon
kerchief light of a morning in March,
the summer-lime underside light
of manna grasses swinging over the bank,
or the white belly-light of swallows
swooping above.

Lovers meet a little like water and light—
one coming down to the other, covering
the other, revealing the naked essence
so caressed and concealed. One yields
to the rocking motion, the pulling gulf
and push of the other. And one receives
the other, as the still depths of a winter
lake receive the revelation of day; and one
knows forever the one entered, as a silver
spasm of rain knows forever the river
it penetrates.

Lungs can take in neither water
nor light. I wonder how it would be
to drown slowly in water and light, yet live,
to know the body swift and seamless
as water, to see the bones as divergent
and willing as light, to recognize in death
the lift of water, the taste of light.

At night, when one watches starlight rise
through water, up from the deepest black
rock crevices and caves at the bottom
of a canyon lake, it might be possible

to forget any concept of surfaces, any fixed
orientation of heaven, to love immediately
the inseparable differences between
the dark soul of water, the thirsting
redemption of light.

INTO THE LIGHT

There may be some places the sun
never reaches—into the stamen
of a prairie primrose bud burned
and withered before blooming,
or into the eyes of a fetal
lamb killed before born. I suppose
the sun could never shine by its own
light back beyond the moment
when it first congealed and ignited.

And Mohammed, it is said, never showed
the inside of his mouth.

But the sun is certainly present
in the black below the earth, shining
inside the surf and thriving minerals
of sycamore, beech and hickory roots.
Blind fishes at the perpetually sunless
sea bottom hold some daylight
in their bodies by the descending
residue of fish particles and plankton
crumbs they sift through and swallow.

Eating Bread and Honey   481

The sun of ten million years previous
holds and glimmers still in the suspended
beat of glacial bacteria, in salt
crystals frozen beneath miles of ice,
a discernible history of light.

Sun off sunflowers gone
for a hundred years is yet here today
in van Gogh's paint on canvas,
just as the radiance of summer trout
watched by Schubert is the sound of sun
now in notes printed on a staff.

And the sun may shine inside a rock
buried on the dark side of the moon,
if I imagine it there. It might illuminate
the buried night existing inside a dead
man's heart, if I say it is so.

If I envision it, could the sun,
shining maybe at first only faintly
like a penny candle or with a light dim
as the light of the Weaver Star, reveal
the outlines of descending salvation
in an icy rain falling at midnight
or the edges of atonement in the potential
luminance of a darkened lamp? I close
my eyes and turn in that direction
to see.

The Eye Has No Will of Its Own

It can only follow wherever the bank swallow
leads it over the sandbar willow upstream,
above the little walnut. Watching that flight,
the eye is bound to swallow-gyre, swallow-
fall-and-sweep.

The eye perusing a yellow locust tree
must turn exactly in the way each pod
has turned. It has always had to move straight
without deviation in order to divine
a streak of slanted sun through forest smoke.

The eye increases when the giant green
anemone spreads, when the ash wings
of the flycatcher open. It must stay still
when the hawk moth it studies is stopped.
An orange banner in a wind, the torn frills
of bull kelp in a surf—both control it
with fluttering currents and curls.

Easily coerced to spirals by the conch
and the periwinkle, it is taken in circles
by a balsam leaf in a whirlpool. It is carried
away suddenly past hedges of ligustrum,
then abandoned, then compelled again
upward to the evening sky, by the whims
of a firefly.

What else can it do to find the form
of the seaside arrowgrasses except submit
to their constant collapse and rolling
resurrections? The marbled spider

Eating Bread and Honey

descends at dusk on its sun–thin tether.
The eye, attendant, becomes one
with the pace of eight-legged descent.

The eye might shut itself, close itself
according to its own choice. But limited
and constrained still behind that blind,
it can only re-envision all the tints
and shapes, the past pacings, the flaring
pauses, all the manipulations and multiple
dictators of its previous histories.

Cause and Effect, Far and Aware

When the flagfish swerved in the sea,
spread her crippled wings and lifted
toward the wavering green water
of the submerged sun, Lena shifted,
turned in the weightlessness of her sleep,
pressed her belly to the bed
as if the dawn light were rising
beneath the sheet and mattress, up
through the boards of the floor.

The running of the bells announcing
a new baby boy born living in June
caused a thousand buds of the prairie solstice
to push themselves forward into blossoms,
thus making a thousand new worlds
for starlight, for cricket pluckings,
for moonsome coyote quarrels to shine upon.

And when Robert put his lips with love
to the breast of a woman for the first time,
a scarcely perceptible glimmer of violet
widened briefly on the corona arc
of Stellar Maris, then thinned
and fell again as he rose.

The moment after the pod of the *Yucca baccata*
broke, spilling a scatter of seeds unseen
against the rocky grasslands, a similar
scatter of northern butterflies hovered
unwitnessed over a shallow of mud-dampness,
became a similar pattern of drift against
the evening, a chord hanging like scattered
notes against the ear of the deaf.

What happened yesterday—a subtle
movement of molecules? a strum or less
of electrons?—that caused the surf to curl
its lather a thread farther up the steel clay
beach, that caused the bend and grip
of the bumblebee to hasten in the building
of her honey pots, that urged the cloudy
salamander to stretch beneath the talus
debris one minute longer?

If the red-legged frog, gorgeous *Rana aurora*,
will simply blink the bronze of its eye
once more quickly, maybe I can watch
and measure what thunder misses a beat
in the poplar's heartwood, gauge what future
fire of vision in the artist's hand
is gathering, glimpse by glimpse,
toward combustion.

Eating Bread and Honey   485

Design of Gongs

Each single spill of rain makes
many ringing water gongs on the pond,
and the calls of the crow are simply one gong
sounding after the other, circling wider
and farther, rippling the sky
above the rippled pond.

Below, a toad bug swivels near the shore,
and many sand grains shiver like cymbals
with the force of that mallet.

The bordering red clover is a gong too,
the way its ruby light spreads, stuns
and echoes in the eye, and the cowpen
daisy—those bold rays of reverberations
fly on and on, clear back to the sun.

The turning wind makes of every quaking
poplar leaf a gong. What a constant
confetti of green percussion that ensemble
of summer aspen creates on the bluff.
Coyote sirens and calls interstice
wildly, override, merge, shrieking,
shaking this entire whining and weaving
design of gongs.

Breathe, breathe. Now the tremblings
and drummings of the early moon spread
through the tambourine thistles, swirl
the bee and beetle dust of the evening,
sizzle the whole heavens and zing
until all crystals of every sense

are struck and dizzy with its continual
white shammerings.

Far away an electron at the edge
of a Sanctus is startled, twirled and redefined
by the solstice gong of the orbiting
earth announcing the first new prayer
of the next season.

THE LONG MARRIAGE: A TRANSLATION

In among the alder's highest black
branches making a complicated map
of depth and elevation against the dull
white sky, winter waxwings in a flock
settle, coming, going.

They depart, altering the design of cold
and season in the tree, return
in gatherings of six or seven, flying
in quick staccato against a largo
of motion relative to one another,
as if they weren't birds alone
but a constantly changing syntax
in a history of place and event.

Several sail together over the fallen
field with an expansion and contraction
of pattern that might sound like a wheezing
of wooden organ or bagpipe, were there sound
to vision. And eleven spiral up, angle

into the evening like eleven dead leaves
with stunted wings and no more purpose
nor will than to illustrate eleven
different motives of the wind at once.

Gliding to gully, to river brush, a wave
of them parts easily, rejoins in crossing
familiarities that might impress like lavender
and sage, were there fragrances
to involution and grace.

Back and forth in ragged unison
through the network of branches, penetrating
and teetering, they leave the dense
scaffolding like torn pieces of broken tree
and veer toward the east; they return
from the west to circle and descend
again into the bare limbs of the alder
back in its place once more. Swerving
and sinking through the light,
they are a hard statement of fact
ameliorating itself midair.

I know evening and alder and waxwings
to one another can never be fixed. No constant
coordinate ever contains them. The new amber
of the sky moves toward darkness. Branches
and birds change places continuously,
as if definition also possessed no certain
form heightening and fading. Night stars,
invisible behind the hour, are bright
in the imagination, silent
with shifting prophecy.

Deep inside the spore-sphere
of a protozoa rising slowly
through cold lulls and currents, blue

with a blue like the under-figment
of early spring waterweed in shadow,

rising in burst and dalliance
past the lurch of a carp's flat
eye, past the fast black trills
of filament-tails in eggs floating

beneath dormant river cress, falling
upward in stutter and eloquence,
drifting netherside up in die

and demand, surrounded by many
flattering wheels circling sideways
toward moon, lapsing, pushing toward sun,

deep inside the spore-sphere
of a protozoa, a small fledge of heat
is asking, in a repetition of the very
first cry and reverie known on earth,
for summer.

INVESTIGATIVE LOGIC IN A STUDY OF LOVE

The field, persistent in its meticulous
study of lantern flies, leaf hoppers, elbowed
antennae and the lightning of sperm,
is the love of the sky made flesh.

To properly study love then,
the sky must be carefully observed
in the act of becoming a curve of yellow clover
or the mouth of an io moth.

The study of the panicled aster and the tent
of the shamrock spider is the invisible love
of the field given sight. Therefore, any fondness
for the rooting of skies can first be seen
in the close examination of Indian grass,
timothy and autumn bluestem alive in the field.

The study of the burrowing habits of the speckled
tortoise, carried out with solicitude,
is obviously an alternative investigation
of the rituals of sky-worship, and the touching
and naming of prairie flower and brush-footed
butterfly is either love studying itself
or the field revealing, piece by piece, the love
of the sky or the love of the mind recognized
as itself through blossom and wing.

The sky has already discovered the white-tailed kite
as the airborne love of such a field study.

The inevitable conclusion is
that the thoroughly studied field will certainly shine

forever afterwards, on its own, like love.
I tell you it will give forth light like the sky
and reflect in all directions like the mind cherishing
the studious glory of a seeded dandelion scattering
its brilliant wind of stars before the sun.

THE WAY I'M TAUGHT BY HEART

The way I'm taught how to move
my hand along the swelve
and lank of your naked back
is by having watched how a pine
in easy wind smooths itself along
the close spine of a summer
night. The way I know how to drink
at your mouth is by remembering
my mouth at the earth once
taking sweet spring water
with my eyes closed.

I learn how to speak to you now
by imitating the cholla blossoms
who, in their hour, speak of lust
and expiation, and I seek you
in the same way the marblewings
opening in dampness at dawn admit
for their own edification every last
probe of sun possible.

Rising and falling inside your arms,
I understand how mosses and cress lose

and gain over and over inside the hold
of a stream. I've seen the headlong
push forward of a trout nudging
upcreek in a current.

Deep sea geographies of spiraling
canyons and cols, sudden stellar-scatters
and the chances beyond—these are the same words
as the words of your body, your name,
as I pronounce it, identical to wind-borne
riflings of rain above desert light.

Here I am, like God, the pulsing
center in a gather of waxwings widening
and tightening in their flock against
the sky, like God, a wayward thread
of cottonwood lifting over fields,
forswearing forever all bones,
every place.

EGG

Perhaps the light inside this temple
is less than a small candle barely
burning beneath a violet shade,
an uncertain diffusion like a glow
of glacier at night without moon,
a presence like morning over a pale
field before dawn, dimmer than day
with no voice to declare it.

Were there ears to hear inside
these halls, then a constant connecting
like scales of organ chords played
in arpeggio by two hands might be heard
as the spine assembles itself, a sound
like the low pizzicato of a cello
as the first faint plicking
of pulse commences.

One could claim a belief in crosses
exists predestined in the pattern
of arteries forming their junctures
yet to appear.

Were a seer present she might say
the attention inside this temple
is like that of rock spurs suddenly
quaked and rebounded by lightning.

Were a shaman present inside
these translucent walls, he might say
the sentiment is like that in a random
meadow of columbine filled
with mountain air before rain.

And were a master in the making here,
he might claim the process witnessed
in the rising and joining of warm wax
cells and oils is god, the exquisite
weaving of salt ropes and red twines
is the presence of god.

Though not one single star
exists in the curved breadth

of this structure, yet the only possible
place where any star might be found
is inside the immeasurable horizon
of the thin-skulled cranium about to be.

Could it be a worship of any kind
beheld in this first absence moving
toward a possible breath of protest
and sacrament?

When the last latching occurs, bringing
the rude kick and the cry, then this temple
must fail, fall, shatter away altogether,
and the world, at once, begin anew.

PUBLICATION CREDITS FOR NEW POEMS

My thanks to the editors of the following magazines in which these poems
first appeared.

Alkalai Flats: "Being Specific."
DoubleTake: "Watching the Ancestral Prayers of Venerable Others."
Connecticut Review: "The Funniest Clown."
Georgia Review: "The Background Beyond the Background"; "Song of the
     Oceans of the World Becoming."
Gettysburg Review: "Afterward"; "Paganini, and Rumor As Genesis";
     "Millennium Map of the Universe (from the National Geographic
     Society)"; "Data from This Line of Light Laboratory."
Gulf Coast: "Variations on Breaking the Faith of Sleep"; "Veneration."
Hudson Review: "Before the Beginning: Maybe God and a Silk Flower
     Concubine Perhaps"; "Almanac."
International Poetry Review: "these horses never cease."
Iowa Review: "The Making of the World"; "The Stars Beneath My Feet."
New Letters: "The Form of That Which Is Sought."
Orion: "Born of a Rib"; "The Blessings of Ashes and Dust."
Potpourri: "Verges."
Paris Review: "The Composer, The Bone Yard"; "Archetype."
Poetry: "On the Way to Early Morning Mass"; "Reiteration"; "Self-
     Recognition of the Observer As Momentary Cessation of Process."
Prairie Schooner: "The Known Unknown."

River Styx: "Born on Noah's Ark"; "Eyes and the Sea."

Tampa Review: "Just to Say It."

Tin House: "Stone Bird."

Washington Square: "Speaking of Evolution: Luminosity"; "Disunion: Moonless Hound Monologue."

Weber Studies: "Fossil Texts on Canyon Walls."

Western Humanities Review: "Peace All Seasons, Each Night."

Wilderness: "The Nature of the Huckster."

"Watching the Ancestral Prayers of Venerable Others" appeared in *Best Spiritual Writing, 1999.*

"The Background Beyond the Background" appeared in *Best Spiritual Writing, 2000.*

"On the Way to Early Morning Mass," "Reiteration," and "Self-Recognition of the Observer As Momentary Cessation of Process" received the Frederick Bock Prize from *Poetry.*

"Before the Beginning: Maybe God and a Silk Flower Concubine Perhaps" appeared in *Pushcart Prize, Best of the Small Presses, 1999.*

"A Very Common Field" and "Once Upon a Time, When I Was Almost Dead with Fear and Doubt" were written during a residency at the Rockefeller Foundation Study and Conference Center in Bellagio, Italy, May 2000.

INDEX OF TITLES

502

504

506

Index of Titles

Index of First Lines

A

516

PATTIANN ROGERS has published seven books of poetry: *The Expectations of Light* (Princeton, 1981), *The Tattooed Lady in the Garden* (Wesleyan, 1986), *Legendary Performance* (Ion Books/Raccoon, 1987), *Splitting and Binding* (Wesleyan, 1989), *Geocentric* (Gibbs Smith, 1993), *Firekeeper: New and Selected Poems* (Milkweed Editions, 1994), and *Eating Bread and Honey* (Milkweed Editions, 1997). She has been the recipient of two NEA grants, a Guggenheim Fellowship, and a Lannan Poetry Fellowship. In May 2000 she was awarded a residency by the Rockefeller Foundation at the Bellagio Study Center in Bellagio, Italy. Her poems have won several prizes, including the Tietjens Prize, the Hokin Prize, and the Bock Prize from *Poetry,* the Roethke Prize from *Poetry Northwest,* the Strousse Award twice from *Prairie Schooner*, three book awards from the Texas Institute of Letters, and five Pushcart Prizes. She is a graduate of the University of Missouri (B.A., Phi Beta Kappa) and the University of Houston (M.A.), has been a faculty member of Vermont College, a visiting writer at the University of Texas, the University of Montana, Southern Methodist University, and Washington University, and, from 1993 to 1997, was on the faculty in the creative writing program at the University of Arkansas. Her papers, including manuscripts, galleys, correspondence, and drafts of poems dating from 1960 to the present, have been acquired by Texas Tech University and are archived in the James Sowell Family Collection of Literature, Community, and the Natural World. The mother of two grown sons and a daughter-in-law, Pattiann Rogers lives with her husband, a retired geophysicist, in Colorado.

MORE POETRY FROM MILKWEED EDITIONS

To order books or for more information, contact Milkweed at (800) 520-6455 or visit our website (www.milkweed.org).

TURNING OVER THE EARTH
Ralph Black

OUTSIDERS:
POEMS ABOUT REBELS, EXILES, AND RENEGADES
Edited by Laure-Anne Bosselaar

URBAN NATURE:
POEMS ABOUT WILDLIFE IN THE CITY
Edited by Laure-Anne Bosselaar

DRIVE, THEY SAID:
POEMS ABOUT AMERICANS AND THEIR CARS
Edited by Kurt Brown

NIGHT OUT:
POEMS ABOUT HOTELS, MOTELS, RESTAURANTS, AND BARS
Edited by Kurt Brown and Laure-Anne Bosselaar

VERSE AND UNIVERSE:
POEMS ABOUT SCIENCE AND MATHEMATICS
Edited by Kurt Brown

ASTONISHING WORLD:
SELECTED POEMS OF ÁNGEL GONZÁLEZ
Translated from the Spanish by Steven Ford Brown

MIXED VOICES:
CONTEMPORARY POEMS ABOUT MUSIC
Edited by Emilie Buchwald and Ruth Roston

THIS SPORTING LIFE:
POEMS ABOUT SPORTS AND GAMES
Edited by Emilie Buchwald and Ruth Roston

EATING THE STING
John Caddy

THE PHOENIX GONE, THE TERRACE EMPTY
Marilyn Chin

TWIN SONS OF DIFFERENT MIRRORS
Jack Driscoll and Bill Meissner

INVISIBLE HORSES
Patricia Goedicke

THE ART OF WRITING:
LU CHI'S *WEN FU*
Translated from the Chinese by Sam Hamill

BOXELDER BUG VARIATIONS
Bill Holm

THE DEAD GET BY WITH EVERYTHING
Bill Holm

BUTTERFLY EFFECT
Harry Humes

THE FREEDOM OF HISTORY
Jim Moore

THE LONG EXPERIENCE OF LOVE
Jim Moore

MINNESOTA WRITES:
POETRY
Edited by Jim Moore and Cary Waterman

EATING BREAD AND HONEY
Pattiann Rogers

FIREKEEPER:
NEW AND SELECTED POEMS
Pattiann Rogers

WHITE FLASH/BLACK RAIN:
WOMEN OF JAPAN RELIVE THE BOMB
Edited by Lequita Vance-Watkins and Aratani Mariko

MILKWEED EDITIONS publishes with the intention of making a humane impact on society, in the belief that literature is a transformative art uniquely able to convey the essential experiences of the human heart and spirit. To that end, Milkweed publishes distinctive voices of literary merit in handsomely designed, visually dynamic books, exploring the ethical, cultural, and esthetic issues that free societies need continually to address. Milkweed Editions is a not-for-profit press.

JOIN US

Milkweed publishes adult and children's fiction, poetry, and, in its World As Home program, literary nonfiction about the natural world. Milkweed also hosts two websites: www.milkweed.org, where readers can find in-depth information about Milkweed books, authors, and programs, and www.worldashome.org, which is your online resource of books, organizations, and writings that explore ethical, esthetic, and cultural dimensions of our relationship to the natural world.

Since its genesis as *Milkweed Chronicle* in 1979, Milkweed has helped hundreds of emerging writers reach their readers. Thanks to the generosity of foundations and of individuals like you, Milkweed Editions is able to continue its nonprofit mission of publishing books chosen on the basis of literary merit—of how they impact the human heart and spirit—rather than on how they impact the bottom line. That's a miracle that our readers have made possible.

In addition to purchasing Milkweed books, you can join the growing community of Milkweed supporters. Individual contributions of any amount are both meaningful and welcome. Contact us for a Milkweed catalog or log on to www.milkweed.org and click on "About Milkweed," then "Why Join Milkweed," to find out about our donor program, or simply call 800-520-6455 and ask about becoming one of Milkweed's contributors. As a nonprofit press, Milkweed belongs to you, the community. Milkweed's board, its staff, and especially the authors whose careers you help launch thank you for reading our books and supporting our mission in any way you can.

Interior design by Dale Cooney
Typeset in Bembo 11/15
by Stanton Publication Services, Inc.
Printed on acid-free 50# EB Natural paper
by Edwards Brothers Incorporated